The Daily Telegraph

BOOK OF SPORTS OBITUARIES

Martin Smith is assistant sports editor of the *Daily Telegraph*, for which he has worked since 1987. He has reported more than 500 football matches for the *Telegraph*, and has compiled the weekly football diary since the 1994 World Cup. He is married with three children, and lives in a Bedfordshire village, ominously close to the churchyard. This is his first book.

Also in this series

The Daily Telegraph
BOOK OF OBITUARIES
A Celebration of Eccentric Lives

The Daily Telegraph
SECOND BOOK OF OBITUARIES
Heroes and Adventurers

The Daily Telegraph
THIRD BOOK OF OBITUARIES
Entertainers

The Daily Telegraph
FOURTH BOOK OF OBITUARIES
Rogues

The Daily Telegraph
FIFTH BOOK OF OBITUARIES
20th-Century Lives

The Daily Telegraph

BOOK OF SPORTS

OBITUARIES

Edited by
MARTIN SMITH

PAN BOOKS

First published 2000 by Macmillan

This edition published 2001 by Pan Books
an imprint of Pan Macmillan Ltd
20 New Wharf Road, London N1 9RR
Basingstoke and Oxford
Associated companies throughout the world
www.panmacmillan.com

ISBN 0 330 37695 0

3 5 7 9 8 6 4 2

A CIP catalogue record for this book is available from
the British Library.

Typeset by SetSystems Ltd, Saffron Walden, Essex
Printed and bound in Great Britain by
Mackays of Chatham plc, Chatham, Kent

In memory of my father

INTRODUCTION

ONE COLD, though mercifully dry Thursday evening in late February, I found myself at the gates of the Boleyn Ground, home of West Ham United. It was an unlikely place to be at that time of night and week: there was no match in prospect, no hot-dog or hamburger stands set up, no fanzine sellers hawking their wares, nor was the ticket office open for business. Yet I was not alone. Others, muffled in overcoats, some bizarrely wearing carpet slippers, had stopped off on their way home from work, or else nipped away from their firesides for a few moments. All human life was there in the half-light: from the rabid supporters, to the mildly interested, right through to little old ladies who had never been inside the ground in their lives, but who always knew the score, and joined in whenever the FA Cup was paraded through the streets, just as they did, say, when the king died. That was the spirit of the East End; they always looked after their own, and rejoiced in their successes. On that night in 1993 the king was indeed dead. Bobby Moore was the King of the East End, a product of the East End, a fitting example of what working-class people could achieve. His subjects came out in droves to pay their respects. They stood with heads bowed, in silence, and looked at the shrine which was taking shape not only round the gates, but also on the approach to the ground which was fast becoming an avenue of remembrance: old photographs and programmes, scarves, flags, shirts, flowers, teddy bears and, most poignantly, messages scribbled on scraps of paper that wished "God speed" and "We'll never forget". It was like visiting an open-air museum, dedicated to one artist.

It was strange to find myself there at all. Yet I had been drawn as if by a magnet. In a typically British way, I find public outbursts of grief particularly embarrassing, if not a little distasteful and unnecessary. They were for those who need emotional crutches, and I didn't count myself in their ranks. But Bobby Moore was dead, had died the day before, and it seemed the most natural thing in the world to do. Perhaps it was the suddenness of his departure, the dignity he had shown in accepting his cancer, or maybe it was an acknowledgement of the unwitting part he had played in my life. It was six years later, while observing a minute's silence for Sir Alf Ramsey, this time inside the ground I was now outside, that I finally understood how important July 30, 1966, had been in shaping my future. It was England's success in the World Cup that fuelled my almost unhealthy obsession with the game of association football, and which led, eventually, to a job in the sports department of *The Daily Telegraph.* As they say, those who can, do; those who can't, write about it.

I was a West Ham supporter by birth — there had been Smiths supporting West Ham from their formation at the turn of the century — so the most obvious place to be on August 20, three weeks after the greatest day in English football history, was on my father's shoulders at the back of the North Bank at Upton Park for the return of the conquering heroes, Moore, Hurst and Peters. Out on to the pitch they strode, a full minute before their team-mates or opponents, to milk the applause of a besotted East End. Typically for West Ham, the script had not included the match itself, and they were duly beaten 2–1 by Chelsea. But a nine-year-old boy was hooked. Line and sinker.

He was nearly 27 years older when he followed the figure of one of his heroes out of the press box at Selhurst Park towards the welcoming warmth of the press room. It was January 30, 1993, and I should have realised things were not well with Bobby Moore OBE. They looked normal at face value, but I remember thinking, as he walked ahead of me, holding open a door, that surely a former captain of England could have found a pair of trousers that would fit properly. It was several days later, when he announced his illness publicly, that the reason for his weight loss became apparent, and the penny dropped. Too soon after, Moore made his last public appearance, providing the expert analysis for Capital Radio of England's World Cup qualifier against San Marino. When he came into the press room at Wembley before the game you could have heard a pin drop as all eyes turned towards him. He walked, as he always walked, with that calm, steady assurance that character-ised his game, and greeted old friends with a smile and a handshake. It was as much as the rest of us could do not to burst into a round of applause. Thankfully it didn't happen: it would have embarrassed him, but it would have embarrassed us more. When he failed to appear in the commentary box for West Ham's match against Newcastle on the following Sunday, we feared the worst. The fears were soon realised, and so we were drawn on a pilgrimage to his, and our, spiritual home.

It was without knowing the consequences that I picked up and flicked absent-mindedly through Barry Hugman's exhaustive record book, which gives biographical and appearance details of everyone who has played in the Football and Premier leagues since 1945. It was during an idle moment that the page flopped open at one William Pitt Cassidy, an early boyhood hero. Next to his entry it read starkly: died 1995. It is at such moments that our childhood dies, and we realise we are getting old, and that, like us, our heroes are not immortal. Bill Cassidy will mean nothing to the majority of readers, nor does his obituary appear within these covers. Like Robin Friday – immortalised in the book co-written by former Oasis bass player Paul McGuigan, *The Greatest Player You Never Saw* – Cassidy would only have intruded on your consciousness if you had supported Rotherham, Brighton & Hove, Chelmsford City, Detroit Cougars or Cambridge United during the sixties. Or perhaps he ruined your Saturday afternoon by scoring against your team. He was a member of the Chelmsford side I watched win the Southern League in 1968, and he formed a memorable striking partnership with Tony Butcher. Yes, Butch (and) Cassidy. At the end of the season he joined Detroit, the Ford-funded team for whom a friend of my parents was European manager. I still have the personally signed photograph upon which Cassidy promised to "look you up next time I'm in England". Hugman's weighty tome suddenly brought home the truth that Bill Cassidy would never come knocking on my door. I was 42. I was almost as mortified as I had been when he returned from the States and promptly joined arch-rivals Cambridge United, and helped them into the Football League. Life is very serious when you are 11. Died in 1995, though. And no one told me. I cannot now ask why he did not pop round for tea, or why his parents christened him William Pitt.

When Dusty Springfield died, Mick Brown, who conducted the last interview with her, told me it had suddenly made him face up to his own mortality. Perhaps when our heroes, or heroines, pass on it makes us realise how vulnerable we are. Whereas we tend to be less concerned about the deaths of politicians and their ilk, it is when we lose our sportsmen, our pop idols, the performers, the entertainers, that reality rushes in. Was it really in 1968 that I last saw Bill Cassidy play?

When, though, do sportsmen and women die? Was it 1995, for instance, aged 55, and after nearly a quarter of a century out of the comparative limelight, that Bill Cassidy passed away? Or did he "die" in 1968, when I last saw him play, or perhaps when he hung up his boots a couple of years later? What happened in those remaining 25 years? And does it matter? Was his *raison d'être*, as far as anyone outside his immediate family was concerned, merely to be a professional footballer and provide the inspiration for a pre-pubescent boy? Should we, perhaps, be writing the obituaries of sportspeople when they retire from their chosen career, rather than 30, 40 or 50 years later when they are half-forgotten memories of an adolescence long past? Or do their obituaries perform a service, allowing us to wallow in a brief act of nostalgia, recalling fleeting moments from our own histories, confirming or correcting our hazy memories, before we shake our heads and say, "Was it really *that* long ago?"

This book was conceived as a celebration of sport in the 20th century through the lives of the people who competed or administered or commentated; the people who shaped sport, played prominent roles, were around at the right time in sporting history, or just had good stories to tell. Sadly, they also had to be dead. That is why such obvious candidates as Muhammad Ali, Pele, Sir Donald Bradman, Lester Piggott, Martina Navratilova, George Best, Ian Botham, Brian Clough, and even our own E. W. Swanton – whose voice resonates through these pages – cannot be included. Mercifully, they were still with us at the dawn of the new millennium, though in Swanton's case sadly only for twenty-two days. Long may the others hang around, not only to remind us of their stirring feats, but to inspire succeeding generations of competitors, watchers and writers, and give us a proper appreciation of sport and its place in our society.

One man who did so was Leon Stukelj: the man who shook hands with history. So ran the headline on a cover story in a Saturday sports supplement in *The Daily Telegraph* in late 1998. It accompanied a piece by David Miller, who had travelled to Maribor in deepest Slovenia to interview Stukelj on his 100th birthday. Despite his six Olympic medals for gymnastics, three of them gold, even his most loyal supporters would not claim Stukelj to be the greatest athlete of the century. Yet, but for 53 days at the end, his life spanned the 20th century, and it is somehow fitting that he should be the 100th, and final, obituary in a book which strives to celebrate sport over the last 100 years. The slightly prosaic headline on the top of Miller's article, for which I plead guilty, refers to the sporting legends Stukelj met while competing at three Olympic Games. "He competed simultaneously with Paavo Nurmi at Paris 1924," wrote Miller. "He applauded poolside when Johnny Weissmuller retained his 100 metres crown at Amsterdam 1928. He shook hands with Jesse Owens, fellow national hero, at Berlin 1936." Three of the biggest names in pre-War sport, two of whose obituaries join Stukelj's in this book.

Remarkably, Stukelj was alive, albeit wearing whatever passed for nappies in 1899 Slovenia, when W. G. Grace played his final Test match for England, thus providing a slightly tenuous link between the start and finish of the book. The good doctor opens our batting here, so to speak, rather cheekily because he played only a smattering of first-class games in what was then the new century, finally declaring on his 58th birthday, in 1906. His obituary, which starts with the mournful "We regret to announce", was written by the magnificent-sounding Lieutenant-Colonel Philip Trevor, and is a veritable gem, redolent of another era, a different set of values.

All the obituaries are contemporaneous and, with the exception of a few minor adjustments, as they appeared in the pages of *The Daily Telegraph*. Unfortunately, during the research for the book, it was found that death notices for some of the more obvious candidates for inclusion – and Jesse Owens springs immediately to mind – were either not available, or too scant for use. During the years of rationing in the 1940s and 1950s, for instance, when newsprint was at a premium, obituaries of even the great sportsmen and women, people who would today merit full-page treatment, were reduced to a few essential paragraphs, or did not appear at all.

Consequently, this book would not claim to be a comprehensive collection of the obituaries of the greatest sportsmen and women of the century. Of necessity they are selective, many of them the personal choice of a West Ham supporter and Essex cricket member, who has dabbled in athletics reporting and has a healthy interest in, and knowledge of, many sports. They are also the personal choice of someone whose sporting memories start, and have been heavily influenced, by the World Cup of 1966. It should be no surprise, therefore, to find here the obituaries of Sir Alf Ramsey, the architect, Bobby Moore, the foundation stone, Gottfried Dienst, the referee, and even Cissie Charlton, who provided important cogs in defence and midfield in the shape of Big Jack and Wor Bobby. She had given them the rudiments of how to play in the backyard and back streets of Ashington, a timely reminder of how and where many of our sportsmen developed their skills in the days before the acceleration of the motorcar, the advent of television, and those mind-numbing computer games that hypnotise the youth of today. In the days when you had to make your own entertainment, I recall reliving the World Cup Final with my mate Gary in the local park with a couple of jumpers for goal-posts – and it was not easy trying to recreate that third goal Herr Dienst so kindly allowed without a crossbar from which the ball could bounce down over the line.

However, if 1966 was my sporting *annus mirabilis*, I have always had a fascination for the Golden Era of sport, the time bordered, loosely, by the two world wars, when the sun seems to have shone continuously, grounds were packed, Bradman had a century by lunch, the dastardly Jardine was plotting how to dislodge him, and Sir Neville Cardus was on hand to record everything in his own inimitable style. Those were the days of such master craftsmen of the cricket pitch as Sir Jack Hobbs, Sir Len Hutton, Harold Larwood and Denis Compton; of golf courses populated by Walter Hagen, Harry

Introduction

Vardon, Henry Cotton, Bobby Jones and Gene Sarazen; of tennis courts lit up by Suzanne Lenglen, Helen Wills-Moody, Kitty Godfree and Fred Perry; of boxing rings resounding to the thuds of punches thrown by Joe Louis, Gene Tunney, Rocky Graziano and Archie Moore. For those of us born too late, we can only wallow in their deeds as described by their contemporaries behind the typewriters.

Reading the obituaries we can spot the changes in sport and society, and note trends and developments. For instance, from Arthur Ashe's experiences growing up in immediate post-War middle America, we can understand how hard it was for black competitors to gain acceptance, or even entry into competition, and how far we have come as a society since then. The role of women in sport has also changed markedly since the days when they were merely there to drape the garlands round the victor's neck. Molly Hide's parents disapproved of her "gallivanting" around the world playing cricket; now Mrs Worthington is as likely to put her daughter in the skin-tight lycra of today's track athletes as put her on the stage. Bobby Riggs probably inadvertently ended the reign of the male chauvinist, and gave women the lift they required, when he lost the Battle of the Sexes tennis match to Billie Jean King in the 1970s. In tennis, again, it seems parents were pushing their teenage daughters on to court long before Mr Williams did so to Serena and Venus: the obituaries of Suzanne Lenglen and Helen Wills Moody bear testimony to that – their fathers laying down training regimes from an early age. Man's penchant for speed is also scattered through these pages, from the early pioneers of record breakers like Sir Henry Segrave, John Cobb and Donald Campbell, to the demons of the circuits, on four wheels or two, like Juan Manuel Fangio, Mike Hailwood, Mike Hawthorn, Graham Hill, James Hunt and Ayrton Senna. What comes through is the development of safety features at the circuits and in the cars, to the extent that Senna's death in the San Marino Grand Prix is considered a freak.

A flick through the contents of the book reveals it to be dominated by football, cricket, golf, lawn tennis, motorsport, rugby of both codes and horseracing: the staples of *The Daily Telegraph*'s sporting coverage. However, in keeping with the paper's policy of reporting just about the whole gamut of sporting activity, 60-plus sports at the last count, there are obituaries of some lesser-known, nay slightly obscure, sportsmen and women who have contributed to our century. Alf Twinn, for instance, boatman of the Cambridge University Boat Club for half a century; Willie Gunn, the ghillie who gave his name to a salmon tie that even the Queen Mother had heard of; Mavis Steele, the matriarch of bowls; and Stuart Parkinson, the skier and bobsleigh driver, for whom camaraderie and sportsmanship were more important than medals.

Perhaps, though, the most poignant obituary is that of Johnny Weissmuller, the Olympic swimming champion who went on to become the most famous movie Tarzan of them all. He fought a long battle against illness in his later years, and was eventually committed to a mental hospital after complaints from the Hollywood home for retired actors, where he lived, that he was upsetting the other patients by spending the nights repeating the famous jungle call he had invented. That's sport, though: from the sublime to the bathetic, tugging at every emotion known to man. Hopefully, this collection of obituaries is a fitting memorial to the 20th century's sporting heroes. The men and women who shook hands with history. Enjoy.

MARTIN SMITH
November 1999

ACKNOWLEDGEMENTS

THE LIST of acknowledgements may read like an Oscar-winner's speech, but the efforts of a great many people have made this book possible. The idea for a sports obituaries book was inspired by Hugh Massingberd, a former obituaries editor of *The Daily Telegraph*, and his excellent series of compilations. It is also important here to acknowledge the work of the "unknown soldiers", the biographers and sub-editors who have written and compiled the unsigned obituaries reprinted within these pages. A considerable number of the obituaries also first saw the light of day on the sports pages, and my appreciation of the work of my colleagues in the sports department must also be recorded. The following, in alphabetical order, provided bylined articles on news and sports pages: Harry S. Altham (C. B. Fry), Harold Atkins (Johnny Weissmuller), Bryon Butler (Ted Croker and Danny Blanchflower), Timothy Collings (Ayrton Senna), James Coote (Lillian Board and Paavo Nurmi), Geoffrey Cousins (Bobby Jones), Leonard Crawley (Walter Hagen), Bill Curling (Fulke Walwyn), Colin Dryden (Graham Hill and James Hunt), Terry Godwin (Sonny Liston), Colin Gibson (Bobby Moore), George Greenwood (Harry Vardon), Michael Kennedy (Sir Neville Cardus), Margot Lawrence and John Parsons (Kitty Godfree), Denis Lowe (Bill Shankly), W. A. McKenzie (John Cobb), Michael Melford (D. R. Jardine and Jim Laker), A. Wallis Myers (Suzanne Lenglen), David Saunders (Tom Simpson), Donald Saunders (Joe Louis, Sir Stanley Rous and Sir Matt Busby), E. W. Swanton (Sir Jack Hobbs and Sir Len

Hutton), Lieutenant-Colonel Philip Trevor (W. G. Grace), George Turnbull (Mike Hailwood) and Michael Williams (Henry Cotton). Others are acknowledged in text.

I must also thank Susannah Charlton, manager of Telegraph Books, who, in sporting parlance, took up the idea of the book and ran with it; Catherine Whitaker, Becky Lindsay and Nicky Hursell, my editors at Macmillan, for their enthusiasm, help and advice; Alex Erskine and her staff in the *Telegraph* library for making the tracking down of obituaries so much easier; Ben Findon for assistance with proof-reading; and, not least, my wife Jane. Her help during the book's conception, elephantine pregnancy and eventual birth was invaluable to the point that it would have been impossible without her. She input the text, mastered the computer and undertook much of the research. Before she entered the arduous world of motherhood, she worked in the court and social section of *The Daily Telegraph*, where one of her many duties included standing outside churches asking people for their names. Several times during the production of this book she was heard to exclaim, "I did his memorial service," or "Ah, he was a nice man." There are, however, a few sportsmen whose deaths would have been greatly exaggerated had her suggestions for possible inclusion not been nipped in the bud. I am thankful that the old adage, "behind every great man there's a great woman", extends to lesser mortals.

W. G. GRACE

We regret to announce that Dr W. G. Grace, the famous cricketer, has died from heart failure, at his residence, Fairmount, Mottingham, Eltham, Kent, at the age of 67. He had been ill for some time past.

CRICKET IS something more than the national game of England; it is an important, even an essential, part of national life. And Dr W. G. Grace was the greatest cricketer who ever lived. We may say of him, as Pope said of Garrick, that he will never have a rival. Some 20-odd years ago an attempt was made to show that in George Giffen, the Australian, "W.G." found approximately his equal as an all-round cricketer. Such a comparison may be dismissed as trivial, and as showing a woeful lack of sense of proportion. National game though it nominally was long before his time, cricket was made by "W.G." It was not until as a boy of 16 he burst upon the cricketing world that the game established its general hold upon, and made its universal appeal to, English people.

Who and what, then, was this man, or rather boy, who came to be better known than any prime minister, and whose features in the days before ubiquitous photography were better known than are those of a popular musical comedy actress today? One of the younger sons of a country doctor, he learnt as practically all great men have learnt – that is to say, he taught himself. "W.G." as a pupil is unthinkable. Today we visit private and public schools, and we witness the spectacle of laborious professionals and unselfish old "Blues" teaching the youth, as the popular song says, "Where to put his feet". At 16 he who lived to be known as the Grand Old Man was what we should now call first class; at 18 he was the best batsman in the world. Experience teaches? No doubt; but you can't make rules for a genius. He succeeds not because he ignores them, but because he deliberately breaks them. Towards the close of his career, when his muscles were stiff and great increase of weight had made him a compulsory adherent of the firm-footed system, "W.G.", no doubt, was overcautious, and indeed, more or less stereotyped. But it was not so when he made his unique reputation. For others, no doubt, he had rules of batting; not for himself. He put the bat on to the ball by instinct; quick-footed, he moved to it by instinct. But by deliberate design did he send it in this or that direction. In the art of "placing" he was, of course, a past master. A famous story in regard to that particular form of prowess will bear repetition. Shaw, at the height of his fame, was asked this question: "Are you the better bowler or is Dr Grace the better batsman?" The reply was that weirdest form of epigrammatic reply – the truth. "Oh! I put 'em where I like, and he puts 'em where he likes."

Let it be remembered that in his toddling days – and he played cricket of sorts directly he could toddle – "W.G." had in front of him a remarkable example of successful unorthodoxy – the batting of his elder brother, "E.M.". In those simple days to "pull" was the unforgivable sin. It was assumed to be a point of honour not to hit the ball on the "wrong" side of the wicket. Young "E.M." Grace took upon himself the responsibility of saying which was the "wrong" side: and, doing so, he made runs by the hundred. The toddling younger brother read, marked, and learnt; then grew up and "went one better". "E.M." was a small man, "W.G." a big one; and what looked awkward when done by a 5ft 5in player acquired dignity when exploited by a hero of 6ft. Moreover, "W.G." did the thing infinitely better then "E.M." Again, "E.M.", as was well said, could not make an orthodox stroke if he tried. "W.G." could make orthodox strokes better than any other man in England, and his own marvellous special strokes he had at his disposal, too. He batted by instinct, and in his best days that instinct was almost faultless. Of course, he had the proverbial eye of the hawk, but more than that, he had dauntless courage. "W.G." was never half out before he was in. It is common knowledge that he was seldom quite satisfied when the umpire's decision was against him, and that he often retired to the pavilion with obvious reluctance. On the other hand, he was ever eager to go in. Facing the music had no terrors for him.

Had the Champion – never was that title better deserved than in his case – been blessed with perennial youth he might have affected cricket much as the exponents of the spot stroke and the nursery cannon have affected billiards. The W. G. Grace of 1871, playing upon modern wickets, and against modern bowling, would, I make no doubt, have caused us to alter the rules. The general public knew "W.G." chiefly as the maker of more than a hundred hundreds, but the Champion became the Champion not because of his knack of compiling three-figure innings – physical capacity largely accounts for that kind of achievement – but because upon wickets upon which no one else could make 10 runs he was wont to make a score of 40 or 50 without a fluke, and often without a bad stroke. On the perfect modern wickets batsmen look reproachfully at a real or imaginary spot in the wicket when the ball gets up a fraction over stump high. "W.G.'s" ribs would often have suffered had he not known how to use his bat. Of course, he had no pet stroke; in other words, he never put the cart before the horse. The bowler bowled the ball, and "W.G." had the stroke to beat it.

One most important practical lesson the great batsman always taught. He made a point of conquering the bowler; it was not enough for him to avoid disaster. Batting with him was the art of making runs in a limited time; he was not there to do so many hours on a treadmill. He was the greatest batsman who ever lived because he made more runs than anyone else. And he made them at a time when bowling was so superior to batting that the customs as well as the laws of the game were unblushingly on the side of the run-getter. Yet "W.G.", and "W.G." alone, was able to profit by the fact. It would not be strictly true to speak of the Champion as a great bowler. That in the Seventies he was easily the best amateur bowler of the day is incontestable. He was eminently successful against young and inexperienced batsmen, especially against opponents meeting him for the first time. But personality more than actual bowling skill helped him on those occasions. The great big man, with the long black beard, and the monstrous red and yellow cap, who rushed up to the wicket, and then tossed the ball up gently, was disconcerting till you got to know him. The very slowness of the flight of the ball suggested guile and wile. Yet the break from leg was small, and sometimes non-existent. For all that some of the best professional batsmen were uncomfortable when the "Old

4

Man" went on to bowl, and that was so even in his later years of cricket. To get catches made on the leg-side was the Champion's main device, but he had also a keen eye for "LBW" possibilities.

In his younger days "W.G." was a smart and reliable fieldsman, while even towards the end of his long career, when he was compelled by lack of mobility to stand at point, he had a safe as well as a big pair of hands. It may be that history will not acclaim the Champion a great captain at any period of his brilliantly and uniformly successful career. It is certain, at any rate, that he never made field captaincy a practical scientific study, in the way in which John Shuter, A. C. MacLaren, J. R. Mason, A. O. Jones and M. A. Noble, for instance, made it one. To the last he retained his boyish enthusiasm, and, valuable in the extreme, as enthusiasm is in the general duties of leadership, it doubtless tends to obscure the critical faculty when a particular situation has to be met. The Old Man – even when a young man – never disguised the fact that he "liked to have a bowl". It was not cheap vanity that so often induced "W.G." to give himself a generous turn of bowling. What he did not know about play and players was "not worth knowing". Knowing what should be done, and how to do it, the Champion was apt to overlook the probability of finding what he wanted in one or other of his colleagues. A fine personal leader is not necessarily the best of directors.

We get back to "W.G." the batsman, and there we have no reservation to make; no superlatives to tone down. Who are his nearest rivals? Few will dispute the names of Ranjitsinhji – happily still with us, though sterner work than cricket claims him now – and of Victor Trumper, that star whom we shall never see again. One might, perhaps, add the name of C. B. Fry. But in reality, comparison is out of place. How would these men have fared on English wickets in the Seventies? It is really mere guesswork to proceed. "Ranji" possibly could have adapted himself and his play to any set of circumstances. But, after all, you cannot argue about wizards, and the things which "W.G." did as a batsman in conditions that the modern player would unhesitatingly call hopeless are a matter of history.

A description of the Champion's batting performance would fill a book; a schedule of them would occupy many columns. The month of May is essentially the bowler's month, and conversely it is just the month which is not to the liking of the veteran batsman, who needs warmth, practice, the relaxing of stiff muscles, and the tiring of bowlers ere he can assert himself. Yet in the month of May 1895, "W.G.", then in his 47th year, scored more than 1,000 runs in first-class cricket matches. This, needless to say, constituted a record, and to it, in the same month, the Grand Old Man added the other unique feat of scoring his hundredth century. The public were delighted by this marvel. From the Prince of Wales "W.G." received a letter of congratulation, and when *The Daily Telegraph* started a shilling fund for a national testimonial to the Champion of the national game, over £5,000 was subscribed by his legion of admirers.

It was in May 1899 that Dr Grace played his last game for England in the Test match with Australia at Nottingham. This was the year in which he left Gloucestershire to captain the London County team at the Crystal Palace – an innovation in first-class cricket which was short-lived. He continued to play in first-class cricket for several seasons, but his career practically ended with the

Gentlemen v Players match at the Oval in 1906. It was a memorable finish, for on this, his 58th birthday, he scored 74 runs. Thenceforward the golf links knew more of his company than the wicket, and his eye and hand did not fail him in the more leisurely game. For nearly 40 years Dr Grace played first-class cricket, and for nearly 30 he dominated it. A great innings is over at last; such another will never be played again.

It will be recalled that the famous cricketer suffered a bereavement in the early death of his eldest son, "the Young W.G.", who got his cricketing Blue at Cambridge and played also for Gloucestershire. Dr Grace is survived by his wife and two younger sons, both of whom are serving their country, Capt. H. E. Grace, RN, and Capt. C. B. Grace, KFRE.

Dr Grace's career in the cricket field can be sharply divided into two portions. His early fame as a batsman culminated in the season of 1876, when in the month of August he scored in three successive innings, 344 against Kent at Canterbury, 177 against Nottinghamshire at Clifton, and 318 not out against Yorkshire at Cheltenham. The second part of his career as a batsman began towards the end of the season of 1880. Following some fine performances for Gloucestershire he played, as everyone will remember, a great innings of 32 at the Oval in the first match in this country between England and Australia. Even then, however, though only in his 33rd year, he laboured under one serious disadvantage. In the four years following his triumphs of 1876 he had put on a lot of weight, and was very heavy for so young a man. He said himself at the time that he was never in better form than in those closing weeks of the season of 1880, and that, but for lack of condition, he would have made many more runs. Against increasing bulk he had to battle for the rest of his cricket life. For a long time he retained his activity to a surprising extent, but as the years went on his once-splendid fielding gradually left him. He kept up his batting, however, in a marvellous way, the success of what one may call his second period in the cricket field reaching its climax when in 1895 he scored 1,000 runs in first-class cricket in the month of May. His batting at that time has never been approached by a man of the same age. He was nearly 47. In 1896 he was still very good, but after that the years began to tell on him.

Of Dr Grace's cricket from the time of his first appearance at Lord's in July 1864, for the South Wales Club against the MCC, down to the end of 1876, columns could be written without exhausting the subject. He was picked for the Gentlemen as a lad of 17, both at Lord's and the Oval in 1865, the honour being conferred upon him quite as much, if not more, for his medium-paced bowling as for his batting. A year later, however, he proved himself, beyond all question, the best batsman in England, two wonderful innings at the Oval establishing his fame. He scored 224 not out for England against Surrey, and 173 not out for the Gentlemen of the South against the Players of the South. An attack of scarlet fever interfered with his cricket in 1867, but after that he never looked back. His best seasons as a batsman were, we fancy, 1871, 1872 and 1873. His play in 1871 far surpassed anything that had ever been done before. During his career he scored in Gentlemen and Players matches 6,008 runs, with an average of 42, and took 271 wickets for a trifle under 19 runs each. He made seven hundreds for the Gentlemen at Lord's, four at the Oval, and one each at Brighton, Prince's, Scarborough and

Hastings. The first of his seven hundreds at Lord's was obtained in 1868, and the last, after an interval of 27 years, in 1895. Of these seven innings the first was, perhaps, the most remarkable. Going in first wicket down for a very strong side, he took out his bat for 134, the total only reaching 201.

As to his connection with Gloucestershire, Dr Grace, with his two brothers, "E.M." and "G.F.", and other fine, though less gifted players, built up a team of remarkable strength in batting and fielding. The county club was established in 1871, and in 1876 the eleven stood ahead of all rivals. Until beaten at Clifton by the first Australian XI in 1878, the team never lost a match at home. After G. F. Grace's death, in 1880, Gloucestershire never seemed quite the same as before, but in 1895, and again in 1898, there was, thanks to W. G. Grace's batting and C. L. Townsend's bowling, a brief revival of old glories.

October 25 1915

SIR HENRY SEGRAVE

SIR HENRY O'NEAL DEHANE SEGRAVE, who died in an attempt on Windermere to achieve a world record for speed in water-craft, was the most famous, and most successful, of the comparatively small band of specialists, colloquially known as "speed kings", evolved by the internal combustion engine. He had since March last year [1929] held the world's record for the fastest speed attained on land. He seemed certain to attain the same honour for speed on water when disaster overtook him.

Tall, slenderly built, erect, with piercing deep-set

eyes and a hawk-like face, he was all that imagination called for in a speed king. He had nerves, but they were nerves of steel; a vivid imagination, controlled by a cool, alert brain.

Sir Henry Segrave, born September 22, 1896, son of Mr C. W. Segrave, of Coombe Court, Witley, Surrey, was educated at Eton and Sandhurst, whence he was gazetted to the 2nd Royal Warwickshire Regiment during the Great War. He was transferred later to the Flying Corps, with whom he spent the latter half of his military life. Being badly wounded, he was attached to the British Embassy at Washington and, while there, started to race motor-cars in 1917. "Every race has its thrills," he once said, "and I started when I returned to England in 1919, and bought an Opel car to run on the Brooklands track. From thence I graduated as a private competitor with a 1914 Grand Prix racer, with which I won a number of races. Then Mr Louis Coatalen offered me a car to drive in the 1921 Grand Prix race in France, and from that date I have always driven Sunbeam racers as an amateur racing driver."

In 1922 he held the 10-mile record at Brooklands at a speed of 114mph, which, though thrilling in itself, was nothing to the joy he felt in 1923 when he won the Grand Prix race in the Sunbeam at Tours, averaging 76mph for the 500-mile race, being the first Englishman and the first English car to win that prize.

By 1924 Segrave's reputation as a racing driver was thoroughly established, and soon afterwards he began his wonderful career as a maker and breaker of records as well as a winner of races. In the summer of 1926 he was astonishing the world by driving a car at a speed of 147mph on the road, and in the following March he set out for his first visit to Daytona Beach, Florida, the stage where he won his greatest fame. That year he had a Sunbeam, fitted with two 500hp Matabele aero engines. The world's record then stood at 174mph.

Segrave said when he set out that he hoped to prove that speeds in excess of 180mph were possible. On March 29 he drove the Sunbeam over the Daytona course at 203.79mph, the first man in the world to travel at over 200mph. At the end of the run the brakes failed to act. He had four miles in which to pull up, but at the end of them he was still travelling at about 100mph, and to avoid being smashed up in the sand dunes he drove into the sea. When he returned he declared he intended to give up motor racing. "As a substitute for the perilous excitement of the track, I shall take up motor-boat racing," he said. But his decision was altered by the events of the following year.

Capt. Malcolm Campbell went to Daytona and raised the record to 206.98mph, and then an American driver, Ray Keech, went a fractional part of a second quicker over the measured mile and captured the honour for his country. The record had to be regained, and Segrave set out to do it. Capt. J. S. Irving, who had been in charge of the construction of his Sunbeam, designed for him a new racer, the famous Golden Arrow. This car had a Napier Lion aero engine, of 12 cylinders, arranged in three blocks of four, developing 950bhp. It was the type of engine with which Lieutenant Webster had won the Schneider Trophy in 1927.

The Golden Arrow, wonderfully streamlined, and by far the most graceful racing machine ever seen, was taken to Daytona early in 1929, and on March 11, at its first serious effort, Segrave drove it to and fro over the measured mile at a mean speed for the two runs of 231.55mph. He was prepared to make another run, but two days later, Lee Bible, a young and rather inexperienced American driver, was killed driving a 36-cylinder challenger, and the meeting was closed.

On his return, Segrave received the honours of a conquering hero. He was accorded an official welcome by the Government, drove in procession through the streets of London, and later was knighted by the King at Bognor Regis, where His Majesty was convalescing.

Segrave, however, had already carried out his intention of taking to motor-boat racing. With the Golden Arrow, there travelled with him to America his first Miss England, a boat fitted with a similar Napier Lion aero engine. With her he hoped to recapture the British International Trophy, which had been taken from us at Southampton by Commodore Gar Wood in 1922, and held by him ever since.

The races between Miss America and Miss England were held at Miami, Florida, 12 days after the Golden Arrow's victory. In the first of the two tests, Miss America broke down; in the second Miss England was damaged by a floating log, but managed to complete the course, though much outpaced. Miss England won the tests on points, but America retained the trophy.

Last autumn in Venice, the battle was renewed. In a series of races off the Lido, Miss England met a new Miss America, and won the Crown Prince of Italy's Cup with a speed of 92.8mph. In another event Miss America, following in the wake of the English boat, struck her wash, and both driver and mechanic were flung into the water. The boat, travelling on uncontrolled, hit another wave, leapt 12 feet in the air, and falling into the water, broke her back. But Commodore Gar Wood and his boat still held the world's record and the international trophy. It was with the object of capturing both that Sir Henry Segrave designed and built the ill-fated Miss England II, undoubtedly the fastest boat put into the water.

June 14 1930

HARRY VARDON

HARRY VARDON, whose achievements are known to golfers throughout the world, died at the age of 66. For some time past he had been in failing health, and recently underwent an operation for internal trouble. He was born at Grouville, near St Helier, Jersey, which has produced many distinguished golfers, among them the Boomer brothers, Edward Ray, the Gaudins, the Renbuis and Herbert Jolly. Vardon's introduction to the game was when a party of strange gentlemen from England descended, one Sunday in 1877, to inspect the ground running along the sea coast. This was the beginning of golf in the island.

The game held a great fascination for Vardon, who made himself a driver from wood cut from the neighbouring hedges and trees. As balls were scarce and far too expensive, white marbles were substituted. Vardon's first real clubs were given him by Major Spofforth, brother of F. R. Spofforth, the Australian cricketer known as the "demon bowler".

While working as gardener for Major Spofforth, Vardon, playing from +3, won a prize in the local artisans' club. He came near to losing this most cherished of all his many trophies in an air raid during the Great War. A bomb, dropped at Vardon's front door at Totteridge, brought down a good part of the house, and his first golf prize, standing in a place of honour on the mantelpiece, was severely damaged.

Vardon's first post as a professional golfer was on the late Marquess of Ripon's estate at Studley Royal, Yorkshire. Later he went to the Bury Golf Club. Aged 21, Vardon was now safely launched on a great and dazzling career, which took him to America and many other parts of the world, where he spread the gospel of golf. For a long time he was invincible, the standard of his play being such that for the space of two years he was never known to be off the course with any shot. No wonder he came to be known as "the greyhound of the links".

He held the record of six Open championship successes, his two great contemporaries, James Braid and J. H. Taylor, having won five each. Vardon paid his first visit to America in 1900, when he won the US Open Championship. On a subsequent visit, in 1920, he was paired with Bobby Jones, then a youth of 18, in the championship. At one hole Jones topped an approach shot across the green into a bunker. Greatly embarrassed, he walked on to the next tee with Vardon, who, up to this point of the round, had not said a word. In an attempt to break the ice Jones said: "Mr Vardon, did you ever see a worse shot than that?" "No," replied Vardon. That closed the incident and the conversation.

Vardon was the originator of the overlapping grip, now the universal method of holding the club. In grace, ease and effortless swing he was the incomparable stylist. Vardon held a strong conviction that the deterioration in the standard of British golf was due, in no small measure, to faulty teaching. He ridiculed the idea of the straight left-arm theory, the practice of which, he claimed, had been the ruin of many promising golfers. For many years Vardon was the professional to the South Herts club, where he was an honorary member.

March 22 1937

BARON PIERRE DE COUBERTIN

BARON PIERRE DE FREDI DE COUBERTIN, who died in Geneva, aged 74, was the Founder and Life Honorary President of the International Olympic Games. He was a philosopher, historian, sociologist and teacher of international repute, but above all he was responsible, more than any other man, for converting Frenchmen to games.

Public opinion was first awakened to the idea of resuming the Olympic Games in 1852, when an archaeologist unearthed a stadium in Athens, the site of the ancient Games. Eleven years later, on January 1, 1863, the man who was to champion these Games successfully was born in Paris. Baron Pierre de Coubertin took up the great mission of his life from his youth and carried on the fight undaunted by reverses.

There was much opposition, but he succeeded in calling an international conference at the Sorbonne, Paris, in 1894. Two years later the first of the modern Olympic Games was held in Athens, with 15 nations taking part.

He was made President of the Games from the first and held that office until 1925, when, at the age of 62, he asked permission to retire. His request was granted and he was named Honorary President for life. At the last Games before his death, held in Berlin, 58 nations competed. For his individual efforts in founding the modern Games the Baron was rewarded with decorations and honours by many nations. In 1928 he was awarded the Nobel Peace Prize.

Half a century ago he began propaganda in favour of English methods of physical education in French schools. He found masters and parents apathetic, so he set about raising the pupils in revolt. The headmaster of one Paris school refused to have anything to do with an athletic gathering of his boys in the Bois de Boulogne. Afterwards he was sorry. The Baron had persuaded President Carnot to come, unannounced, to present the prizes. In those early days Baron Pierre de Coubertin taught French schoolboys to play rugby football.

September 3 1937

SUZANNE LENGLEN

MLLE SUZANNE LENGLEN, whose death occurred in Paris at the age of 39, was not the youngest champion Wimbledon knew – that distinction was held in 1887 by an English girl of 15, Miss Lottie Dod – but she was its greatest artist and its most magnetic personality. By her prowess and publicity she was to prove the unconscious author of a revolution in the physical development of her sex.

Before the French girl's reign began, the women's game, while attracting talented players, many of them perhaps steadier in execution and shrewder in tactics than those who keep press photographers busy today, was subordinate in public interest to the men's game. It was Suzanne's grade and genius, her complete control of the ball in motion, the effortless ease with which she dominated all her opponents, reducing them to impotency, that not only brought fame to this young girl from Picardy, but fired an athletic trail among her sex throughout the world.

Born in Compiègne on May 24, 1899, she was a delicate only child, and if her father, M. Charles Lenglen, had not been himself a keen athlete, showing his stamina on the cycle track, his theory that strength can be invoked by methodical training would never have been illustrated in his own daughter.

There were Lenglen legends even in those early days. One of them concerned the iron discipline to which she was subjected in training. The stories were exaggerated. M. Lenglen was not a martinet, but he was a clever and practical coach, and determined that his daughter should not defy the laws of physical mechanics and play lawn tennis, as so many girls do, to the detriment of success, with anatomical strain.

Mlle Lenglen's first prize was won in the handicap singles at Cannes, when she was 12 years old, and the fact that two years later, when she was only 14, she carried off the championship of Picardy and won the open singles at Lille reveals the measure of her father's training and her own instinctive skill. In May 1914 she celebrated her 15th birthday by winning the world's hard court championship at St Cloud, an event open to all comers.

It was my misfortune, [writes A. Wallis Myers] when opposing her in the semi-final of the mixed doubles, to realise the truth of the proverb, "a child's service is little, yet he is no little fool who despiseth it". For one found that if one attempted to place the ball in a position where older legs might not have reached it, this child of the bounding stride could do so.

Mlle Lenglen won her first championship at Wimbledon in 1919, after a dramatic challenge round against Mrs Lambert Chambers, at which King George V and Queen Mary, watching with Princess Mary, later the Princess Royal, from the committee box, were as excited as any member of the packed crowd, except M. Lenglen, the father of the heroine. Before she came within a stroke of defeat in a contest indelibly marked in the annals of the Old Wimbledon – for there was never a loose shot in it and both competitors were as level as could be – the French girl had shown signs of physical collapse. From the covered stand her agitated father admonished her to go on, throwing down a brandy ball on to the court to sustain his daughter.

When the long tension was at last over the winner swept off her soft white hat and rushed forward, with streaming locks, to shake hands with her opponent. Kissed on the court by one of her countrymen, she was overwhelmed by her parents when she emerged, pressed on all sides, through the corridor. In M. Lenglen, the Svengali of the act, the deliverance of France's lost provinces did not produce stronger emotion than the deliverance of Suzanne from what looked like certain defeat.

Lionising Lenglen was the outcome of this triumph. In her joy she called Wimbledon the wonderland of the world, and promised to come again next year. She came, and this time beat Mrs Lambert Chambers with the loss of only three games. In 1921, making the last stroke on the old ground, she won 11 games in succession against the challenge of Miss Ryan.

For five successive years she was invincible at Wimbledon, until, in 1924, she was forced by illness to retire when playing in the semi-final against Miss McKane, who went on to become the holder. In 1925, however, Suzanne returned, to defeat Miss McKane in two love sets. That was her year of zenith, for she won all three championships both at Wimbledon and St Cloud.

Twelve months later, when Wimbledon was celebrating its Jubilee, her bright-hued bandeau was seen for the last time on the Centre Court. She retired in the third round of the singles, and two months later she abandoned her amateur status and undertook a professional tour of the United States. Her career as an "exhibitionist" was brief, and later she found a more acceptable medium for expressing her vivacious personality, and for imparting her intuitive knowledge of the game, by founding an academy of lawn tennis in Paris. Here, both on outdoor and covered courts, she conducted lessons for the younger generation on novel and persuasive lines.

Of her famous matches three will live in lawn tennis history. That of 1919 at Wimbledon, her first appearance on a turf surface, has been mentioned. The second was at Cannes in the spring of 1926, when she met Miss Helen Wills, later Mrs Moody, in the final of the Carlton tournament. The sporting interest of Europe and America was roused to almost fever heat by this trial of strength between the reigning champion and her Californian girl rival. Suzanne was victorious in two closely contested sets, but the writing was on the wall. I do not doubt that, realising that spartan training was demanded if her sovereignty was to continue, the intention was then formed in her mind of abandoning tournament play.

The third match was in the second round of the American championship at Forest Hills, in 1921, when she met Mrs Mallory, the reigning American champion. Suzanne was forced, through illness, to retire from the match after Mrs Mallory had won the first set 6–2. There was a furore from the disappointed crowd and some hissing as Suzanne left the court. But Suzanne did not consciously outrage the American public, though she was the target of many taunts. Her training and temperament were at that time irreconcilable to a New York crowd. To surrender a match in Europe through indisposition was not a misdemeanour: in America money paid at the gate means a fight to the finish. The unaesthetic milieu of Forest Hills repelled the visitor.

She had no practice on American courts or with American balls; she did not appreciate that Mrs Mallory, preferring these accessories, would be nearly 15 better than in Europe. The shock of surprise reacted on a nervous system already shaken by the voyage; the absence of her father, who was opposed to her trip, completed her dismay. When the victim of this tragedy next engaged Mrs Mallory, on Suzanne's home court at Nice, the American champion did not win a game; and at Wimbledon in the final she defeated the American champion in 26 minutes with a conclusive score.

As a player Suzanne Lenglen was incomparable. She had no weakness in a finished game. She was like H. L. Doherty in that, by the faultless rhythm of her stroke and the perfect timing of the ball, she got the maximum of effect with the minimum of effort. By her exquisite balance and poise she could make her racket a shield or shock-absorber for stronger blows, and by her agility of hand and foot she could open the court serenely for the finishing stroke. Her service, judged by the standard of Miss Marble, was unprovocative, but she could place the ball at will. Like H. L. Doherty, when he defeated Norman Brookes, armed with a dynamic service, her sweet answer could turn away the wrath of the enemy. But skill and artistry are not necessarily allied. Suzanne had both these qualities and though she won her championships with the first, it was the second that brought her universal homage.

July 5 1938

JOHN COBB

JOHN COBB had one fear about the jet-powered Crusader in which he lost his life on Loch Ness. In the last talk I had with him during trials on the loch [writes W. A. McKenzie] he told me what it was. From the eye-witness reports of the crash it appears that the thing he feared took place. "At high speed," he said, "one kicks up a lot of water in front. There's always a risk that it will get thrown into the intake orifice of the engine and – put the fire out . . ." The emphasis he gave the last words, and the pause which followed them, were eloquent of what the result might be if the power were suddenly to be cut off.

I saw the death, 22 years ago, of Sir Henry Segrave, who also died attacking the world's marine speed record on Windermere. The two men's lives were as similar as the circumstances of their deaths. Both were old Etonians.

Both had seen service in the RAF. Both, when they died on the water, were holding the world's land speed record, and no man has lived to hold both records. There was a further link between the two men, for Cobb was awarded, in 1947, the Segrave Memorial Trophy for the "most outstanding demonstration of the possibilities of transport by land, sea and air", in that year.

John Rhodes Cobb was 52 when he died. He was a fur expert in the City, a member of a long-established business of fur brokers. Motor racing and record-breaking formed a lifetime hobby which he financed largely out of his own considerable wealth. However, in his last attempt he had the backing of nearly 40 industrial concerns. More than 6ft 2in tall, 15st in weight, he was a genial giant who, in a racing car, became a changed man with a brain and reflexes working with a lightning precision.

His early racing days at Brooklands are best remembered for the successes he had with a huge old Delage in the days of Birkin, Howe, Campbell, Eyston, Kay Don and other great personalities of the track. Later he got Railton to build him an aero-engined 500hp car in which he took many records in time and distance up to 234 hours. He held the lap speed record at Brooklands at 143.4mph.

Cobb's fame, however, rests chiefly on his fantastic achievements in taking the world's land speed record. With another Railton-built car he went to the Utah Salt Flats in 1938 and put the record up to 350.2mph. At that time he had not previously driven a car at more than 180mph. It was a short-lived glory. The next day Capt. George Eyston in his Thunderbolt car raised the record to 357.53mph. But in 1939 Cobb went out again, and recaptured the record with a speed of 368.85mph. At the

same time he took the world's records from five kilometres (three miles) to 10 miles, which still stood at his
death.

He returned to England to join the RAF and was in
Bomber Command when he appeared in the "briefing
scene" as an operations officer in the *Target for Tonight*
film of War-time fame. Later, he transferred to Air
Transport Auxiliary and spent two years ferrying aircraft
from factories to squadrons.

After the war he planned to be the first to travel on
land at 400mph. He achieved his ambition at Utah in
1947 when, in his Railton car, he raised his own world
record to 394.2mph, covering the mile in one direction
at 403.135mph. His aim to take the water speed record
of 178.4mph from the American Stanley Sayres was to
have been his last speed venture. It was not entirely the
thrill of the achievement that attracted him. He believed
that Crusader, of revolutionary design, would add an
important chapter to man's conquest of time and space.

September 30 1952

C. B. FRY

HAD CHARLES FRY, who died aged 84, been born half
a century later, he must surely have been for some years a
focus for all the resources of modern sporting publicity.
As a boy at Repton, he had, before he was 17, played for
the Casuals in the FA Cup, had captained both cricket
and football teams and had twice won the personal
athletic trophy.

At Oxford he set up a world record for the long

jump, made a century in the University match, played four years against Cambridge in football and was prevented only by injury from gaining a fourth Blue as wing three-quarter in a very strong Oxford XV.

A few years later, in 1902, he played for Southampton against Sheffield United in the final of the FA Cup on a Saturday in April, and on the following Monday made 82 runs at the Oval for London County against Surrey. Most of these runs were made in partnership with W. G., with whom three years earlier he had opened the innings for England against Australia in what was his own first Test match and the "Old Man's" last. In 1912 he captained England to victory in the only Triangular tournament played against Australia and South Africa.

These years have been called the Augustan age of English batting; certainly as a spectacle the game can never have been more worth watching; nor have there been so many batsmen who could without serious criticism have been chosen to play for their country, or who, if they played and made runs, would have been more certain to give pleasure to those who watched them.

Among these, Charles Fry was one of the elect. He could not rank with his great friend "Ranji" for wizardry, with Jessop for sensation, or with MacLaren, Jackson, Spooner or Johnnie Tyldesley for ease and brilliance of stroke. But in the making of runs – after all, the primary function of batting – and in making, on all wickets, the bowlers opposed to him look, to use a phrase of his own coining, "plainly playable" he could hold his own with any rival.

In advance of most of his generation he relied for defence almost entirely on back play rather than on the "bridge-building" forward stroke which had for so long been *de rigueur*. He was therefore, especially on turning wickets and against the best bowling, far more secure than his fellows. In attack he could play all the strokes, but he was above all a driver, hitting the over-pitched ball past or over mid-off, the bowler and mid-on with certainty and truly formidable power.

In all first-class matches he made over 30,000 runs with an average of over 50, and it must be remembered that he did not play so long or so regularly as many others. His greatest season was 1901, in which he scored 3,147 runs and made 13 hundreds, six of them in succession.

Fry's athletic distinction, unparalleled in its versatility, reflected only one side of an astonishing endowment. Elected senior scholar at Wadham on a roll that included P. E. Smith, later Lord Birkenhead, he gained a first in Classical Moderations, though later a variety of distractions denied him similar distinction in "Greats".

After a short spell on the staff at Charterhouse he spent some years in Fleet Street, first as athletics editor to that admirable boys' magazine, *The Captain*, and later as creator, director and editor of *C. B. Fry's Magazine*. Two of his books, written in collaboration, *Great Batsmen* and *Great Bowlers and Fielders*, though now more than 50 years old, not only present an incomparable and fascinating gallery of a great generation of players in action, but still constitute the most acute analysis of cricket mechanics achieved. His later study on *Batsmanship* carried that analysis to still greater depths.

In 1930 he initiated a new style in cricket reporting, in the form of a running commentary, which made him within a month the most eagerly read and the most widely acclaimed of cricket journalists. However, it was neither in his writing nor even in his athletic achievements that he found the chief interest of his own life and made the greatest contribution to the lives of others. In 1908, on the death of Charles Hoare, the banker who founded H. Hoare, he took over, as an act of faith and in circumstances of great uncertainty, and indeed hazard, the control of the training ship *Mercury* on the Hamble.

There, until his retirement a few years ago and in perfect partnership with his wife, who died in 1946, he devoted all his great resources of mind and personality to developing its establishment and to the training of generations of boys for service in the Royal and Merchant navies. He was an honorary captain to the Royal Naval Reserve. Surely the long retrospect of his *Mercury* command must have given him the best of all reasons for the title he chose for his lively and challenging autobiography – *Life Worth Living*.

September 8 1956

D. R. JARDINE

DOUGLAS ROBERT JARDINE, who died aged 57, captained England in the "Bodyline" Test series in Australia in 1932–33. The general public will remember him mostly for his share in that England victory, for his austere approach and his uncompromising use of the fast bowling of Larwood and Voce. However, he was also a cricketer of outstanding ability, the leading amateur batsman of his day. He made 35 centuries in first-class cricket.

Jardine evolved the bodyline policy himself and in

Larwood had the perfect instrument to implement it. He did not himself agree that short bowling at the body constituted physical intimidation of the batsman. In a book later he described such charges as "stupid and patently untruthful". When he himself was confronted with it he did not flinch. One of his most famous innings was his 127 for England at Old Trafford in 1933 against the West Indian fast bowlers Constantine and Martindale.

However, the later matches of the 1932–33 tour were played in an atmosphere of unparalleled tension and hostility which induced a series of cables between the Australian Board of Control and MCC. The first Australian cable stated that bodyline bowling had assumed such proportions that physical defence of the body was becoming the first consideration. MCC replied that they had all confidence in Jardine. They confirmed their confidence not only by appointing him captain in India but by congratulating him when he returned from Australia on his able and determined captaincy.

In time, however, official and public opinion began to change until bodyline was generally accepted as having been a pernicious influence on the game. Legislation since the War has made bodyline bowling on these lines impossible: "The persistent bowling of fast, short-pitched balls at the batsman is unfair if, in the opinion of the umpire at the bowler's end, it constitutes a systematic attempt at intimidation."

The son of M. R. Jardine, of Oxford University and Middlesex, Jardine was one of the few Scots to reach the highest class of cricket. Born in Bombay, he was educated at Winchester, where he was three years in the XI, and at Oxford University.

Six feet tall and strong of wrist and forearm, he was a graceful, thoroughly sound batsman, particularly fluent on the off side. He won his Blue at Oxford as a Freshman in 1920 and played against Cambridge in 1921 and 1923. A knee injury kept him out of the side in 1922.

After he began to play for Surrey, Jardine improved steadily and played for England for the first time against West Indies in 1928. In all, he played 22 times, the last 11 times as captain. In Australia in 1928–29, he averaged 61, scoring centuries in his first three matches, but in the next two English seasons played little first-class cricket.

The MCC team Jardine led in Australia in 1932–33 curbed Bradman at the height of his power, played some of the best cricket by a touring side and won the series 4–1. Yet the bitterness surrounding the tour robbed the victory of much of its sweetness. Jardine returned to England a figure of controversy. He had succeeded P. G. H. Fender as captain of Surrey in 1933. But while in India the following winter captaining another MCC side he resigned and dropped out of first-class cricket.

In 1939 he was appointed cricket correspondent of *The Daily Telegraph*, but by September of that year was on active service with the Royal Berkshire Regiment. He had been an active Territorial. After the War he was President of the Oxford University CC and played for the Authors in the annual match in Vincent Square against the Publishers. Jardine was a barrister and a director of several companies. He was taken ill with a tropical fever while visiting Salisbury, Southern Rhodesia, to inspect land he owned there. He married, in 1934, Miss M. I. Peat, who survived him with a son and three daughters.

June 20 1958

MIKE HAWTHORN

MIKE HAWTHORN, who was killed in a road accident, had many escapes on the race track during his spectacular progress to the forefront of British drivers. World champion at the age of 29, Hawthorn announced just a month before his death his retirement from Grand Prix racing. In a Ferrari he won the title at Casablanca in 1958 by a single point after coming second to his friend and rival, Stirling Moss, in the Morocco Grand Prix.

In eight years as a race driver Hawthorn won prize money estimated at £40,000. In the course of collecting it he suffered mishaps which included: the collapse of a rear spring at Goodwood which threw him out of the car at more than 100mph; failure of brakes at Aintree which sent him careering into a ploughed field; the dislodging of a bonnet-top which blew off and hit him in the face during practice at Silverstone; a skid at Oulton Park which caused his car to do a triple somersault and throw him 40ft; and a collision with two other cars while racing in Sicily which caused his car to burst into flames. He was badly burnt and spent several weeks in hospital.

In 1955 Hawthorn, driving a Jaguar, won the 24-hour Le Mans race in which 85 spectators were killed when a Mercedes driven by a Frenchman ran into the crowd at 150 mph.

Hawthorn was deeply affected by the death of his friend and fellow driver, Peter Collins, in the German Grand Prix in August 1958. Hawthorn, driving in the race, saw Collins hit a bank and turn over. Many felt that the loss of his friend was a factor in Hawthorn's decision to retire.

Tall, fair and genial, Hawthorn was immensely popular with his fellow drivers. His father, Mr Leslie Hawthorn, himself a racing driver, bought him a motorcycle while he was still at Ardingly College. By the age of 18 he had won a cup. By 1950 he owned his first sports car, a 1934 1,100cc Riley "Ulster Imp", and drove it successfully in speed trials. In 1952 he leapt into prominence by beating the great Argentinian driver, Juan Fangio, at Goodwood. Hawthorn drove B.R.M. cars for a time, but in 1956 signed for Ferrari, the Italian firm, and with victories in race after race in many parts of the world established himself as a fearless and first-class driver.

W. A. MacKenzie writes: Mike Hawthorn was the most colourful and unpredictable personality in post-War motor racing. He was practically unheard of until the Easter Holiday meeting at Goodwood in 1952. In a Cooper Bristol, and in the company of many of the world's leading drivers, he won two races and in a third finished second to the Argentinian Gonzales.

His entry into Grand Prix racing was just as precipitate. He joined the Ferrari team and won the French Grand Prix at Rheims in 1953. For over 150 miles Hawthorn and Fangio were never more than a length apart. Hawthorn won, though the race was so close that Fangio and the equally famous Ascari and Gonzales all finished within three seconds of the winner. One knew then that the big, flaxen-haired young Englishman had the courage and skill of a champion. He was 23 at the time.

Hawthorn was in the news again at Le Mans in 1955,

when his car was involved in an accident with Leveigh's Mercedes Benz which disintegrated and killed 85 spectators. I think that is the only time I saw Hawthorn's nerve shaken. He leapt out of his car, jumped across the tarmac and started to run wildly away, saying that he would not drive again. He was almost dragged back, and with the Mercedes Benz opposite the pits an inferno, he went on to win the race.

Five months before his own death, he lost his closest friend Peter Collins, who was killed on the Nurburgring. His team-mate Luigi Musso crashed fatally a few weeks earlier and Archie Scott-Brown, another friend, lost his life during the season. Finally Peter Whitehead died in a high-speed car trial.

January 23 1959

SIR JACK HOBBS

SIR JACK HOBBS, who died aged 81, was the greatest English batsman since W. G. Grace, a supreme master of his craft, and the undisputed head of his profession. Born on December 16, 1882, the son of the groundsman at Jesus College, Cambridge, he made his way to the Oval at the age of 20. Half a century later, long after his retirement but when his name was still a household word, he accepted the honour of knighthood.

John Berry Hobbs learnt his cricket, as so many Cambridge men have done before and since, on that sublime stretch between Fenner's and the Town, called Parkers' Piece. Tom Hayward was his mentor there, and it was Hobbs's luck, after Hayward had persuaded him to qualify for Surrey, that he should serve his apprenticeship at the Oval as opening partner to that great batsman.

There have been three men, as one surveys the history of cricket as a whole, whose genius and influence have transcended all others: W. G. Grace, Jack Hobbs and Don Bradman. Like most of the truly great – it was the same with Hutton and Compton, Hammond and Woolley – Hobbs proclaimed his promise beyond all argument more or less right away. He made 155 in his second match for Surrey, scored 1,300 runs in his first season of 1905, and improved considerably on that in his second. The next year he was chosen for the Players and also won a place in the MCC side to Australia of 1907–08. It was then already said of him that there was no better professional batsman in England bar Hayward and Johnny Tyldesley.

It was the second of his five visits as a player to Australia that brought him right to the top of the tree. In that series he averaged 82, scored three Test hundreds and, with Wilfred Rhodes, made 323, which was the longest opening partnership for England against Australia. Noting the consistency of his scoring and the speed with which the runs generally came in those days, one can appreciate the remark of Frank Woolley: "They can say what they like about him, but only those of us who saw Jack before 1914 knew him at his very best." However that may be, he was and remained the world's premier batsman until, when nearer 50 than 40, his gradual decline coincided with the advent of Bradman.

The long span of Hobbs's career made it probable that he would corner most of the aggregate records. Thus no one can match his number of runs, 61,221, any more than they can compete with his 197 centuries. No doubt he was lucky in his opening partners – compared with, say, Hutton. Nevertheless, his figure of 166 stands of a century or more for the first wicket sets an almost unassailable target. Even more conclusive may seem the consistency of his performances. He averaged just under 50 in England over his whole time, stretching from 1905 to 1934. In Australia his average was 51, in South Africa 68, and in Tests alone it stood at 56.94.

Hobbs had two great Surrey partners, Hayward and Sandham, two even more famous for England, Rhodes and Sutcliffe. It was he and Sutcliffe who decided the Oval Test of 1926 that brought back the Ashes after many crushing defeats by their wonderful partnership of 172 on a bad wicket. In the next series in Australia these two paved the way to the victory that kept the Ashes safe by scoring 105 together on a Melbourne glue-pot, one of the classics of bad-wicket batsmanship. On A. E. R. Gilligan's tour of 1924–25 Hobbs and Sutcliffe, going in against a score of 600, batted the entire day for 283.

If one summer marked his peak it was perhaps 1925, when, at the age of 42, he scored 3,000 runs, including 16 centuries, and with two hundreds in the match against Somerset at Taunton, first equalled and then surpassed the 126 hundreds made by "W.G".

Early recollections of Hobbs are confined in my own case {writes E. W. Swanton} to inessential things like the frequent spinning of the bat in his fingers before he settled into his stance, and the way he pulled down the peak of his cap, so that it slanted almost parallel with his slightly beaky nose. Before I knew enough to admire his batting it was his fielding which fascinated most. He would walk about at cover in an innocent preoccupied sort of way in between times, hands often deep in pockets.

If the ball were pushed wide of him, and the batsmen made to run, he would usually move at a quite leisurely speed to cut it off. Then suddenly an apparently identical stroke would be repeated, and this time the relaxed figure would spring into action with cat-like swiftness – there was a dart, a swoop, and the quickest of flicks straight at the stumps, with the batsman pounding to the crease as if for dear life. Australians as a rule are good between the wickets, but on one tour Hobbs at cover point ran out upwards of a dozen of them.

It has been written of him often enough that he was the bridge between the old batting and the new. When he entered the scene it was the age of elegance, and the best professionals absorbed, and were caught up in, the classical style based on the swing of the bat from the shoulders, driving, and the off-side strokes. There were, of course, strong back players, notable Fry, and more and more men came to practise the art of working the ball to the on side. Hobbs was quickly identified with this school. Then, when he was still climbing to the top, came the revolution in technique, that was made necessary by the arrival of the googly and the advance of the wrist spinner. At the same time the faster bowlers were exploring the possibilities of swing.

Neville Cardus has described him as "the first batsman really to master the new bowling". He combined with the classic freedom of forward play, and full swing of the bat, the necessary adaptation to defeat the googly and late-swerve – legs and pads over the wicket with the hands held loosely on the bat in order to scotch the spin and bring the ball down short of the close fieldsmen, virtually in the crease.

Enough of technique, though. In the last resort the

difference between talent and mastery is a matter of character. Hobbs brought to his cricket an ascetic self-discipline which in tight corners expressed itself perfectly in his play. He was a man of conspicuous personal modesty; but his pride in his position as – in every sense – England's No. 1 gave to his batting an aura of serenity equally communicable to his opponents and to his fellows. No one saw Hobbs rattled or in a hurry. And if he was anxious it never showed.

There was a quiet dignity about him, which had its roots in mutual respect: for others as for himself. He had the natural good manners of a Christian and a sportsman, and the esteem in which, in his day, his profession came to be held owed much to the man who for the best part of a quarter of a century was its undisputed leader.

December 23 1963

DONALD CAMPBELL

DONALD MALCOLM CAMPBELL, who was killed, aged 45, broke his own water speed record less than nine hours before his deadline, the end of 1964, and became the first man to set up land and water speed records in the same year. He raised the water record to 276.33mph. Fulfilment of his 10-year ambition to bring off the "double" in the same year came on the 16th anniversary of the death of his father, Sir Malcolm Campbell, who once held both records. Donald Campbell's 276.33mph was set up in two runs on Lake Dumbleyung, Western Australia, in his jet boat *Bluebird*. His previous record was 260.35 on Coniston in Lancashire, in 1959. In July 1964, he had attained 403.1mph on Lake Eyre Salt Flat, Australia, in his gas turbine car *Bluebird*, and this was recognised as the land record.

Donald Campbell's high courage and doggedness enabled him twice to beat the world water speed record in 1955, to raise his own record in 1956, to beat it again in 1957, and to raise it in 1958 and 1959. On Ullswater in July 1955, he made two runs over the measured kilometre at an average speed of 202.32mph and became the first man to breach the "water barrier" and survive.

Campbell crashed in Utah in 1960. Afterwards he said: "I can tell you most definitely my nerve has not been affected." In 1957 he came within an ace of losing his life during an attempt on his own water speed record. His hydroplane hit another boat's wake while travelling at 240mph on Lake Canadiagua, New York State.

In 1951 his boat *Bluebird* sank at speed on Coniston Water, but Campbell and his mechanic were rescued by motor launch. He gave his views on fear in 1963. "When I am no longer afraid I shall know it is time for me to pack in," he said. "Fear is a natural safety valve."

Mr Campbell was educated at Uppingham. At the beginning of the 1939–45 War he underwent training as a pilot in the RAF, but was invalided out because of the after-effects of rheumatic fever. He was appointed CBE in 1957. His reminiscences, *Into the Water Barrier*, were published in 1955. His first marriage, in 1945, to Miss Daphne Margaret Harvey was dissolved on her petition. There was one daughter. He married in 1952 Miss Dorothy McKegg, daughter of a New Zealand dentist. He divorced her in 1957, and in 1958 married Miss Tonia Bern, a Belgian-born cabaret singer.

Donald Campbell

Colin Dryden writes: So Donald Campbell has joined the proud but melancholy roll of honour of great men who have died keeping Britain to the forefront in world water speed attempts. None knew the risks better than they did, but all were patriots.

For Campbell there was also the desire to emulate his famous father, Sir Malcolm, and it was obsessional. But later, as his father's records were surpassed, this tended to be replaced by a fierce brand of patriotism, no longer fashionable. In a letter to *The Daily Telegraph* in 1952, he wrote: "Surely any endeavour, whatsoever it may be, that is calculated to enhance and further one's country's prestige is more than justified."

Like all men of great achievement Campbell had his detractors. The inevitable delays and setbacks attending his land and water speed attempts in Australia, America and the Lake District, and disputes with backers, gave ammunition to his critics. But the fact remains that however large the sum involved in the record attempts — and it ran into millions — one man only repeatedly looked death in the eye and that was Donald Campbell. Like all racing drivers who must always wear the same crash helmet or carry a lucky charm, Campbell was intensely superstitious. His final run must have called for even more courage than usual, in view of the premonition of disaster he had received.

January 5 1967

TOM SIMPSON

TOM SIMPSON'S death at the age of 29, and at the height of his racing career, shocked the whole cycling world. His name had become a legend among cyclists in this country and the measure of his achievements is hard to evaluate in the cold light of day. Always a fighter, sometimes foolhardy and impetuous, he brought an entirely new look to the Continental idea of an Englishman.

His cycling life was dogged with bad luck throughout. Even in his amateur days crashes upset his chances. A spill in the World Amateur Championships in 1958, when he dislocated his jaw, possibly prevented him from taking his first world title. Simpson's courage was beyond question at all times and he fought through for another seven years before his dream came true and he won the world professional road title at San Sebastian in 1965. Even then the fates were against him for, only three months later, he broke his leg in a skiing accident. His world title win made history, but that was just another chapter for this splendid rider.

He had already made his mark in the pages of sport by being the first Englishman to hold the Yellow Jersey in a Tour de France, to win the Belgian Tour of Flanders, the Italian Milan–San Remo and Tour of Lombardy classics, and countless other events both home and abroad.

He began his cycling career at the age of 14 with the Harworth and District Cycling Club, in Nottinghamshire. Although born in Durham, he lived most of his life near Harworth, and was always determined to be a great rider. His first real chance came in 1956 when, at the age of 18, he rode for Britain in the Olympic Games in Melbourne. He gained a bronze medal in the team pursuit event, and back in Britain, went from strength to strength, eventually winning the British pursuit title in 1958, and then moving to France to seek fame and fortune the following year.

His first appearances abroad were sensational, and he won no less than 60 events that season, culminating in his turning professional and finishing fourth in the world road championships. After victory in the French Tour of the South-West in 1960, he rode his first major tour without any great success.

Despite all the other major races and his countless victories, it was the Tour de France which was always the centre of attraction for him. I remember him telling me [writes David Saunders] not long ago that it had always beaten him in the end, but one day he would win it. That day will never come now, but, knowing him personally, as a friend for many years, I think he would be happy at going the way he did. In his own humorous way he would surely have commented that he had abandoned for the third successive year.

He leaves a wife, Helen, and two small daughters. He will be sadly mourned in cycling circles the world over and it will be a long time before this country can produce an equal both in terms of ability and courage.

July 14 1967

WALTER HAGEN

WALTER HAGEN, the great American golfer who died in Traverse City, Michigan, at the age of 76, may well be said to have been the founder of a new generation of professional golfers, and both British and American professionals owe him a debt of gratitude that nothing can repay.

Walter Charles Hagen first appeared in Britain at the age of 27 in 1920, not only a very fine player but an extraordinary, picturesque figure. His groomed black hair, high complexion and perfectly chiselled features gave him a noble appearance, and he was a man of whom it was hardly possible to take a neutral view. One either liked or disliked him, but his character and flavour were such that they compelled attention.

The sum of his golfing achievements is so large that it is possible to set down only a few. He won numberless big money tournaments in his native country and had the happy knack of winning when there was most at stake. He won two American Open championships (1914 and 1919), and four British Opens (1922, 1924, 1928 and 1929), but his most remarkable feat was the winning of four American PGA Matchplay championships in a row, from 1924 to 1927, to make it five in all.

There have been more skilful and more faultless players than Hagen, but none with greater sticking power or temperament more ideally suited to the game of golf. He was strictly well mannered, and yet showed a certain suppressed truculence towards his opponents. He was so supremely confident, particularly near the hole, that they felt him to be a killer and could not resist being killed by him.

"The Haig" was the first golfer to make a million dollars, and he spent them all as they came. His career was a very long one and towards the end, when his powers of winning began to fade, he was sounder through the green than when at the height of his money making.

One of the most remarkable features of his great character was his ability to forget failure. In 1928 at Moor Park he lost a 72-hole challenge match to Archie Compston by the huge margin of 18 up and 17 to play, and yet a fortnight later he won the third of his four Opens, at Royal St George's, Sandwich. It was difficult to know whether to damn his eyes or fall about his neck, lost in admiration.

It was in his pitching and his putting that his great strength lay. But it was his putting, when he had become a much sounder golfer at the end of his career, that let him down, when he would have preferred to have gone on for at least another five years. To those who watched him all over the world his memory will never be allowed to fade.

Enid Wilson writes: Walter Hagen was one of the idols of my youth, and close on 40 years ago I had the delight and privilege of partnering him in a charity exhibition match in Scotland.

He had an uncanny and devastating facility of getting down in two from any difficulty. This was before the advent of the wedge, and when such shots had to be manufactured by the player himself. No man was more certain than Walter to hole a long putt in a crisis. He was the supreme showman of his generation, and full of wit and wisecracks. In his early days, Walter was reported as having said: "I don't want to die a millionaire, I merely want to live like one." His sartorial elegance set standards for his profession.

Walter will go down to posterity as one of the greatest competitors in the game, and to all of his generation his memory will remain evergreen.

October 7 1969

LILLIAN BOARD

LILLIAN BOARD, who died in a Munich hospital, combined a rare athletic brilliance at every event from 100 to 800 metres with beauty and a vivacious personality. She was just 22. That she had only just started to nibble at the honours she would inevitably have gained was demonstrated by the manner in which she won two European gold medals in 1969 with limited training after injury. In a three-year spell she finished fifth in the 1966 Commonwealth Games 440 yards, won the women's AAA title in 1967, the Olympic silver medal for the 400 metres in 1968, and finally the 800 metres and 4x400 metres in the European Championships in Athens.

Miss Board and her twin sister Irene were born in Durban and returned with their Manchester-born parents to live in West London in 1950. At 14½ she had already made her mark by winning the English Schools junior long jump, and her coaching was taken in hand by her father George, who dedicated his spare time to supervising her athletics, attending every training session in fair weather or foul.

When she was only 17½ the dividends from the endless hours of hard work and perseverance paid off. She was selected to run in the Commonwealth Games in Jamaica and did better than expected. The following year she defeated Judy Pollock, the world record holder, in Los Angeles during the United States v Commonwealth match in 52.8 sec, a second faster than she had run before.

After a brilliant season in 1968 she went to Mexico as favourite for the Olympic 400 metres and confirmed the rating with two good preliminary runs. In the final, however, after a nervous start and a too-fast first half she was pipped by the French girl Colette Besson by a mere 7/100ths of a second. She gained ample revenge in Athens with an enthralling last leg in the 4x400 metres. This was possibly her greatest run, for by then she was an 800 metres specialist and had scarcely prepared for the 400 metres. Even though she had won the 800 metres with a surprising facility she was by no means at her fittest as a result of a combination of a persistent back strain and an early-season dental operation.

Despite her youth she did not allow the fame, acclaim, and awards that came her way to turn her head. She was voted Athlete of the Year in 1967 and 1969, Sportswoman of the Year in 1968 and was made an MBE in 1970 when she was also voted *Daily Express* Sportswoman of the Year. In an effort to retain a vestige of her private life her telephone number was changed and made ex-directory. Yet she was unhesitatingly courteous to callers, even when often it must have been inconvenient.

During the early part of the 1970 summer it was obvious things were not quite right for she was in pain whenever she trained. By mid-June her ability to complete the season was in doubt. She ran her last race on June 20, finishing third in the 800 metres at the women's championships. On June 29 she said she would have to withdraw from England's Commonwealth Games team. Shortly afterwards she entered hospital, which she left on October 23. Her desperate last hope flight to Munich came on November 7.

Her loss is a more than usually tragic one. She had started to show flair as a dress designer and her future seemed assured. As charming off the track as she was single-minded in the pursuit of victory on it, she never let us forget that she loved to be considered part of the swinging Seventies, mini-skirts and all – not just an athletic freak. The sporting world will mourn her.

December 28 1970

SONNY LISTON

CHARLES "SONNY" LISTON, who died in Las Vegas, aged 38, was one of the most remarkable heavyweight champions boxing has known. In his career he was labelled great and unbeatable, and also coward and faker. Remarkable, too, in that he emerged from poverty and illiteracy, deprivation and imprisonment to earn riches and respect from winning the richest prize in sport.

A son of an impoverished Arkansas cotton picker, he was always a refugee from his past, and he never quite escaped it. That is why now some could argue that his two inglorious defeats by Cassius Clay present him not as a fraud or coward or a fighter who took a "dive", as a victim of a background of early hardship, brushes with the law, robbery and violence. It is inarguable that Liston will be remembered more for his fiascos with Clay than anything else. Yet his record is outstanding, his reputation at his peak was as high as any previous champion.

Liston was taught to box by the Chaplain of Missouri State Penitentiary. He turned professional in September 1953 and ran up a sequence of wins that stands comparison to Marciano's early record. Only eight of 34 opponents had lasted the distance with him when he was matched against Floyd Patterson for the world title in 1962. The bear-like, 6ft 1in Liston overwhelmed Patterson inside a round. He repeated the dose a year later, and now a dollar millionaire he stood like a colossus over world boxing. Unbeatable and seemingly impervious to pain, he earnt the title of the most fearsome and feared heavyweight of all time.

Shame and indignity, though, were just round the corner. Seven months after beating Patterson again he was matched with the unbeaten youngster from Kentucky. Liston was 1–7 when he climbed into the ring in Miami Beach for what everyone thought would be the slaughter of an innocent named Clay. Six rounds later he sat dejectedly defeated in his corner, claiming an injured shoulder. The return at Lewiston, Maine, saw Liston beaten in a round to evoke angry cries of "fake".

For over a year, with controversy and argument raging, Liston stayed away from boxing. He came back to win 14 straight victories before Leotis Martin ended his career, finally, with a knockout in 1970. So Liston, believed to be 38, but who many thought much older, had reached the end of the road. His death not only closed a book of controversy, it inevitably left unanswered many questions about one of boxing's strangest heavy-weight champions.

January 7 1971

BOBBY JONES

BOBBY JONES, who died in Atlanta, Georgia, at the age of 69, was an infant prodigy who became a colossus in maturity. Yet he never sacrificed modesty or courtesy to the demands of fame, and wore his many honours with dignity and gentility.

Every generation of golfers has provided its great men, and it is often reasonable to hail some outstanding player as the finest of his time. That distinction, of course, belonged to Jones; but in his case one could go further and suggest that he was the greatest golfer the world has seen. The facts are in the record book. In eight seasons from 1923 he won 13 national titles on both sides of the Atlantic, culminating in his *annus mirabilis*, 1930, when he won in succession the Amateur and Open championships in Britain and the Open and Amateur titles of the United States. This had been picturesquely described as "the impregnable quadrilateral", and surely, in these highly competitive days, it is safe for all time from emulation.

Robert Tyre Jones, Jnr, born in Atlanta, Georgia, on March 17, 1902, became not merely a winner of championships but also the exponent of a style superior in quality, artistry and durability to that of his most stylish contemporaries. Every movement he made was easy, graceful and rhythmical. He was almost the greatest exponent of the short game. And, above all, his approach to all that he did on the golf course was uncomplicated and natural.

All this, of course, was in accord with his character. Bobby was a gentleman, and so conscientious about his golf, as indeed about everything else, that playing in championships imposed on him severe mental and physical strain. He would lose many pounds in weight in a week's hard golf; and when, in 1930 at the age of 28, he decided to give up championship golf, his decision was that of a man who knew exactly how he stood. His mind opened and shut freely like the breech of a gun. Championship golf at any lower level was beyond his comprehension.

For seven years after he astonished the American golf world by reaching the last eight of the United States Amateur Championship at the age of 14, Bobby wore the mantle of an infant prodigy without quite fulfilling his great promise. However, all that time, during a succession of near misses, which for any lesser golfer would have ranked as triumphs, he was perfecting his competitive technique and, most of all, conditioning a youthful turbulence of temperament to the introspective calmness essential to greatness.

It was during this period that he made his first visit to Britain, in 1921, with almost disastrous results. He played without distinction in the Amateur Championship at Hoylake, then paid his first visit to St Andrews and tore up his card in the third round of the Open after taking 46 to the turn. Two years later came the breakthrough. He won the United States Open after a play-off with Bobby Cruickshank, and was to win that title thrice more. He tied twice and lost the play-off and finished second on two other occasions. In 1924 he won the first of five United States Amateur championships.

Two years later he came to Britain again and won the Open at Lytham after playing the famous bunker shot at the 17th which is marked by a tablet at the spot. In 1927 he successfully defended the title at St Andrews, and, in great contrast to his first experience there six years earlier, beat the field and the championship record aggregate by six strokes. Then came the grand slam in 1930, and retirement. But only retirement from the championship arena. His interest in golf never faded.

In his student days Jones had gained first-class honours at three different universities in law, English literature and mechanical engineering, and eventually he passed top in his law finals.

He settled down to his attorney's practice in Atlanta, and conceived and helped to develop the idea of the great Augusta National Links. During the Second World War, Jones served as an officer with the Army in Europe. In 1948 he competed in the Masters for the last time. Soon afterwards he was stricken by the illness which made him physically inactive but could not quench his spirit, dull his intellect, nor dim his interest in golf and golfers.

In 1958, when acting as captain of the United States team in the Eisenhower Trophy at St Andrews, he was made a freeman of that city. Some who attended that impressive and emotional ceremony, and who had seen this splendid golfer at the height of his fame and power, admired the brave smile with which he drove his electric buggy down the aisle of the hall, with the Provost of St Andrews as his passenger. The applause marked the homage not only of St Andrews, but also of the whole golfing world. For Bobby Jones will be remembered wherever the game is played as not only a great golfer, but also a great gentleman and a great sportsman.

December 20 1971

SIR FRANCIS CHICHESTER

SIR FRANCIS CHICHESTER, who died aged 70, crowned a unique career as navigator *extraordinaire* by his lone voyage round the world in *Gipsy Moth IV*, which began on August 27, 1966. Arriving at Sydney, Australia, on December 12, after a 13,750-mile voyage from Plymouth, he contemplated the journey home through some of the worst seas in the world around Cape Horn.

"I am not as confident as I could be," he said. "I would be tempting the gods if I asked to lay odds on my chances of survival." But survive he did, to receive a hero's welcome at Plymouth. The Queen had sent him a *bon voyage* message, and, with Prince Philip, another to welcome him home.

Sir Francis had a running battle against cancer during the latter part of his life. In 1957 he survived the verdict of doctors who had given him only three weeks to live. Five of them confirmed that he had cancer of the lung, and one believed it was too late to operate. There would have been an operation had his wife, Sheila, not refused permission. She believed that in his condition at the time an operation would kill him. With intense faith in the power of prayer, she willed him to live. And after her prayers for his recovery Sir Francis survived to go on to his greatest fame as a world sailor.

Illness, though, eventually forced him to turn back

from his last voyage, in the year of his death. He recalled, from his hospital bed, that after returning from his round-the-world trip in 1967, it was discovered that he had a malignant growth near the base of the spine. The tumour spread to the spine, and later to other bones. He fought the disease with the help of treatment. As the bones became increasingly affected, they became more painful, and pain from hitting the side of his bunk when the yacht rolled ended his voyage. He had realised that, under the influence of the pain-killing drugs he had to take, his mind was no longer functioning normally.

The voyage round the Horn was a perilous adventure. "You have no conception of what goes on in those Southern waters," said Chichester. "You only survive down there with good luck." He arrived at Plymouth on May 28, 1967, 119 days out from Sydney. He had been away for nine months and a day, and almost the whole of that time, for 28,500 miles, alone in his boat. South of the equator the heat was so intense that he poured buckets of water over himself every hour or two, and on the cockpit floor to prevent burning his feet.

On January 27, 1967, he was appointed a Knight Commander of the Order of the British Empire "in recognition of his individual achievements and sustained endeavour in the navigation and seamanship of small craft". In the following July Sir Francis, who had sailed on from Plymouth after an illness, knelt before the Queen to receive the accolade in the grounds of the Royal Naval College, Greenwich. At Tower Bridge he was greeted by the Lord Mayor and driven in an open car through crowded City streets to lunch at the Mansion House.

In 1960 Sir Francis evoked world admiration by his single-handed crossing of the Atlantic in a 13-ton yacht.

Equally remarkable were his flying adventures 30 years earlier, which included the first solo flight across the dangerous Tasman Sea from New Zealand to Australia. Modest in achievement, blessed with a great sense of humour, and completely fearless, he developed such remarkable gifts as a navigator that the methods he evolved were adopted as the basis of training in Coastal Command during the 1939–45 War.

Born in North Devon, the son of the Revd Charles Chichester, he was educated at Marlborough. When he was 19 he emigrated to New Zealand, where he built up a successful land agent business. In 1929 he returned to England, learnt to fly at Brooklands, and promptly set off for Australia in a Gipsy Moth. This was a daring under-taking at the time, and he had some exciting experiences.

A few months later he became the first man to fly the Tasman Sea, doing so in three hops over a course of 1,400 miles. For this purpose his machine was converted into a seaplane so that he could descend for refuelling on two tiny specks in the Pacific, Norfolk and Lord Howe islands. His only aids were a sextant and a pocket compass.

By supreme navigational skill he found the first island and with similar exactitude reached the second. Disaster followed. A fierce gale blew up at Lord Howe Island and his Gipsy Moth, torn from its moorings, overturned and sank to the bottom of a lagoon. Though lacking any knowledge of aircraft construction he rebuilt the machine so skilfully that he was able to fly the remaining 500 miles to Australia.

A little later he flew to Japan, but in attempting to alight in a small harbour crashed into a maze of telephone wires and, though injured, escaped death. It was five years before he started flying again. He flew from Sydney to England, via Peking, and established himself in London as a map publisher.

When the 1939–45 War broke out the Air Ministry took eager advantage, for instructional purposes, of the authoritative knowhow he had employed on long-distance flights. As Chief Navigational Officer at the Empire Central Flying School his methods were particularly valuable.

After the War he took up yacht racing, but in 1958 his health caused such concern that he was told he had not much longer to live. Two years later, fully recovered, he helped to organise an extremely hazardous solo race across the Atlantic. At 58 he was the oldest competitor. Single-handed, he set off in his 40ft *Gipsy Moth III*, which normally required a racing crew of six. A succession of heavy gales constantly threatened disaster and he had to sail under bare poles for a total of 48 hours.

He fought his way against headwinds and groped through fog with constant danger from icebergs. In the midst of all this, soaked to the skin because he was unable to dry his clothing in a boat which more often than not was plunging wildly in terrific storms, he methodically kept a diary that ran to 50,000 words. This was the first yacht race across the Atlantic from East to West, and he won it by a handsome margin in 40½ days.

The name *Gipsy Moth* seemed to fascinate Chichester. With it he linked his aerial exploits with his many challenges to the sea. *Gipsy Moth I* was a De Havilland biplane, *Gipsy Moth III* a 40ft yacht, but *Gipsy Moth IV* was the giant of them all – an enormous yacht for single-handed sailing – 53ft in length.

In her the intrepid adventurer, within three weeks of

his 65th birthday, set out from Plymouth to sail along the route once taken by the *Cutty Sark* and the other tea clippers. To guard against what he declared was a real danger on such a voyage – scurvy – he grew wheat in his bathroom and ate the green wheat shoots at sea. When he entered Sydney Harbour the voyage had taken 107 days. Among the honours Sir Francis received were the Freedom of Barnstaple and election as an honorary member of the Bench of the Middle Temple.

In May 1971, Sir Francis returned to Plymouth from an attempt to sail 4,000 miles in 20 days across the South Atlantic. He failed by two days, though he set pretty tall targets for others to aim at.

After battling for 13 days with bad weather and ill-health in the *Observer* Transatlantic Single-handed Race in 1972, Sir Francis returned to Plymouth on July 3 in *Gipsy Moth V* and went to hospital, where doctors told him he must have a complete rest. Anxiety had been felt for him following days of radio silence after he started in the race against doctors' advice.

Sir Francis was appointed CBE in 1964. His life story is told in his autobiography *The Lonely Sea and the Sky* which was published in 1964. His books also included *Gipsy Moth Circles the World* and *The Romantic Challenge.* Once asked: "Why do you want to do it?" he replied: "Because of the excitement and the satisfaction that comes with a sense of achievement." His first wife died in 1929, and a son also died. In 1937 he married Sheila Mary Craven and had a son.

August 28 1972

PAAVO NURMI

PAAVO NURMI, the "Flying Finn", who died at the age of 76, could lay powerful claims to be the greatest runner of all time. He revolutionised training methods, breaking 28 world records in 10 years from distances of one mile up to 20 kilometres. He also set innumerable indoor records, some of which stood until as late as 1963, so far ahead was he of his time.

Of his many outstanding athletics achievements the greatest without any doubt came in 1924 when he won four gold medals in the Paris Olympics in the 1,500 metres, 3,000 metres team, 5,000 metres and cross-country events. During his career, which started before the end of the 1914–18 War and ended in 1935, he won seven Olympic gold medals and would certainly have added to the total in 1932 had he not been barred on the eve of competition for allegedly taking excessive expenses during a trip to Germany. He ran in Finland for another three years as a "national amateur", since Finland found him not guilty of the charges.

Athletics ruled Nurmi's life. From his early teens he undertook a Spartan regimen, dedicating himself to a life of fitness; he became vegetarian, did not smoke, drink, take tea or coffee and, whenever he had spare time from his 30 miles a day training, walked and walked. Around 1920 he began his famous "stop-watch training". He realised the necessity for level-pace running, setting a fast enough tempo to kill off the opposition from the start, and would train carrying a watch. He continued the habit into competition. Shy and retiring, Nurmi refused constantly to give interviews, both during and after his athletics career. In 1967 he broke his rule for the first time. He followed athletics with interest but would watch only from seats where he thought he would not be recognised. In 1952 he was persuaded to light the Olympic Flame, marking the opening of the 15th Games in his home city of Helsinki.

October 2 1973

SIR NEVILLE CARDUS

SIR NEVILLE CARDUS, who died aged 85, was a critic and essayist of music and cricket. It can be said of him that he raised sports reporting in his chosen field to the status of an art form. His best descriptions of cricket and cricketers rank among the most distinguished examples of the English essay. His flair for the telling phrase which caught the fleeting moment and gave it permanence never deserted him. Though his detractors have said that he sometimes dealt in fantasy rather than fact (a charge he did not wholly deny), he was a great journalist, and the facts and figures were there.

He was born in the Manchester suburb of Rusholme (in a street appropriately, though courageously, named Summer Place), the son of a violinist and a Lancashire woman who took in washing which Neville delivered in a push-cart. He learnt his cricket in the streets, his literature in the Free Library and his music at the Halle concerts of Richter's day. A voracious reader, he was truly self-educated.

He delivered newspapers, sold chocolates in Miss

Horniman's Gaiety Theatre and, at 15, became a clerk in a Manchester marine insurance office. At 23, in May 1912, he became assistant cricket coach at Shrewsbury School and also secretary to the Headmaster, the Revd C. A. Alington. When Dr Alington went as Headmaster to Eton, Cardus returned to Manchester, worked for the *Daily Citizen* as music critic, became agent for a burial society and then, in 1916, worked as secretary to C. P. Scott, editor of the *Manchester Guardian*. In April 1917 Scott transferred him to the reporting staff.

Cardus had a physical breakdown in 1919. When he returned to work, W. P. Crozier suggested that he could recuperate by going to Old Trafford to watch cricket, sending in a report if he liked. So, by chance, came fame. For the next 20 years, under the pseudonym "Cricketer" he wrote about cricket for his newspaper, not hesitating to compare cricketers with Dickensian characters, to use musical metaphors and to match the game's poetry with his own prose-poetry. His style was inimitable, though it has not lacked imitators.

He was fortunate in that his ascendancy coincided with Lancashire's greatest period. The cricketers whose prowess he described were his friends off the field and his mind was richly stored with anecdotes about them. They live beyond their short playing span in the pages of his books *Days in the Sun*, *The Summer Game*, *Good Days*, *Australian Summer* and others.

Yet it was music which Cardus loved more than the summer game. He understudied Samuel Langford in Manchester until Langford's death in May 1927, when the initials "N. C." soon became as familiar as those of "S.L."

Cardus gloried in the gibe which his friend Ernest

Newman once flung at him, that he was a "sensitised plate" critic. He was frankly a romantic at heart, believing in the emotional rather than the intellectual responses to music.

The composers he loved most – Wagner, Strauss, Elgar, Bruckner, Schubert, Delius and, above all, Mahler, for whose works he was a pioneering champion in Britain – bear this out.

From 1939 to 1948 Cardus worked in Australia where he wrote on music for the *Sydney Morning Herald*. Returning to Britain, for a time he severed his connection with the *Guardian*, but returned to it until the end of his life, though he contributed freely to many other papers and periodicals. He was made CBE in 1964 and, in his 76th year, published the first volume of his study of Mahler's symphonies. His frank and amusing *Autobiography* first appeared in 1947.

In April 1966, on completion of 50 years in journalism, he was paid the tribute – for a music critic remarkable, if not unique – of concerts given in his honour in Manchester and London by the Halle. Naturally, they played a Mahler symphony. In 1967 he was knighted for services to cricket and music.

As can be imagined from his writings, Sir Neville was a brilliant raconteur and wit. Above all, he enjoyed life and people. Never mind if the conversation sometimes became a monologue, it was usually worth hearing.

He was married in 1921 to Edith Honorine King, who died in 1968. They had no children.

March 1 1975

GRAHAM HILL

GRAHAM HILL, known to millions throughout the world as a world champion racing driver, used his fame to help the less fortunate. After giving up competitive driving he devoted much time and effort to causes like the Disabled Drivers' Association and the Springfield Boys' Club in the East End. His record on the circuit will probably never be surpassed: twice world champion, in 1962 with BRM and in 1968 with Lotus, winner of the Indianapolis 500 and Le Mans and participant in 176 Grands Prix, including five victories at Monaco.

To survive appalling race crashes and die on a routine flight returning from a testing session in the South of France with members of his Embassy Hill Formula 1 team is a tragic irony. The motor-racing world had heaved a sigh of relief in July 1974 when Hill, married with three children, formally announced his retirement just before the British Grand Prix and decided to stick to team management. As Jackie Stewart said: "He had retired from motor racing to be safe, grow old and be with us for the rest of his life." Hill's death away from the track which claimed so many of his fellows parallels that other great English world champion, Mike Hawthorn, who retired only to die in a road accident on the Guildford bypass in 1959.

Not a natural driver like his friend Jim Clark, who was killed in a racing crash in 1968, Graham Hill epitomised grit and determination. This was never more evident than his fightback from a terrible crash in the 1969 American Grand Prix when both legs were shattered. Confined to a wheelchair for months – some thought for ever – Hill willed himself back to the cockpit. Asked about his greatest achievement Hill described it as "coming sixth in the South African GP after my accident".

Even an iron will cannot completely heal severed nerves and sinews, however. Hill walked with a limp, and was often in pain, but would never admit to it. His many friends urged him to retire after he had proved he could drive again. The spectacle of a world champion no longer able to be ultra-competitive seemed inappropriate. Though destined never to win another Grand Prix after his 1969 accident, Hill answered his critics by winning the 1971 International Trophy Formula 1 race at Silverstone, and crowned a great career with victory in the 1972 Le Mans 24-hour endurance classic.

As he said in his autobiography *Life at the Limit*, Hill did not know what he wanted to do with his life even at the age of 24, when he had just bought his first car, a 1934 Morris 8. As a young man rowing was his sport. He stroked the 1953 London Rowing Club eight in the Grand Challenge Cup at Henley and afterwards wore their blue and white colours on his racing helmets. Rowing gave him a physique which was to stand him in good stead for the rigours of motor racing. One pounds-worth (four laps) of Brands Hatch in a 500cc Formula 3 car in answer to an advertisement was enough to decide Hill. He was bitten by the motor-racing bug there and then. Having given up his job at Smiths Industries, he was on the dole and later worked as a mechanic to get into motor racing.

He won his first World Championship with BRM in 1962 and was runner-up in 1964 and 1965. Then he won Indianapolis in 1966 and bought a twin-engined aircraft with the winnings. The following year he joined Jim Clark in the Lotus team and in 1968 held the team together – severely shaken by Clark's death – and went on to win the World Championship.

The fact that he had been able to fight his way out of a wheelchair left him with very real compassion for those condemned to immobility for life. He became an ardent campaigner for better transport for the disabled, describing the official-issue invalid tricycle as "the worst thing I have ever driven". At a test session in 1973 for *The Daily Telegraph Magazine*, he likened the tricycle to a "motorised bathtub". He took part in deputations to Downing Street, calling attention to the invalid tricycle's defects with the help and support of the Earl of Snowdon. As well as giving his time Hill paid some of the bills for the Disabled Drivers' Action Group and gave £500 to launch the Invalid Tricycle Action Group.

Whatever cause Graham Hill took up received his full attention and energies. President of the Springfield Boys' Club in Upper Clapton, he was no figurehead. Despite a hectically busy life Hill still found time to attend management committee meetings at the club. Since running the Embassy racing team left him with even less spare time, Graham and Bette Hill had boys from the club to camp at their country home in Hertfordshire.

With the death of Hill's promising young driver Tony Brise, tipped as a future world champion, designer Andy Smallman, team manager Ray Brimble and two mechanics, the Embassy Hill Formula 1 team was wiped out.

December 1 1975

HAROLD ABRAHAMS

HAROLD ABRAHAMS, who died aged 78, was one of Britain's foremost athletes in the 1920s and was the first British runner to win a gold medal for the 100 metres with his victory in Paris in 1924. He took part in the 1920 and 1924 Olympics and was captain of the 1928 British Olympic team.

His association with athletics was life-long, for when a long-jump fall which broke his left leg ended his own athletics career, he became a noted sporting journalist and radio commentator. Indeed he broadcast the first running commentary in 1926 – they had not been allowed before. He was athletics correspondent of the *Sunday Times* from 1925 to 1967 and an athletics administrator for more than 50 years. In 1976 he became President of the Amateur Athletic Association and the British Amateur Athletic Board, having served in various offices since 1926. From 1950 to 1963 he was secretary of the National Parks Commission.

As one of the most likeable personalities in sport he had a great following during his athletics career. From Repton he went up to Gonville and Caius College, Cambridge, and represented Cambridge against Oxford in 1920, 1921, 1922 and 1923, on the last occasion winning three events, the 100 yards, 440 yards and long jump.

Called to the Bar in 1924, he worked at the Ministry of Economic Warfare during the 1939–45 War, and in 1946 became an assistant secretary at the Ministry of Town and Country Planning. His elder brothers, Sir

Adolph Abrahams, the physician, and Sir Sidney Abrahams, former Chief Justice of Tanganyika, were both active in sport before him. Sir Sidney, a long-jump champion, represented Britain in the 1908 and 1912 Olympics when Sir Adolph was medical officer to the Olympic team.

Harold Abrahams married Miss Sybil Evers, the light opera singer, in 1936. She died in 1963. At 75 he was still an exceptionally fit man, despite a permanent limp from his long-jump mishap. His advice for staying fit was "get rid of your car and walk – and take an hour's nap after lunch".

James Coote writes: Harold Abrahams distinguished himself in diverse fields, dominating the sprints and long jump in four years at Cambridge. In the 1920 Olympics he represented Britain in the 100 and 200 yards, 4x100 relay and long jump but with middling success.

Four years later he was selected for the same four events, but in the interim had applied himself to training using a scientific approach that an athlete of the 1970s would not be ashamed of. He showed excellent form a month before leaving for the 1924 Games in Paris by setting a British long-jump record which stood for 33 years.

He did not tackle the long jump at Paris, where he started by equalling the Olympic record of 10.6 seconds in the second round and repeated this in the semi-final despite a poor start, defeating the reigning champion and world record holder, Charley Paddock. He won the final by a yard, again in 10.6 seconds and went on to add a silver medal to his laurels in the relay. He was awarded a CBE in 1957 for his services to the National Parks Commission.

January 16 1978

JOE DAVIS

JOE DAVIS, the man whose name was synonymous with snooker for 50 years, died aged 77 at a Hampshire nursing home. Born at Whitwell, a village near Chesterfield, he took up billiards after watching customers play at his father's hotel. By the time he was 12, he had compiled his first 100 break.

In the mid-1920s, when already established as an outstanding billiards player – he was world champion four times – he was the first to foresee snooker's possibilities. Though the game was invented in 1875, it was still being played as a lighthearted fill-in by the professionals. Davis soon realised that it was a crowd-pleaser and, in 1927, persuaded the then governing body, the Billiards Association, to sanction the first world professional snooker championship. Acting as promoter and organiser as well as competitor, Davis took the title and cash prize of £6 10s.0d (£6.50). He held the championship, unbeaten, for 20 years.

During those two decades, the game increased in popularity to the extent that, after the 1939–45 War, it had overtaken billiards. The top players had made billiards too easy-looking and repetitive, and the public turned to snooker. Davis himself constantly worked on his own game and developed the techniques now taken for granted in modern break-building and positional play.

His mastery of the delicate stun shot, and ability to think many moves ahead in the manner of a chess master, were unequalled.

His first 100 snooker break came in 1928, his 100th in 1939, his 500th in 1953, and his skill was often employed for charity, for which he raised nearly £1 million. Many of his major triumphs were scored with a cue he bought for 7s. 6d (37 pence) at a church institute in 1931. He offered £50 for its return when it was lost in 1948 – and got it back.

He retired from championship play in 1947, having won the snooker championship on all 15 occasions it had been held. He was the only player to hold both this and the world professional billiards championship simultaneously. Still playing competitive snooker, usually giving away large handicaps and still winning, he had to wait until 1955 to achieve the snooker player's "Everest", the first snooker maximum break of 147 (15 reds, 15 blacks and all the colours), in public under championship match conditions.

Davis, who was made a member of the Order of the British Empire in 1963, retired completely in 1964, but remained very much in evidence at major tournaments. At the world professional snooker championship in April 1978 Joe Davis collapsed after watching his younger brother, Fred, playing in the semi-finals. Two days later he survived a six-hour heart operation and was convalescing when he developed a chest infection. He is survived by his wife, June.

July 11 1978

FRANK WOOLLEY

FRANK EDWARD WOOLLEY, who died aged 91, at Halifax, Nova Scotia, was one of the great cricketers of history and, in particular, the pride of Kent. He was as graceful a batsman as ever played. The beauty of his play was in spite of a quite apparent stiffness of limb and gait. As with Denis Compton, one tends not to notice a certain awkwardness of movement in the joyous contemplation of the stroke. Familiarity and affection breed a blindness to such a detail.

However, if Woolley, coldly analysed, was hardly a graceful figure, he was a supremely rhythmic, stylish, debonair striker of a cricket ball. Charm is a difficult virtue to dissect. The late R. C. Robertson-Glasgow began his *Print of Frank Woolley*, in that delightful series of his, by saying that "he was easy to watch, difficult to bowl to, and impossible to write about".

The key to his play, as with all the very greatest, was an extraordinary refinement of timing, and that, again, seemed to derive from the severe simplicity and correctness of his method. Here was this extremely tall, slim figure, swinging his bat in the fullest and truest pendulum through the line of the ball. There were no kinks or ornamentations – no one surely was so free from mannerism? Here comes the ball, there goes the foot, down she comes and through. Naturally enough, Woolley was a glorious driver, while to the slower straight one he played a perpendicular back stroke with a power which could be generated from the easiest, laziest swing.

But of the more delicate strokes, he was equally the

master, and here was to be seen his amazing keenness of eye. He was a glorious cutter, and no one turned the ball more finely and prettily off his legs. Such is a brief technical appraisal of his batsmanship, but what endeared him to the ringside, and at the same time made him so devastating an opponent, was his whole approach to batsmanship.

The modest, self-effacing companion of the dressing-room quickly became an utterly disdainful, aloof antagonist at the wicket. Mr Robertson-Glasgow, in his article, went on to say that Frank Woolley was never known to express a particular liking or distaste for any bowler. He seemed superbly indifferent to who was bowling, or how they were bowling. The bowler, you might say, was an anonymous privileged contributor to his art. He sometimes got out, I believe [writes E. W. Swanton], because he had refused to recognise a particular trap set for him. He certainly paid the penalty, now and then, for taking to himself a bowler whom a comrade did not relish, seeking to knock him off. The thing he never seemed to contemplate, let alone fear, was getting out himself. He was the antithesis of the calculating, bread-and-butter run collector. He played the ball on its merits, and he played for his side.

In the nineties he batted precisely as he would bat after the century was reached — which perhaps is why he was comparatively often got out just those few runs short of what to most cricketers is the important goal. Perhaps the more astute of his opponents tempted him to risks at this time.

He was a Kentish cricketer of the county's golden age. In his first year, as a lad of 17 in 1906, he played with K. L. Hutchings, J. R. Mason, C. J. Burnup and

R. N. R. Blaker in the team who first brought the championship to Kent. "We were never allowed to play for averages in the Kent side," he wrote in *Wisden* on his retirement, and went on to say that it was the policy that the pitch *must* be occupied all day after winning the toss. Such was his early environment, the influence of which so firmly shaped his attitude throughout his cricket life.

I trust to have given a faint picture of Woolley as a batsman to those who never watched him play. Those who saw him even in the closing years of his life on the Kentish grounds, white-haired but spare and upright, looking like a retired bishop, will not easily forget his natural dignity and handsome appearance. As to his bowling, I have not attempted a description, for his serious efforts ended in the early Twenties, and I have only the memory of an occasional over, of the easy slanting run, left hand behind the back, and the poise of the high action.

But it is as well to remind the young that before the 1914–18 War he was not only the best all-rounder in England, but very nearly the best slow left-arm bowler; likewise, too, and right up until middle age, one of the finest slip fieldsmen. He took 1,017 catches, more than any man. He cared little for figures, yet only Hobbs narrowly bettered his aggregate of 58,969 runs (including 145 centuries). Only 25 bowlers have taken more than his 2,068 wickets.

The innings one has seen from his come readily to mind in swift kaleidoscope: two brief but perfect gems at Lord's, both, oddly enough, scoring 41 runs, one against Australia in the second Test of Bradman's first tour, the other his farewell in Gentlemen and Players at the age of 51; several prolonged and severe chastisements of the Champion County bowlers at the Oval – he averaged a hundred in this annual fixture; a lovely piece of play that enriched a cold Trial Match at Old Trafford; and, for Kent, a century before lunch against Nottinghamshire at Canterbury after rain, on a nasty, flying pitch.

Alas! That one knows so many of the greatest only at second hand, the classic 95 and 93 at Lord's against Armstrong's Australians, in his own view the best innings he played. He was quite active into his late 80s, and in January 1971 flew to Australia to watch the last two Tests. Nine months later, in Canada, he married for the second time, his first wife having died 10 years earlier. His second bride was Mrs Martha Morse, an American widow.

October 19 1978

GENE TUNNEY

GENE TUNNEY, former world heavyweight champion, died, aged 80, in hospital in Greenwich, Connecticut. His son John, a former senator from California, said that the cause of death was blood poisoning. Tunney won two of the most famous fights in history – his battles with Jack Dempsey in 1926 and 1927. Tunney retired as first undefeated champion after another fight, in 1928. He knocked out Tom Heeney in New York and retired with 56 wins. He later said: "I knew if I were knocked out, I'd be licked by the game. I wanted to quit before being victimised by it."

Dempsey had been world champion for seven years at

their first meeting and Tunney, former American light-heavyweight champion who had only moved into the heavyweight class in 1925, was given no chance against the "Manassa Mauler", still reckoned the hardest-ever puncher. But Tunney's logical ringcraft outsmarted the champion and he won on points over 10 rounds. The match was fought in Philadelphia in a blinding rainstorm and the crowd of 120,000 were drenched. For the Chicago return fight Thomas Cook laid on the first air tour, flying patrons from New York to Chicago and back, with ringside seats and an overnight hotel, for £125. The £1,350,000 receipts paid by 104,943 were a record until the Spinks–Ali fight in September 1978.

It was also the fight of the famous "long count". In round seven, Dempsey floored Tunney with a series of blows but, sensing victory and desperately eager to reclaim the title, stood over Tunney and failed to go to a neutral corner as the rules stipulated. The referee did not count for five seconds, until Dempsey had complied with the rule and Tunney, who rose on the count of nine, was on the canvas for 14 seconds. He won on points.

The merits of the "long count" are still debated, but it was another example of Tunney's calculating approach. Later he maintained that Dempsey was the greatest fighter in history. Of the "long count" dispute, Tunney used to say: "I know I was the beneficiary but it wasn't my idea. I first heard the count at two and I could have got up any time after that, but I preferred to take the benefit of the full count." He maintained that this was the only round Dempsey won. "Everybody forgets that I knocked him down with the first punch in the next round," he said. For this fight he was paid $990,000 (£198,000) and he paid the promoter $10,000 to receive a $1 million cheque. He earnt £105,000 from his fight with Tom Henney before retiring.

Three months later, in October, 1928, he married Polly Lauder, a £10 million heiress to the Carnegie steel fortune. He became a socialite, meeting the Prince of Wales and Shaw in London and giving his views on Shakespeare at interviews and lectures. During the 1939–45 War he was American director of physical training, with lieutenant commander rank. He had three sons – a judge, an oil magnate and a Californian senator. In 1970 his daughter, Mrs Joan Wilkinson, was ordered to be detained in Broadmoor after pleading guilty with diminished responsibility to killing her husband.

Tunney became director of a bank, coalmine, paper firm and two insurance companies. It was a long haul from his boyhood ambition to become a Catholic priest. His father, a New York docker, gave him boxing gloves when he was 10, and his first work was as a shipping office typist. After serving with the marines in the 1914–18 War – he was the regimental boxing champion – he tried the ring. He had 70 professional fights and lost one – in 1922 to the American light-heavyweight champion, Harry Greb, whom he beat in a return match.

Despite his rank as an immortal, Tunney was unpopular for many years among the boxing fraternity. It was felt that he had quit early and had grown socially ashamed of his trade. For many years he turned his back on the ring, but for his last 20 years he was a regular attender at heavyweight championship fights and loved to talk of his days as a boxer.

November 9 1978

MIKE HAILWOOD

MIKE HAILWOOD, 40, who died from injuries received in a car accident in which his daughter was also killed, was universally regarded as the finest and most popular exponent of the art of motorcycle racing. Hailwood had been fighting for his life at Birmingham's accident hospital since suffering severe head injuries in the crash. His nine-year-old daughter, Michelle, was killed and his son David was slightly hurt. Hailwood, who was fetching fish and chips, collided with the back of a lorry on the A435 at Portway, near the Warwickshire–Worcestershire border, only two miles from his home at Tanworth-in-Arden, Warwickshire.

In a career spanning some 21 years and at a time when competition was at its toughest, Hailwood, known as "Mike the Bike", won nine world championships and a record 14 Tourist Trophy races over the notorious mountain course on the Isle of Man. His world championship tally would have no doubt been much higher, but for the decision at the height of his motorcycle racing career to switch to car racing.

It was said that Stanley Michael Hailwood was born to race motorcycles. Certainly with a millionaire father he had no need to enter such a demanding and dangerous sport. However, even as a youngster at Pangbourne Nautical College, he declared his intentions of becoming a motorcycle and racing car driver and from the day he made his debut at a 17-year-old at Oulton Park on Easter Sunday 1957, it was evident that Hailwood had followed his right instincts. Less than two months later, he won his first race, a 125cc event, and from that point his flair and rapidly developing natural talents took him to Grand Prix championship successes. He won the 250cc World Championship in 1961 and was double 250 and 350cc champion in 1966 and 1967. In between, he won the supreme title, the 500cc championship, four times in succession.

Hailwood achieved the rare distinction for a motor-cyclist of becoming a household name worldwide. But success and fame never rested easily on his shoulders. An extremely modest, even shy man, he was continually embarrassed by praise and tended to reply to compliments with a quip which was often misunderstood for aloofness.

Having won nearly all there was to be won, Hailwood retired from full-time two-wheel racing in 1968 and turned to cars, and though he became a competitive Formula 1 driver he never achieved the success he sought. A 100mph crash brought his car career to an end at the Nurburgring in 1974, two years after he had been awarded the George Medal for bravery in pulling fellow driver Clay Regassoni from his blazing car during the South African Grand Prix. Typically he never talked about this.

His countless fans, however, had not seen the last of Hailwood. Ten years after being awarded the MBE for services to motorcycle racing he returned from New Zealand to enter the 1978 TT, just for the fun of it. Amid jubilant scenes never before witnessed on the Isle of Man he won the Formula 1 race after an 11-year absence. A year later he won the senior TT and ended an extraordinary career a few days later with a win at Mallory Park.

March 24 1981

JOE LOUIS

JOE LOUIS, who died aged 66, was probably the greatest heavyweight of all time. Many would rate him even higher than his fellow Negroes, Jack Johnson and Muhammad Ali, and above the supreme white champions, Jack Dempsey and Rocky Marciano. A master craftsman and devastating puncher, Louis won 68 of his 71 contests between July 1934 and October 1951.

Of those victories, 54 were earnt inside the distance and in no fewer than 27 of the bouts he was either defending or challenging for the world title. Two of his three defeats were suffered when he was making a comeback in the Fifties in a belated effort to reduce tax debts that had accumulated during his heyday, and which were always to pursue him. Ezzard Charles outpointed him in a championship bout in September 1950, and Rocky Marciano knocked him out in the eighth round of his last fight 13 months later.

His only other conqueror was Max Schmeling, who created one of the biggest surprises in ring history by knocking out the "Brown Bomber" in the 12th round, on June 19, 1936. Though Louis went on to win the world title by defeating James J. Braddock in the eighth round one year and three days later, he did not regard himself as a worthy champion until he had avenged that defeat by Schmeling. This he did, at the Yankee Stadium, New York, on June 22, 1938, by destroying the German in two minutes four seconds, before a crowd of 70,000, who had paid £210,000 to watch the slaughter of the man Hitler had described as "the next champion of the world".

Many years later, Louis became a close friend of Schmeling, by then a successful businessman in West Germany. He also had the warmest regard for Tommy Farr, the former British champion, who took him the full 15 rounds in his first title defence, in New York, on August 30, 1937. It was during that period that Louis was at his busiest and greatest. Having outpointed Farr, he then defended the championship 20 times before volunteering for the armed forces in March 1942, and apart from Arturo Godoy, none of those challengers lasted the distance. But for the four-year intervention of the War, Louis probably would have scaled even greater heights. As it was, he defended the title on four more occasions, then announced his retirement as undefeated champion in March 1949.

Alas, like many a boxer before him, he had failed to hold on to the fortune his fists had earnt. So he returned to the ring and, after a series of exhibition bouts, unsuccessfully challenged Charles for the title in September 1950. Still determined to regain his old place, he won a handful of contests before being mercilessly thrashed by the up-and-coming Marciano. He was then more than 37 and, though he took part in a number of exhibitions with American servicemen during the Korean War, he reluctantly accepted that this illustrious career was over.

Perhaps at times, as he made his rounds of gymnasiums and arenas, he sighed over that lost fortune. Wherever he went Joe Louis, one of the gentlest, kindliest men, was acclaimed on all sides as a great American hero. Only hours before his death, Louis had attended the WBA Championship fight between Larry Holmes and Trevor Berbick. As had been the practice at Las Vegas championship fights, Louis watched the fight from his wheelchair at the ringside after being introduced to the crowd.

He was so feted the night Muhammad Ali was humiliated by Holmes in October 1980 that it was doubtful whether he was really aware of what was going on in front of him. As Donald Saunders, *The Daily Telegraph*'s boxing correspondent, wrote at the time: "Louis travelled to the ringside in his wheelchair, staring unseeingly ahead, unheedful of the chants of 'good old Joe', his body wrecked, his mind seemingly frozen by a series of strokes." It was a sad sight indeed, for those who would prefer to remember him as the "Brown Bomber", that superb athlete who so often demonstrated that boxing can be "the noble and manly art".

April 13 1981

BILL SHANKLY

IN THE world of professional football, where the word is frequently misused, Bill Shankly was unique. There will certainly never be another quite like him. Others have his legendary passion for the game; others can lay claim to inclusion among the greatest managers. But no one was cast in the mould of Shanks, football folk hero to the core.

Shankly, who died in Broadgreen Hospital, Liverpool, at the age of 67 following a heart attack, will best be remembered as the driving force behind Liverpool. In 15 glorious years as manager at Anfield, he made them into one of the world's most famous and respected teams.

Three Football League championships, two FA Cup Final victories and one UEFA Cup remain as monuments to Shankly's magnificent work at Liverpool, where he built two great sides before his retirement in July 1974. Bob Paisley, his eager lieutenant throughout those years, subsequently steered Liverpool to even greater success, but the admiration football folk have for his predecessor goes far beyond the Merseyside boundaries.

Born in the Ayrshire mining village of Glenbuck into a family where brothers and uncles became professional footballers, Bill Shankly started as a League player with Carlisle United before making his mark with Preston in the 1930s. A tenacious, dedicated wing-half, he would have won many more than five full caps for Scotland but for the War. After RAF service, he returned to Preston for a couple of seasons in company with Tom Finney – a footballer he revered – and then turned to management with Carlisle, Grimsby Town, Workington and Huddersfield Town.

The call to Liverpool came in 1959, and Shankly, after signing men such as Ian St John and Ron Yeats, took the slumbering giant back into the First Division and on the road to 18 successive seasons in European competition. A tremendous motivator of men, Shankly filled his teams with inspiration, and helped to make players such as Kevin Keegan – recruited from lowly Scunthorpe – into some of the world's top footballers. Shankly became the idol of the Kop, developed a closer relationship with supporters than probably any other manager in history, and was awarded the OBE in 1974.

Shanks, as he was affectionately known throughout football, had a sharp, dry and sometimes abrasive wit, as many players and journalists came to know. But he was a soft, warm-hearted man. He never bore a grudge and buried many a hatchet by sharing a cup of tea, his favourite drink. Impulsive and loquacious words poured from Shankly in a crisp Scottish accent, and he gained the reputation as a showman and public relations expert, and launched a thousand quips. "Football is not just a matter of life and death – it's much more important than that," he once pointed out, a saying that could well serve as an epitaph for one of the game's most fascinating and colourful characters. He leaves a wife, Nessie, and two daughters.

September 30 1981

JOHNNY WEISSMULLER

The death of Johnny Weissmuller in Acapulco came after years of physical and mental decline especially tragic in a man who will be remembered as the epitome of healthy masculinity. The screen's legendary Tarzan had fought a losing battle with infirmity since a stroke in Los Angeles in 1977 affected his nervous system. In 1979 he was committed to a mental hospital after complaints from the Hollywood home for retired actors, where he lived, that he was upsetting the other patients by spending the nights repeating his jungle calls.

After moving to Mexico in 1979 with his German-born sixth wife, he suffered lung trouble and pneumonia. A kidney ailment forced him to give up his beloved swimming. In 1982 he secured a discharge from hospital, saying he wished "to die like a man" rather than be kept alive artificially in hospital.

He spent most of his time indoors, unable to talk after a growth was removed in an operation to insert a tube in his throat for breathing. Friends said he suffered periodic depression, including a pitiful spell when he would pace the garden trying vainly to emit the Tarzan cry. He was 79 when he died at his home.

He enjoyed two outstandingly successful careers: first as a superlative swimmer, then as the greatest Tarzan of them all. Yet he came to the role accidentally, and soon found it monotonous. He was visiting his friend Clark Gable at the Metro-Goldwyn-Mayer studios in 1932 when someone said, "They're testing for Tarzan", and he went along and got the job. He was the sixth film Tarzan and the first to talk, starting with *Tarzan, The Ape Man*, and he became more celebrated than any of the other dozen or so "lords of the jungle".

He wrestled with lions and alligators, manhandled elephants, fought cannibals and deadly spiders and frustrated tribes of apes, and even flocks of flamingos, in the rescue and defence of Jane, his mate, usually played by a flimsily dressed Maureen O'Sullivan. With a 6ft 4in frame befitting an Olympic swimmer, he swung from tree to tree and over canyons, and took rivers and lakes in his stride. He was supposed to look dumb but good, and his main conversation was "Me Tarzan, you Jane" and "Come with me to the jungle".

Edgar Rice Burroughs, who in 1914 created Tarzan, the lost boy brought up by apes in the African jungle, pronounced it "Tar-zan" with the first syllable accented, originally made his hero a young English milord, Viscount Greystoke, lost in childhood. But the story took variagated turns as it was filmed from 1918 onwards, starting with Elmo Lincoln as Tarzan.

Weissmuller, son of a Viennese brewer, was born in Chicago in 1904 and educated at Chicago University. A sickly child, he learnt to swim at 12 after doctors recommended it for his health. He went on to win three gold medals at the Paris Olympics in 1924, followed by two more (and a silver for water polo) at the Amsterdam Olympics in 1928. He broke 67 swimming records and won 52 United States championships. When he retired from amateur swimming at 25 he had never lost a competition. In 1922 he smashed every world record between 50 and 500 yards.

Three years later he was making a living by selling swimming suits and had appeared in one or two short sports films when he had the sudden chance of a film test. He said later that he was asked whether he could run, climb a tree and pick up a pretty girl. He replied, "With pleasure," and got the part. His popularity was widespread as the prototype of unspoilt man and the noble savage, though the part gave little scope for acting, though he did everything that was asked of him.

He soon found it very monotonous and longed to be a Wild West star. He said he never saw a script and uttered only a few sentences. The "Me Tarzan, you Jane" line originated, he said, in an off-duty joke between himself and Maureen O'Sullivan, mocking the primitive nature of the whole thing. Cheetah the Chimp formed an integral part of the Tarzan–Mate–Son menage. Asked after he had finished his career as Tarzan if he had any advice for successors, he said: "The main thing is, don't let go of the vine when you're swinging through the jungle."

By 1945 Brenda Joyce had succeeded Miss O'Sullivan as Jane and in 1949 Weissmuller gave up the role, being succeeded by Lex Barker. By that time he was starring as a white hunter in the *Jungle Jim* series for Columbia, making 75 episodes. This became a TV series in 1958. He made a total of 19 Tarzan films between 1932 and 1949, most in a forest 10 miles north of Hollywood. He was paid about $100,000 a performance. But in later years he admitted nothing remained of his film fortune. "I blew it on boats and good living," he said. His financial interests included real estate, a chain of swimming pools and 75 health food stores in America.

He was working as a celebrity greeter for Caesar's Palace in Las Vegas when he was cut down by a stroke in 1977. When a judge appointed his wife as his guardian, his estate was valued at $738 a month. He had a son and two daughters from his six marriages, the third of which was to the actress known as the "Mexican Spitfire", Lupe Velez.

January 23 1984

JIM LAKER

JAMES CHARLES LAKER, who died aged 64, was one of the finest off-spin bowlers in the history of cricket, perhaps the finest. Certainly he holds a record never likely to be equalled. His 19 wickets against Australia in the Old Trafford Test of 1956, for which he will always be remembered, are two more than had been taken before in a first-class match, let alone in a Test match.

Jim Laker's career coincided with an era of uncovered, slow turning pitches, but no one else brought to them the same unrelenting accuracy, allied to considerable powers of spin. A quiet, reserved thinker on the game, with a somewhat flat-footed walk, he did not give the impression of great vitality on the field, but caught many good catches, usually in the gully; he was also a hard-hitting batsman at No. 8, good enough to make 63 at Trent Bridge against the 1948 Australians.

His origins will seem strange to later cricketers. A Yorkshireman who played in the Bradford League for Saltaire before joining the Army in 1941, he began to make his name later in the War in good-class cricket in the Middle East. He had been more of a batsman in the League, but now began to concentrate on off-break bowling, and while awaiting demobilisation in London in 1946, joined the Catford club. From there it was a short step to the Oval and Surrey – with Yorkshire's permission.

At the end of the 1947 season in which he played his first Championship matches, he was picked for the tour of West Indies under G. Allen, and was the most successful bowler despite his lack of experience. He was one of those bowlers who suffered while Australia made their 404 for three to win at Headingley in 1948, but in May 1950 he upset a Test trial at Bradford by taking eight wickets for two runs.

In August 1953, his partnership with Tony Lock had much to do with England's recovery of the Ashes at the Oval. Just over a year later, he was surprisingly left out of Len Hutton's team who retained the Ashes in Australia, but he remained an important part of the strong England bowling side of the 1950s until he retired in 1959 when still a very good bowler.

The publication of Laker's autobiography, including criticisms which he much regretted subsequently, led to the withdrawal of his MCC honorary membership. However, in another publication he put the record straight and returned after two years to play for Essex for three seasons. The MCC membership was restored and he moved on eventually to a successful career as a television commentator on cricket. Though he had not always been in good health, his sadly premature death was a particular shock to viewers who though not remembering him when he was a great bowler, had long been accustomed to his sound, unflappable interpretations of television matches.

April 24 1986

SIR STANLEY ROUS

SIR STANLEY ROUS, who died aged 91, will be remembered as football's greatest administrator, the man who having forced the FA to face reality then guided FIFA safely through their most difficult period. As an accomplished goalkeeper, highly respected international referee, forthright secretary of the FA and enlightened FIFA president, the former schoolmaster contributed more to the world's most popular game than probably any other person.

After refereeing more than 30 international matches, and the 1934 FA Cup Final between Manchester City and Portsmouth, he took over at Lancaster Gate as secretary of the Football Association. Between 1934 and 1961 he patiently changed this old-fashioned, insular organisation – obsessed with their position as the homeland of football – into an enterprising, powerful voice in the international game. Having played a major role in the maintenance of club football throughout the Second World War, he then used his considerable influence to make sure England became members of FIFA.

Meanwhile, under his guidance, Walter Winterbottom was establishing a national coaching scheme that eventually enabled England to catch up with developments taking place elsewhere in the football world. Not surprisingly, Sir Stanley's growing prestige, especially abroad, did not always meet with the approval of lesser men on the FA Council. Some clearly resented the fact that he was regarded in domestic and international circles as far more important than any of them, and accordingly treated with much greater respect. They got their revenge in 1962 by refusing to appoint his protégé, Walter Winterbottom, as his successor at Lancaster Gate.

FIFA treated him with rather greater respect, at least at first. His dominant presence and distinctive voice helped him become one of the most powerful men in international sport. Sir Stanley used his power skilfully, sensibly, not for self-aggrandisement but to make sure that the politicians did not get as firm a grip on football as they eventually did on the Olympic Movement. Though he failed to keep South Africa in FIFA, he did prevent some of the more politically motivated black African nations from exerting undue influence.

Eventually in 1974 he was voted out of office after Joao Havelange, a Brazilian lawyer, had promised third world nations a brave new world. Despite his bitter disappointment, Sir Stanley remained close to the game. Right up to the last season he was attending at least two games a week, anywhere in the world. Indeed, he was spotted at Tel Aviv airport five months before his death when the England party arrived for a friendly match against Israel. His spirit of independence was as buoyant as ever. "I'm not with them (the FA)," he was at pains to explain. "I am here as a guest of the Israelis."

July 19 1986

SIR GORDON RICHARDS

"The most beautiful sight in the world," the late Quiny Gilbey wrote, "is Gordon Richards two lengths in front and his whip still swinging, when you have bet twice as much as you can afford." However large or small your bet, the news of Sir Gordon Richards's death at the age of 82 will bring a lump to many throats from which the cry "Come on, Gordon!" welcomed that "beautiful sight" between 1925 and 1953, when the most consistently successful British Flat race jockey hung up his boots for good.

Coincidentally, two days before his death was the 100th anniversary of another great jockey's death, the day Fred Archer shot himself at Newmarket, aged only 28. Archer was champion 13 times and rode over 200 winners in seven different seasons. Only one other man reached 200 before Gordon Richards beat Archer's record total of 246 in 1933. That year was the seventh of his 26 championships, but this is no time for futile statistical comparisons. Unlike Fred Archer and Lester Piggott, Gordon Richards – never troubled by weight – could eat what he wanted throughout his riding career; but unlike them, too, he had neither racing nor riding in his blood.

Born into a family of eight (his mother had 12 children, but four died), he was the son of strict Primitive

Methodist parents who might well have been expected to object when their son answered an advertisement for stable lads. But not a bit of it. Gordon's mother had already refused to let him go down the mines and his father, a mining contractor, said: "Go and ride, if you want. If it does not work at least you'll have learnt a lesson."

If you look to your left travelling up the M4 towards London, you can still see the two places, Foxhill and Russley Park, where Gordon learnt his first and most important racing lessons, at the feet of Steve Donoghue, then Jimmy White's stable jockey. It was there, too, that his genius first became apparent, and from Russley, his first season out of apprenticeship, weighing 6st 11lb, he first headed the list with 118 winners.

However, just because he was a natural lightweight, let no one suppose that this extraordinary sportsman "had it easy". Before the next season started, the champion jockey was found to be suffering from tuberculosis, still in those days very often a fatal disease. Though, after missing one whole season, Gordon's recovery was rapid and complete, there were several other periods when falls, injuries or losing runs damaged his surprisingly fragile confidence. Truly brave men, though, are not the ones who have no fear and Sir Gordon, highly intelligent and imaginative, was one of that much rarer breed, those who have doubts but overcome them.

He must also have overcome numerous temptations because his retirement came well before the modern era of huge prize money, multi-million-dollar stud syndications and the gift of stallion shares to successful jockeys, which puts them among the world's best-rewarded sportsmen. Sir Gordon Richards was certainly not a poor man when he retired, but his rewards did not begin to compare with those of his successors.

In a sport which daily redistributes millions of pounds tax free, *any* top-flight jockey was – and still is – the object of many and various seductive approaches. However, throughout his long career, and even in the gossip-ridden world of racing and betting, Sir Gordon's integrity was unquestioned. He was a rock in an often treacherous sea and his universally popular knighthood in 1953 was awarded at least as much on account of the example he set as the 4,870 winners he rode.

Though Sir Gordon became a successful trainer and later a tireless and skilful manager of Lady Beaverbrook's good horses, it is – needless to say – as a jockey that he will be remembered.

Throughout his career, the one infallible recipe for making a dull day enjoyable was "Watch Gordon Richards". Trainers lucky enough to employ him have described the wonderful feeling of confidence that short, square figure inspired with its rolling sailor's walk. Though the price was often on the short side, hopeful punters felt the same.

There were no starting stalls in those days but you knew that Gordon would get off precisely where he wanted. Then, though he preferred to be up near the leaders, any horse who needed relaxing could be "put to sleep" just as effectively as Pat Eddery lulled them in more modern times. And then, best of all, you would see the shoulders start to hunch and the whip begin to wave, and even if someone else was sitting motionless, you would know you still had hope. Because, with a longer rein and much longer stirrups and a much more upright back and an altogether different method from the modern masters, you *knew* the horse would run home straight and as fast as he was able.

That was "the most beautiful sight in the world", and many devotees will always be grateful to Sir Gordon for creating it, and proud that we were there to cheer him home.

November 11 1986

HENRY COTTON

HENRY COTTON, who died at the age of 80, was the father figure of British professional golf. His three Open Championship victories in 1934, 1937 and 1948 earnt him a respect without parallel in this country. This was reflected by the players, young and old alike, who invariably addressed him as "Mr Cotton". They recognised all he had done for the game.

Cotton's enthusiasm for the game was quite inexhaustible. Until only a year or so before his death a day seldom passed without his playing a few holes. It was his whole life and even when he finally put his clubs away, he still followed the game closely. "To be a champion," he once said, "you must act like one," which echoed the sentiments of that great American, Walter Hagen, who felt that it was not necessary to be a millionaire, "only to live like one". Cotton was true to his word. There was a style about almost everything he did.

In his early days he was the epitome of practice making perfect. As a young man he would practise until his hands bled. It was his ambition to be the best in the world and for a time he was. Success nevertheless did not come easily, or without suffering. When he won his first Open at Royal St George's, Sandwich, in 1934, he set a record score of 65 in the second round. It was not beaten until 1977 when Mark Hayes had a 63 at Turnberry. Cotton's 36-hole total was another record, 132 (he played the first round in 67). After three rounds that year he led by 10 strokes. But as he waited for the final 18 holes, a nervous stomach cramp started to play him up and for a time it looked as if he might lose. However, despite a 79 he won by five strokes.

A final round of 71, in awful weather at Carnoustie three years later, was a much better reflection of Cotton's golfing mastery and he always regarded this as his finest moment because it was gained in the face of the entire visiting American Ryder Cup team. His third Open win came at Muirfield in 1948, and but for the intervention of the War there would surely have been others. The strength of Cotton's game was his driving. In his prime, it was said, it was impossible to tell whether he had driven down the left side of the fairway or the right, so straight was he.

Cotton won the Belgian Open three times, the German Open three times, the Czechoslovakian Open twice, the French Open twice and the Italian Open once. He was three times matchplay champion and three times a beaten finalist. His successes in professional tournaments in Britain were numerous, while he also had victories in America and Argentina, the home of his wife, Toots, who was also his greatest supporter. Cotton made three appearances in the Ryder Cup and was non-playing captain at Wentworth in 1953. He was made an MBE for his services to golf in 1946. In his last years, Cotton spent much of his time on the Algarve, designing the Penina golf course and spending the winter months in the hotel there. Architecture was just another of his interests, but Penina he looked upon as his home and it was there that he will be buried on Boxing Day next to his wife, who died on Christmas Day, 1982.

December 24 1987

SIR GUY CUNARD

SIR GUY CUNARD, 7th Bt, who died aged 77, was a legendary gentleman-rider popularly known as the "Galloping Major". An intrepid steeplechaser and rider to hounds, he rode 268 point-to-point winners and 60 under National Hunt rules – including the 1948 Liverpool Foxhunters' Chase over the Grand National course on San Michele.

A tall, lean man, he seemed a typical Yorkshireman: lugubrious, taciturn and with a dry sense of humour. Endearingly, for one so apparently world-weary, he found the novels of his fellow steeplechaser, Dick Francis, "too steamy".

Cunard had an unfortunate tendency to put on weight and so had to devote much time to its reduction by gruelling physical exercise. He had numerous falls, some of them serious, such as those at Catterick Bridge in 1948 and at Perth in 1950, when he fractured his skull. Injury could not keep him out of the saddle for long, and he astonished his friends by the quickness of his return to competitive riding. But in 1968, after yet another serious fall, his riding career came to an end.

He was then granted a trainer's licence and, among other fine horses, produced Calypso Mio and Bountiful Charles. Though his licence came late in life he had been winning races since his schooldays; and training them from his time as a cavalry subaltern. His most famous horse was Venturesome Knight, who made a good showing in the 1940 Grand National. In 1948 he won the Cheltenham National Hunt Steeplechase on Bruno II.

Guy Alick Cunard was born in 1911, the son of a cavalry officer and the great-great-grandson of Sir Samuel Cunard, 1st Bt, who founded the transatlantic shipping line. He succeeded his brother in the title in 1973. After education at Eton and Sandhurst, Cunard was commissioned into the 16th/5th Lancers in 1931, but transferred to the 4th/7th Dragoon Guards two years later.

In 1940 he went to France with his regiment, but the German Panzer thrust from Sedan towards Abbeville necessitated a hasty return, and Cunard was evacuated from Dunkirk. Later he served in the Western Desert and Italian campaigns. At the end of the 1939–45 War Cunard was commanding a prisoner-of-war camp in North Yorkshire, where he settled and continued his distinguished riding career. He was also a capable and successful farmer, played cricket for Old Malton and hunted with the Middleton. Sir Guy was a bachelor and there was no heir to the baronetcy.

John Oaksey writes: The first time I saw Guy Cunard he was parking a fully loaded horsebox in Jermyn Street. En route from Yorkshire to Wye and Fontwell Park, he had called at the Turkish baths to remove a few more pounds from his already emaciated frame. Then, in his late forties, Guy was still a resourceful and formidable amateur rider. He trained his own horses, drove them tirelessly all over the country – and gave them every possible assistance when they reached the racecourse.

Though much too tall to be stylish, he was extremely hard to beat, and absolutely impossible to outmanoeuvre. Only the foolhardy or the uninformed attempted to overtake on his inside. Even later in Guy's long career, I was unable, on account of some minor contretemps, to ride a horse of my own in the Eton and Harrow Point-to-Point. When I offered Guy the ride, he asked none of the usual cautious, probing safety-first jockey's questions. "Of course. I'll be down tonight," was all he said – and sure enough he turned up with his own portable Turkish bath, a canvas contraption under which he sat sweating all evening. The horse, alas, fell at the last fence – "knocked over by some idiot of an Harrovian!"

David Turner may have ridden a few more point-to-point winners than Guy Cunard, but in any case, neither Turner, nor anyone else I heard of, dedicated himself more completely to the thrill of riding horses across country, as fast as they can be ridden. The price in pain and broken bones – neck, back, both arms, both legs – would, for any normal man, have seemed unbearably high. Guy not only paid it without complaining, he thought it infinitely well worthwhile.

January 23 1989

STUART PARKINSON

STUART PARKINSON, who died aged 60, was a gifted skier and bobsleigh driver, and probably the only Englishman to represent his country in those two quite different sports. With strong nerves, a wiry physique and a reckless love of speed he was a most dashing racer – in fact he raced much better than he skied. As a result he frequently injured himself, though he was never off the snow for long.

Parkinson's heyday was in the 1940s and 1950s, the time of post-War austerity and strict amateurism. Unless one was in the services, training for an Olympic or world championship meant giving up two weeks' annual holiday. If a competition in the Alps finished on a Sunday it meant that most British athletes had to scurry back across Europe to be back at work on Monday morning.

"Parky" had a wonderful equilibrium and exceptional reactions, which would have ensured his success in almost any sport, but he was reluctant to involve himself in training, which he found boring, and concentrated on sports involving gravity rather than excessive energy. Throughout his bobsleighing days he wore a long, black astrakhan overcoat. Unless the race was particularly important he would jump into the bob after the start still wearing his coat, tuck the tails between his knees and the steering wheel, and disappear round the first corner like some holidaying Armenian diplomat out for an Alpine drive.

William Stuart Parkinson was born in 1929 and started skiing at Haileybury. On a National Service commission he won the Army ski championship in 1947, and the next year went straight into the British team for the Olympic Games at St Moritz; in 1950 he won the British championships. On coming down from Queen's College, Cambridge, Parkinson joined Sir Lindsay Parkinson's civil engineering contractors and building firm, based in East Lancashire.

He no longer had the time for competitive skiing, so he turned to bobsleighing. After a creditable second place in the 1953 European Junior Championships, for the rest of the decade he often made the British team and invariably finished in the top third of the world championship entry. Indeed, Parkinson was eighth in the 1955 world championship four-man bobsleigh event and 10th in the two-man bob race at the Olympic Games at Cortina d'Ampezzo in 1956.

Away from the snow and ice, one of Parkinson's lifelong passions was his formidable 1,000cc Vincent Black Shadow motorcycle. He covered enormous distances on this machine, thinking nothing in his younger days of riding to London for the evening and then back up to Lancashire in time for breakfast next morning. He had a rather rakish "tough guy" image, with an urbane, mocking cynicism and a slightly cadaverous charm. Well over 6ft tall and of slim build, he sometimes gave new acquaintances the impression of a "stretched-out Humphrey Bogart".

With the ambition of most of today's athletes, Parkinson would have been an international champion; instead he preferred to do his work and live his life, giving what time he could to sporting competition, but never taking it too seriously. What mattered more to him was that his friends and sporting rivals knew him for his camaraderie and sportsmanship.

He left the family firm in the late 1970s and set up his own company in London. He retained his interest in amateur winter sports and in 1987 was back at the wheel of an old bob in Switzerland. Parkinson was recently appointed president of the Les Avants Bobsleigh and Toboggan Club in recognition of his services to the sport. He is survived by his wife, Susie, and four children.

October 31 1989

SIR GEORGE "GUBBY" ALLEN

SIR GEORGE ALLEN, universally known as "Gubby", who died aged 87, had a stronger influence on the world of cricket and for a longer span of years than anyone since the 4th Lord Harris. Allen played the first of his 25 Tests in 1930. He captained England both at home and in Australia; and was elected to the committee of MCC in his early thirties, and served the club as both treasurer and president, as well as on successive committees, for more than 50 years.

Harris, who led England in the first Test in this country in 1880, and was a dominating influence in the game until his death in 1932, had trodden all these paths and when it came to mastery of argument on important issues those who sat in committee with both probably accorded them equal attention and respect.

George Oswald Browning Allen was born in Sydney on July 31, 1902, of a family with deep roots in Australia. His great-grandfather emigrated in 1816, was the first

94

man in Australia to serve his articles as a solicitor there, and founded what became the oldest legal firm in Sydney. Gubby's father, Walter, brought his family to England in 1909, and at the outbreak of the 1914–18 War joined the Metropolitan Special Constabulary, eventually becoming Commissioner and earning a knighthood.

From his private schooldays at Summerfields, Oxford, young Allen showed that he had cricket in the blood. An uncle had played for Australia and it was said his father might have played for Cambridge in the era of Ranji and Stanley Jackson if he had exerted himself rather more. That was a charge which could never have been made against his son.

When Eton and Harrow resumed their rivalry at Lord's in 1919, Allen was run out in the first over on the first morning without receiving a ball. However, things turned out well for him – as they generally did – in the second innings, his 69 not out helping Eton to an easy victory. He was lucky in having for a housemaster C. M. Wells, formerly of Cambridge and Middlesex, who ran the cricket, and for a coach the celebrated George Hirst. By the time their mettlesome protégé left Eton, his promise as a fast bowler, with a beautiful action and late out-swing, was clearly recognisable, whereas he was correct and determined as a batsman.

Allen walked into Hubert Ashton's powerful Cambridge side of 1922 and his nine wickets in the university match for 78 runs sped Oxford to an innings defeat. After two years he left Cambridge for the City, where he became a successful stockbroker, and thereafter became his own brand of amateur, playing never even half a season for Middlesex and, despite this, reaching the top of the tree as an all-round cricketer. Commuting, so to speak, between the Stock Exchange and Lord's, he rarely failed to make an impact for Middlesex whenever he turned out, either as batsman or fast bowler, or both.

The first of his 25 appearances for England was against Australia in the famous Lord's Test of 1930 when, substituting for Harold Larwood, he bowled expensively but, with A. P. F. Chapman, made 125 for the sixth wicket in the second innings. The following year he and L .E. G. Ames, against New Zealand at Lord's, combined in a stand of 246, a world record for the eighth wicket in Tests, both making hundreds.

His choice for D. R. Jardine's MCC team to Australia in 1932–33 was strongly criticised. Yet he was one of the successes of the tour, taking 21 wickets in the Tests and averaging 23 with the bat. It is a matter of history that though entreated by his captain to do so he declined to bowl "bodyline", and was always frank in his disapproval of it.

Allen first led England in the 1936 series against India, in obvious preparation for the captaincy in Australia the following winter. After winning the first two Tests there, England were defeated in the following three – thanks chiefly to some phenomenal scoring by Bradman.

In 1938 Allen was commissioned into the Territorial Army and after serving in the City of London Yeomanry ("the Rough Riders") he joined an anti-aircraft battery who defended RAF Fighter Command HQ at Stanmore and Canvey Island. He was invited into Dowding's celebrated "ops" room and developed a close relationship with the RAF which led to a posting as flak liaison officer at Bomber Command's No. 5 group. Determined to assess enemy anti-aircraft fire in action, Allen flew over the Ruhr in the air gunner's seat of a Handley Page Hampden in the autumn of 1940. His increasing flak expertise was then used, first as GSO2 of MI 14E and then as GSO1, in the rank of lieutenant colonel, with MI 15 (as the War Office centre for collating intelligence on German air defences became known). He was awarded the American Legion of Merit.

Just as Allen's leadership in Australia before the War had come in for the highest praise on all counts, so it did again in 1947–48 in the West Indies, even though Allen was now 45 and, with a weak side, MCC could not match the emergent brilliance of the "three Ws", Worrell, Weekes and Walcott. He was a model touring captain in that he took infinite trouble over every member of his side. At his best Allen was a valuable Test all-rounder, a fast bowler whose speed stemmed from a perfect action, a sound bat and excellent close fielder.

He took 81 wickets in Tests at an average cost per wicket of 29.37, and made 750 runs, average 24.19. His first-class record was 784 wickets at 22.24; 8,866 runs, average 28.05, including 10 hundreds. Allen's most notable feat was in 1929 at Lord's when he took all 10 Lancashire wickets for 40 runs, this after arriving late on the field (by arrangement, naturally) and so missing the new ball. In county cricket at Lord's it was a unique feat, and so it remains.

The Lord's Committee Room was the scene of his work for cricket from 1932 to 1985, an unprecedented span interrupted only by the Second World War. In 1963–64 he was president, and from 1964 to 1976 held the club's key post of treasurer. An amateur in the most complete sense on the field, Allen was very much a professional in committee. No one had a wider knowledge of every facet of cricket politics and administration. No one was better briefed, nor, it should be added, more tenacious, in his opinions. He had more time than most, and he could show infinite patience in order to win his point. It was sometimes whispered that the easiest way to get a thing through was to persuade the *eminence grise* that it had been his own idea. There is no doubt he could be difficult. Likewise, it generally had to be admitted in the end that "Gubby is probably right".

Allen was the chief instigator of the national post-War movement in cricket for the involvement and teaching of the young. This was hitherto an uncharted field, but now there are associations covering every area. It led to Allen's authorship with H. S. Altham of *The MCC Coaching Book*, a best-seller for many generations.

When England and Australia were very much at odds over the perilous issue of throwing after the MCC tour of 1958–59 it was Allen who, with Sir Donald Bradman's eventual strong co-operation, devised a successful formula for eliminating the "chucker". He performed no more important service than this. Not the least of his labours was his seven seasons' chairmanship of the Test selectors from 1955 to 1961.

Allen was not only a shrewd judge of a cricketer, but he was also, on the testimony of all who served with him, an admirably fair and thorough chairman with a flair for finding the man for the occasion. In all he did there shone his great devotion to the game and helpful, unfailing friendliness to all cricketers. He was awarded the Territorial Decoration in 1945, appointed CBE in 1962 and knighted in 1986. Gubby Allen never married. His family said he was always wedded to cricket.

December 1 1989

GEOFFREY GREEN

GEOFFREY GREEN, the former football correspondent of *The Times* who died aged 78, was a much-loved figure in the press boxes around the world, a gifted amateur in a world increasingly given over to dour professionals. Not for him the typewriter, word processor or fax machine. When time permitted he wrote elegantly with pen or pencil. Otherwise, he would calmly *ad lib* his lyrical prose over the telephone amid the tumult of the stadium.

Green, whose own football-playing career was cut short by a knee injury after he had won a Blue at Cambridge as a centre-half of great promise, loved the open, flowing football of the Brazilians and of Matt Busby's Manchester United. His heroes were Pele and Bobby Charlton, who remained a close family friend to the end.

He also wrote with knowledge and affection about cricket and lawn tennis. Nothing pleased him more on a long, overseas football tour than to sit in a smoke-filled room, discussing over a whisky or two with a few friends the relative merits of, say, Frank Woolley and Denis Compton. Green lived life to the full. He believed that "every day is Christmas Day" and never ceased searching "over the rainbow" for true happiness. Inevitably, this philosophy, combined with the demands of his job, led to domestic difficulties. His marriage broke up, as did a number of subsequent relationships. But the last of these gave him a daughter, Ti, who brought him much happiness. In his retirement he lived in an 18th-century cottage at Twickenham, where he continued to write books and articles into the late 1980s.

Geoffrey Green was born in Madras, on May 12, 1911, and educated at Shrewsbury and Pembroke College, Cambridge. He tried teaching and selling insurance and then in 1938 persuaded Major Bob Lyle, racing correspondent and sporting editor of *The Times*, that he was destined to be a journalist. Barrington-Ward, assistant editor of *The Times*, allowed Green three months' training as a sub-editor, without payment. This led to the offer of a job as a holiday relief sports sub-editor at £5 a week. "Chaps returned from holiday, but no one asked me to leave," Green later said. He was still at *The Times* in 1940, when he joined the RAF.

Though the old football injury ruled him out of flying, he progressed steadily, on ground duties, to the rank of squadron leader, was mentioned in despatches and appointed MBE. Returning in 1946 to Printing House Square, Green was asked to cover the first post-War FA Cup Final, between Charlton and Derby County. Shortly after he became football correspondent.

In 1953 Green was persuaded, against his better judgement, to become Sports Editor. "Deep down, I knew I had done wrong," he explained later. "At heart I was a gypsy, a beachcomber, who wished to be free and meet people. I felt trapped. I stood it for eight months, then gave it up."

Despite an increasing programme of domestic, European and international games, Green wrote several books, notably an excellent history of Manchester United and a revealing autobiography. His husky voice and laid-back style made him for many years a favourite with listeners to Saturday afternoon *Sports Report* on BBC Radio 2.

Green was appointed OBE in 1976, shortly after he had covered his 31st consecutive FA Cup Final.

May 15 1990

ROCKY GRAZIANO

ROCKY GRAZIANO, who died in New York aged 71, was world middleweight champion from July 1947 to June 1948, a period when the toughest middleweights in the history of the game were in action. Graziano had 83 professional bouts and won 67, 52 of them by knockouts. He is best remembered in boxing circles for his three bloody and bruising encounters with Tony Zale, though he gained wider fame with his best-selling autobiography *Someone Up There Likes Me*, later made into a film with Paul Newman playing Graziano.

His first encounter with Zale, who was then the middleweight champion, was at Yankee Stadium in September 1946. A tremendous battle – described by one spectator as "a small war" – ended with a knockout win by Zale in the sixth round. The effect of the knockout punch was described later by Graziano: "It is a big left hook, and I see it coming, but I can't stop it. It was like the ground exploded up and hit me in the stomach . . . I tried to yell, but I can't make a sound, I am deaf, and I can't talk, and I can't lift my arms, and I am falling. For the first time in my life I know what it's like to be KO'd."

A return match, for which the whole of New York, solidly behind the local boy, was baying, took place before a crowd of 27,000 in July of the next year. This time Graziano won the title by knocking out Zale in the sixth. But he enjoyed a reign of only a year before losing once more to Zale, this time in three rounds.

Notable practitioners in the middleweight division in those post-War years also included such formidable fighters as Jake "Raging Bull" La Motta, Marcel Cerdan and Sugar Ray Robinson, who effectively ended Graziano's career by knocking him out in a title bout in three rounds in April 1952.

Son of a boxer known as "Fighting Nick Bob", Graziano was born Thomas Rocco Barbella in "Little Italy" on New York's Lower East Side. He grew up as a street-fighter and learnt to steal before he could read. "I quit school in the sixth grade because of pneumonia," he joked, "not because I had it but because I couldn't spell it. We stole everything that began with an 'a' – a piece of fruit, a bicycle, a watch, anything that wasn't nailed down." At the age of 12 he was arrested for the first time when he was caught breaking into a chewing-gum machine; while on probation he stole a bicycle and was sent for the first of three trips to reform school.

In 1939 a friend took him to Stillman's Gym to see if he could put his street-fighting instincts to use in the ring. When a seasoned pro named Antonio Fernandez beat up the lad, Barbella swore he would never box again. Two months later, though, he was back in the ring, this time fighting under the name of his sister's boyfriend, Rocky Graziano. He went on to win the Metropolitan AAU welterweight championship. There followed a spell in the Army, where Graziano was sentenced to a year in military prison for striking an officer. On his discharge he won the Amateur Golden Glove Championship and in 1942 turned professional.

Then the gangsters moved in, offering a $100,000 bribe and a promise not to reveal his prison record if Graziano would "take a dive" in a bout against "Bummy" Davis. He refused the bribe and knocked out Davis in the fourth round, but the New York authorities suspended his licence for not reporting the incident. The Chicago authorities thought better of him, and though he refused to go there at first, it led him on to take the title. After his humiliation at the hands of Robinson, Graziano had just one more fight, which he lost on points to Chuck Davey, and he retired from the ring in 1952.

In retirement Graziano dabbled in painting for a time and developed an admiration for the style of Picasso. He then took up writing before embarking on a lucrative career as a television actor. He was comedienne Martha Raye's sidekick for a while, and in recent years was much in demand for commercials.

May 24 1990

ALF TWINN

ALF TWINN, who died aged 74, was boatman of the Cambridge University Boat Club for 50 years. He coached countless college crews and covered many miles on the towpath, first on a horse and later on a bicycle. He had a sound sense of technique, and his knowledge of the relative qualities of potential Blues in college crews made him an indispensable ally to the CUBC coaches.

Twinn kept the boats and oars in immaculate condition, and took great trouble over mixing the paint for oars and riggers so that it was the exact tint of Cambridge blue, a notoriously difficult colour to get right. He was a fanatical supporter of Cambridge rowing, and it was unwise to make a joke about the Light Blues in his presence.

Alfred Charles Twinn was born on October 7, 1915, and at the age of 14 was appointed assistant to "Cooie" Philips, the Cambridge boatman whom he succeeded in 1933. He served in the Second World War in the Royal Artillery. He was a Freeman of the Company of Watermen and Lightermen of the River Thames, and in 1989 coached Ralph Humphrey to win the Doggett's Coat and Badge. He is survived by his second wife, Ruby.

May 28 1990

SIR LEONARD HUTTON

SIR LEONARD HUTTON died at Kingston Hospital, Surrey, following an operation for a ruptured aorta, the main artery of the heart. He was 74. Though the end came suddenly he had been in frail health for some years. At the Oval Test a fortnight before, his appearance saddened his friends. The quizzical smile peculiarly his own, as though he were enjoying some private joke – the expression by which many will remember him – emerged now and then, but keeping cheerful was plainly an effort.

He was an essentially quiet, reticent man, though capable of sudden shafts of humour. From his earliest days with Yorkshire there was a natural dignity about him which remained through life. Through the most stressful moments he appeared outwardly unruffled. The good name of cricket meant much to him, and he was only caustic about those who sullied it.

Sir Leonard Hutton holds a secure place among the household names of cricket. He will be remembered as in lineal descent from the great players who, before him, wore the white rose of Yorkshire, as the holder of the record score, of 364, in Tests between England and Australia, and as the captain who recovered the Ashes in 1953 and retained them "down under" 18 months later.

The strain of leadership on a sensitive, introverted personality, coupled with the responsibility of continuing to open the England innings, led shortly after these successes to what was then considered a premature retirement six months short of his 40th birthday. The award of a knighthood closely followed, the second bestowed upon an English professional cricket.

His predecessor was Sir Jack Hobbs, still remembered as "The Master", whose last days with Surrey in the early summer of 1934 coincided exactly with Hutton's first with Yorkshire. Hutton, like his great forerunner, was far from robust in physique. Each had reached the peak of his skill when war interrupted his cricket, in Hobbs's case for four years, in Hutton's for six. The course that their careers subsequently took reflects the respective demands made upon them. After the First War Hobbs made only three tours, all to Australia, before his retirement 15 years later at the age of 51.

In the decade after the Second War Hutton's shoulders were burdened with 16, at home and abroad. He toured Australia three times, the West Indies twice and South Africa for a second time during this period. In all but his last tour he was the mainstay of England's batting. In the Australian series of 1950–51 and 1953 his average was almost double that of anyone on either side.

If Hobbs be acknowledged as the greatest of all

professional batsmen, Len Hutton by common consent must rate pre-eminently with two others of equal pedigree, Denis Compton and Walter Hammond. These two were more flamboyant in style than he as befitted their place at No. 4 in the order. There was more self-denial about Hutton's opening role, a characteristic inherited in full from his mentor and partner Herbert Sutcliffe. But he too could dazzle when he deemed the time was right.

Leonard Hutton was born a mile from the celebrated cricket nursery of Pudsey in the adjacent village of Fulneck. Several generations of Huttons had belonged to the self-sufficient community which the mid-European Moravian sect had established there in the 19th century. His father and grandfather were builders. Naturally the village had its cricket ground, where the minister bowled to him as well as his father, uncles and brothers. All were dedicated cricketers.

Moving on to Pudsey St Lawrence, Len was only 13 when he was bidden to the Yorkshire nets at Headingley. Len never forgot what George Hirst said after he had first seen him bat. "Well played. Try and improve on that."

Another great Yorkshire cricketer, Sutcliffe, was much more effusive in his comment, so much so that the question was whether Len had been burdened with prophecies too extravagant for a youngster's good. However, this one always kept a clear head on his shoulders.

He recovered from a duck in his first innings for Yorkshire shortly before his 18th birthday, and from another (his scores 0 and 1) on his debut for England a few days after his 21st. There had never been any doubt about his method, while as his career unfolded his temperament proved equally reliable. He made the first of his 19 Test hundreds in his second match against New Zealand, while both he and Compton scored hundreds in their first Tests against Australia at Trent Bridge the following summer.

In the fifth Test, in August 1938, the first and the last "timeless" Test to be played in England, he produced the ultimate marathon of endurance, an innings of 364 which was both the highest Test score and, at 13 hours 20 minutes, the longest played. As a boy young Len had seen the making of the score he had now surpassed, the 334 at Headingley by Don Bradman, who was thereupon installed as his hero.

The first of his seven MCC tours followed, to South Africa. In 1939 he made 12 hundreds, two for England v West Indies, 10 for Yorkshire. When War came, Hutton was at the top of the tree, a well-nigh ideal model for imitation. Perfect positioning of the feet and fault-less balance at the moment of impact gave him the timing that a modest physique demanded. These attri-butes became the more important when in 1941 he suffered a serious gymnasium accident, falling on his left arm during Commando training. This resulted in several operations, the arm in question emerging from 14 months in plaster emaciated and three inches shorter than the right. The lengthy recuperation period naturally involved also an adjustment of his batting technique.

Hutton was at the centre of the pictures in all England's post-War Test series along with Compton, and notably in the duels against the Australian fast bowling pair of Lindwall and Miller. In 1952, as the most seasoned and level-headed among the leading professionals, he was promoted to the captaincy of England, the first of his kind since the early missionary tours in Australia in the 1870s.

He wore the mantle of leadership with unruffled dignity if little indication of comfort. India were disposed of easily in England in preparation for the Australian visit following. After four fluctuating draws Hutton, himself playing the highest innings of the match, brought the Ashes back home at the Oval after a record absence of 19 years.

So far so very good. In that 1953–54 winter was due another visit to the West Indies, against whom England had already lost two post-War rubbers. Dubious though many were at the prospect of his handling all the problems of a tour to fervent and politically emerging countries, MCC made the cardinal error of departing from established custom, appointing not an experienced tour manager but a player-manager in C. H. Palmer, a younger member of the team who had not hitherto played for England. Wholesale defeats in the first two Tests saw English prestige at its lowest, both on the playing field and off it. The subsequent recovery, to the point of halving the series, owed most to the captain, who, draining himself to the furthest point of nervous and physical exhaustion, played successive innings of 169, 44, 30 not out and 205. If it was not a happy tour, much was redeemed by its ending.

In the following English summer, when Pakistan were the visitors prior to the MCC tour of Australia and New Zealand, Hutton's hold on the captaincy did not go unquestioned. In his absence because of "acute neuritis due to overstrain", the selectors turned to D. S. Sheppard, a batsman of clear leadership credentials, but who was at a theological college at the time, and soon to be lost to

the game. The implications implied in this move caused
a rare clamour and a press outcry lasting until Hutton's
appointment late in July.

Up to a point England's fortunes in Australia followed the West Indies course in that the first Test ended
in wholesale defeat. Now, however, two young amateur
batsmen, Peter May and Colin Cowdrey, saved their side
in successive Tests, while Frank Tyson emerged as a
match-winning fast bowler. A narrow victory in the
second Test was followed by two by wider margins, the
second of which secured the retention of the Ashes.
Hutton had handled his side with quiet, shrewd assurance, though it has to be said that the tactic of slowing
down the over-rate dates from this tour.

The captain returned home to a hero's welcome. He
was appointed captain for all five Tests against South
Africa, an unprecedented mark of confidence, and by
passing a new rule MCC were able to make him an
honorary cricket member while still a player. However,
in personal terms the cost of Len's three-year span had
now to be accepted. His batting in the Australian Tests
had been an unaccustomed struggle, and in the MCC–
South African match in May he was stricken with
lumbago and forced to withdraw, as he did soon afterwards from the England captaincy.

He managed 10 matches for Yorkshire, in between
aches and pains, and in the penultimate one came his
129th, and last, hundred, against Nottinghamshire at
Trent Bridge. After reaching a characteristically flawless
unhurried hundred in about three hours he suddenly
blossomed into a stream of the most brilliant strokes, so
that his last 94 runs actually came in 65 minutes. As at
Sydney and Brisbane, for instance, in Test matches, the

Roundhead had revealed a Cavalier struggling to burst forth.

Hutton needs no figures to illustrate his mastery as a batsman. Confined to 16 home seasons and seven in the sun and heat of tours, his tally of 40,140 tells its own story. In Tests his 6,971 runs were made at an average of 56. Given a full career without intermission or accident who can tell what his record might have been? After retirement he covered Test matches for the *Observer* newspaper and served as a Test selector between 1975 and 1977. A former president of the Forty Club, he was president of Yorkshire at the time of his death.

September 7 1990

FULKE WALWYN

FULKE WALWYN, CVO, one of the great racehorse trainers and a former trainer to Queen Elizabeth the Queen Mother, died aged 80. Walwyn was one of only two men this century to have ridden and trained a Grand National winner. He was champion trainer five times, and won four Cheltenham Gold Cups, a Grand National and two Champion Hurdles.

His wife, Cath, said: "The Queen Mother was here on Monday and Fulke talked to her. He died very peacefully. He had a wonderful life and wonderful success. I think of all the horses Mandarin was his favourite."

Michael Oswald, the Queen Mother's racing manager, said: "He was the greatest trainer of chasers of his time, and perhaps of all time. He had infinite patience and his results speak for themselves. I think his training of

Special Cargo was brilliant. The horse had appalling leg problems and to have got him back on a course, and then win a Whitbread Gold Cup and the Grand Military Gold Cup three times, was a most remarkable training performance." Fellow trainer Nick Gaselee, an amateur rider for Walwyn and his former assistant, described Walwyn as "the best National Hunt trainer there's ever been. A great era in National Hunt racing has come to an end."

One of the best amateur riders of the last 60 years, Walwyn, a Welshman, won his first steeplechase at the age of 19, defeating five leading professionals in a race at Cardiff in 1930. At the end of the 1932 season he became leading amateur. In an injury-troubled career, Walwyn had several very bad falls, and in 1938 fractured his skull severely and was forced to give up race-riding. He took out a trainer's licence the following year, having his first winner, Poor Duke, at Buckfastleigh, just before the outbreak of War.

Cheltenham was his favourite course, and Walwyn trained four Gold Cup winners: Mont Tremblant, Mandarin, Mill House and The Dikler; two Champion Hurdle winners: Anzio and Kirriemuir; and 200 winners there – a remarkable feat.

In that first post-War jumping season, Walwyn won more races than any of his rivals bar one, and when, the following year, Dorothy Paget decided to send him most of her large string of jumpers, he finished leading trainer. Walwyn's first big-race winner was in the Scottish Grand National with Rowland Roy, who went on to take the first post-War running of Kempton's King George VI Chase eight months later – Walwyn's first of five winners of the Christmas feature race.

The year 1952 was to be an important one in his life.

His first wife, Diana Carlos Clarke, had died young, and in 1952 he married Catherine, daughter of Sir Humphrey de Trafford, who bred Parthia to win the 1959 Derby. Cath was to prove an outstanding wife, and but for her great support he would have had to retire as a trainer some time before he did. That same year, he saddled his first outstanding chaser in Mont Trembland, winner as a six-year-old of the Cheltenham Gold Cup and runner-up, under top weight, to Early Mist in the 1953 Grand National.

Taxidermist and Mandarin were the next stars to emerge from Saxon House. Mandarin's success in the Grand Steeplechase de Paris at Auteuil in 1962, with Fred Winter up, in spite of losing his bridle early in the race, was a most remarkable victory. Mandarin had been just beaten in the first running of the Whitbread Gold Cup in 1957, but the next year Taxidermist made amends when admirably ridden by Mr John Lawrence, later Lord Oaksey. Taxidermist was the first of Walwyn's seven successes in the race, Mill House, Charlie Potheen, The Dikler, Diamond Edge (twice) and the Queen Mother's Special Cargo being the others.

In 1964 Walwyn saddled his only Grand National winner with Team Spirit, who was running in the race for the fifth successive year. Team Spirit, a thorough stayer, was only fourth at the last fence but, beautifully ridden by Willie Robinson, he got up to win almost at the post.

Though Walwyn will be best remembered as a trainer of chasers, he also saddled two Champion Hurdle winners. If the victory of Team Spirit in the National had been impressive, Walwyn's first Champion Hurdle winner, Anzio (1962), was equally so, and again Willie Robinson shone. He took Anzio the shortest way round and they squeezed through on the inside at the last hurdle to beat Quelle Chance by three lengths.

Two years later, Walwyn saddled a small four-year-old called Kirriemuir, a novice hurdler who had won seven consecutive hurdle races, to run third in the Champion Hurdle. Kirriemuir was beaten in his first five races of the following season before winning the Champion Hurdle at 50–1 with the stable first-string, Exhibit A, fourth. However, the success came as little surprise to Walwyn, who had backed the horse before Christmas.

Mill House was an imposing animal to look at and was Walwyn's outstanding chaser of the mid-1960s. In any normal era, he would have been an undisputed champion. But he had the misfortune to come up against the legendary Arkle. The winner of the 1963 Cheltenham Gold Cup, Mill House also twice finished second to that great horse.

The Dikler and Charlie Potheen were the chief Walwyn winners of the next decade and then, when on the death in 1973 of Peter Cazalet, Britain's most popular National Hunt owner, Queen Elizabeth the Queen Mother sent most of her horses to Walwyn, another great era began. The Queen Mother's last big favourite Walwyn trained was Special Cargo, who won the 1984 Whitbread Gold Cup at Sandown Park by inches. Sandown was Special Cargo's happy hunting ground. He won seven races on the course including three Grand Military Gold Cups. Walwyn's final winner for the Queen Mother was The Argonaut in the 1990 Grand Military. He saddled over 2,180 winners in his time – 115 for the Queen Mother.

February 20 1991

R. J. O. "JACK" MEYER

R. J. O. "JACK" MEYER, who died aged 85, was the most remarkable and arguably the most successful headmaster in Britain in the years after the Second World War. His foundation, Millfield in Somerset, began with a sprinkling of Indian princes in 1935, and grew into an outstanding public school. In particular it gained a reputation for sending forth a stream of first-class athletes.

"Jack" Meyer himself had been a formidable all-round games player, and his school reflected his versatility. There were Olympic gold medallists such as David Hemery and Mary Bignal Rand, a lorry driver's daughter who was obliged to leave the school because of an infatuation with a Siamese prince; tennis players such as Mike Sangster; golfers such as Brian Barnes; the swimmer Duncan Goodhew; and, most illustrious of all, the great Welsh scrum-half Gareth Edwards.

However, Millfield was, and remains, far more than a sporting nursery. The school also produced an annual clutch of Oxbridge scholarships, occasionally achieved by candidates who had come to the school after failing the 11-plus. It was Meyer's credo that, no matter how indifferent the material, there was always talent to be elicited. He liked to call Millfield "the only comprehensive school that really works" – the kind of phrase that never failed to irritate the zealots of left-wing educational theory. It was true, though, that there was no entrance examination to Millfield. If Meyer liked a boy or girl he took him or her in, and with no regard to rank, riches or class.

He never scrupled to demand outrageous fees – and even "entrance" charges of, say, £10,000 – from those who could afford them, a policy which allowed him to educate children of the poor for nothing. "I don't mind taking money off the rich," he explained. "If I didn't have it they'd only spend it on drink or motor-cars or something."

The story goes that a duke once approached Meyer, a shade diffidently, to take his son into the school. The boy had failed to gain entrance to Eton, despite the fact that generations of his ancestors had graced the school. Meyer explained the peculiar character of his school to the duke: that it had girls as well as boys, that it was not exclusive to the rich, and that he made a point of taking talented children from the local town. The duke looked doubtful. "One has to think carefully about this," he said. "What if my son were to meet and get attached to a chimney-sweep's daughter? What would I do then?" "What makes you think a chimney-sweep's daughter would *want* to get involved with a boy who had failed entrance to Eton?" Meyer returned. The duke sent his son to Millfield.

The school's success certainly could not be explained in terms of the physical environment. For years its buildings were lamentable: Nissen huts, with pupils in their overcoats huddled round a stove, and "chicken runs" as they were called, no better than wooden sheds. From the start, though, Meyer grasped the overwhelming importance of good teachers – both David Cornwell (John Le Carré) and Robert Bolt served on his staff. He made a point of seeking out and recruiting mature staff, whether ex-servicemen or outstanding public school masters who were on the point of retirement, men who still had 10 years or more of good teaching in them, not least as coaches for Oxbridge.

Meyer also insisted on small classes, with a teacher–pupil ratio never greater than one to eight. Much of the teaching was one-to-one, and not simply for scholarship preparation; Meyer made a speciality of taking in dyslexic children and other public school rejects. "A backward boy is like a broken-down lorry," he explained. "You can push him up the hill by brute force – that's cramming. Or you can try and get his engine started, and that's what we do at Millfield."

Meyer was not a sentimentalist, though; he resisted any idea of disguising from children that some were less able than others. Life was a battlefield, and all must be taught to fight for their place in the sun. It was important to turn the attention of backward children towards other activities – be it bird-watching, climbing, photography, gardening, or whatever. The confidence gained would bear fruit in their academic studies, or, in the case of Tony Blackburn, in an ability to jabber between gramophone records.

However, Millfield's conspicuous success did not earn it much support from other public schools. Meyer was never invited to join the prestigious Head Masters Conference (HMC). Equally, when the school governors tried to join the Governing Bodies Association, they were told that the school was "not up to our standards". Yet in that same year Millfield received a glowing report from Her Majesty's Inspectors – "the best school we have seen in years".

Meyer believed that the hostility was based on deliberate prejudice against him because of the unconventional nature of his school. He also thought there was a great deal of jealousy because his school attracted an impressive array of celebrities' offspring – Haile Selassie's grandson, Dame Margot Fonteyn's stepson, the 1st Earl Attlee's son ("I am sending him to your school because of my socialist principles," the Labour statesman told Meyer) – and many others.

Elizabeth Taylor sent her children by Michael Wilding to Millfield, though Richard Burton, when he met Meyer, professed that he found him "disappointing . . . I had imagined a much wiser, more authoritative man. This man was tall, thin, very English, nervous in gesture and a compulsive talker. One white liar recognises another and I found some of his stories too highly polished . . . still, he's obviously good at his job."

Meyer's own memories of meeting Richard Burton were that the actor was so drunk that the head waiter was obliged to put a screen round their table. His relations with Miss Taylor declined sharply when he insisted that she should herself deliver her son to Millfield.

Meyer's views on education were by no means uniformly progressive. With his conviction of the moral and educative function of games, he expressed outrage that the standard of public school cricket should be sacrificed to the quest for marginally higher standards at A Level. Known in the school as "Boss", he was a stout defender of the cane, believing that it was necessary to resist the natural tendency of children to probe for the weak spots in authority. "The young should be made to realise that behind the work of reproof is something hard that hurts."

Meyer worked for the school day and night, claiming in 1968 to have gone 17 months without going to bed. But his headmastership ended unhappily. In 1953 he had made the school over to an educational trust, which meant that his own position became dependent on the continued support of the governors. He had always had a weakness for the gaming tables, and in 1970 the governors were obliged to demand if he had been playing the casinos from fees which parents had paid. "Of course," Meyer returned; and the school had gained handsomely from his speculations. The answer was not deemed satisfactory and the headmaster was demoted to the office of warden, being succeeded by another Somerset cricket captain, Colin Atkinson.

A canon's son, Rollo John Oliver Meyer was born in Bedfordshire on March 15, 1905, and educated at Haileybury, his loathing for that school becoming a forcing house for his educational ideas. He then read History and English at Pembroke College, Cambridge. On the games field Meyer was at once brilliant and unpredictable. When he opened the bowling against Oxford at Lord's he sent down a lemon first ball and professed himself most satisfied with the amount of swing obtained.

After Cambridge he thought of becoming a school master, but finding himself in the embarrassing position of having accepted offers from Eton and Harrow simultaneously, escaped to India as a cotton broker. When this first career was ended by the stockmarket crash of 1929, Meyer turned to tutoring Indian princes. In 1933 he returned to England and took a house at Millfield to prepare six Indian princes and three English boys for various kinds of further education: Sandhurst, the Civil Service and Oxbridge entrance. "I didn't mean to found a school," he later reflected, "it was all a mistake." But once Millfield was launched Meyer never doubted that he would succeed, despite numerous difficulties with the bank.

Even in retirement Meyer remained irrepressible. After toying with a scheme to found a new Millfield on Francis Noel-Baker's estate on Euboea, in 1973 he became president of the Campion International School in Athens, and spoke highly of the help he received from the Greek military junta – "the Colonels have helped in every way". Meyer appointed a sociologist as headmaster – "I told him straight that hogwash was not one of my subjects." In two years the school was thriving, but when the governors sacked a woman teacher without consulting him, he resigned.

He said that he would like his ashes to be spread on the Millfield wicket: "It's a pretty fast pitch as it is . . . and a few ashes should make it even faster." Meyer was appointed OBE in 1967. He married, in 1931, Joyce Symons; they had two daughters, one of whom predeceased him.

E.W. Swanton writes: The personality, imagination and energy which had enabled him to found Millfield were reflected in Meyer the sportsman. He was a rackets Blue and on coming down from Cambridge became a good enough golfer to be made a member of the Oxford and Cambridge Golfing Society. But it was as a cricketer that his qualities found special scope.

An outstanding bowler and captain at Haileybury, he played all his three years in the strong Cambridge sides of 1924–26, in his last year shaking the Australians by taking six of their wickets for 65 with a versatile mixture of swing and spin. Following 10 years of first-class cricket in India, he returned in 1936 as a fully fledged all-rounder for Somerset. With a remarkable 202 not out in 3¾ hours at Taunton he deprived Lancashire of victory.

Two years later, for the Gentlemen against the Australians, he had five, including Don Bradman's wicket, for 66 runs. He was very much a man for the occasion. Meyer could only be an intermittent player for Somerset except in 1947 when, aged 42, he took on the captaincy. He had to battle courageously through the summer with back trouble while the solid professional core of the side could not always keep up with his theories. His admiring contemporary R. C. Robertson-Glasgow, recounting how Meyer experimented with every variety of slow bowling, including the occasional, enormously high leg-break known as the "Spedigue Dropper", quotes him lamenting that he really needed 12 or 13 fielders. " 'It works,' he said in his philosophical way, 'but like the earlier models of the motorcycle it needs a lot of attention.' "

Undoubtedly Meyer's most valuable contribution to cricket was the beckoning finger he extended throughout his long headmastership of Millfield to potential cricketers, including many whose parents had to have generous help with the school fees. No one expressed better the *mens sana* ideal.

March 11 1991

JOHN ARLOTT

JOHN ARLOTT, who died aged 77, turned the routine business of cricket commentary into something approaching an art form, so that for 34 years his rich and mellow Hampshire tones became an integral part of the English summer. His style was instantly recognisable not merely by the accent but also by an incomparable blend of poetic imagination, verbal resource, shrewd judgement of character and ready humour. Arlott was essentially an impressionist, with an eye for the telling irrelevancy; he never descended into mere punditry.

As a phrase-maker he was unmatched. "Consider Lillee in the field," he once observed. "He toils mightily but he does not spin." Lillee, incidentally, claimed that it was listening to Arlott that had first made him interested in cricket: "He really made me want to play." An authority of another kind, Dylan Thomas, described Arlott's commentaries as "exact, enthusiastic, prejudiced, amazingly visual, authoritative and friendly".

Apart from the quality of his broadcasts, in sheer volume of output no one approached him. From the first Test of 1946 against India at Lord's he covered an unbroken succession of Tests at home until he retired after the Centenary Test against Australia in 1980. He also commentated on Sunday League games for television, though he never seemed quite at home in the medium that obviated the necessity for word painting.

Arlott the wireless commentator signed off for the last time as though it were a normal occasion – "and now, after comment by Trevor Bailey, it will be Christopher Martin-Jenkins". But first his fellow commentators, then (after a loudspeaker announcement) the fielding Australian side and the entire Lord's crowd stood and applauded him – a gesture that was almost too much for this deeply emotional man.

Arlott reverenced the gods of cricket, in particular Sir Jack Hobbs, in whose honour he founded the Master's Club, but he was also a connoisseur of the county game. He delighted to celebrate the journeymen of cricket, forgotten players like Jack Mercer, who represented

Glamorgan from 1922 to 1939 and "bowled more overs, conceded more runs, took more wickets, scored the fastest 50, made more ducks and was Not Out more often than anyone else in the county's history".

Arlott loved the fellowship of cricket, and held the players, as a group, in rare esteem. His warm feelings were reciprocated, and the distinction which probably meant more to Arlott than any other was his presidency of the Cricketers' Association. His part in steering the professional players' trades union from their foundation in 1968 to a position of respect within the game must rank as one of his greatest achievements.

Arlott's contribution to cricket profited from his sense of proportion about its place in the general scheme of things. "Anyone for whom cricket was everything," he said, "wouldn't half be a limited chap." He was a man of letters, a passionate collector of books, aquatints and glass, a Liberal candidate (at Epping in 1956 and 1959), a lover of France, and, above all, an oenophile strong on theory and even stronger in practice. These other interests meant that for Arlott the loss of a Test series, far from being a national catastrophe, was simply another phase in the history of a game which existed in the last analysis simply for the purposes of entertainment.

However, this kind of awareness also implied a reciprocal responsibility. Arlott had been shocked by what he saw in South Africa when covering MCC's tour of 1949, and thenceforth he fiercely opposed any suggestion that cricket should lend itself to the sustenance of apartheid. He condemned players on the unofficial tour of 1982 as "cynical, mercenary and completely selfish". Conversely, he regarded the part he had played in bringing Basil d'Oliviera to England as the most important thing he did.

Leslie Thomas John Arlott was born on February 25, 1914 at Basingstoke, in the lodge of the cemetery where his grandfather had been registrar. He won a charity scholarship to Queen Mary's Grammar School, where he nurtured a deep loathing for the caning headmaster, who had decreed that the young Arlott should never play for the school again after being convicted of violent play in a football match.

In 1926 he went to the Oval to watch the first day of the Test match against Australia, conceiving his devotion to Hobbs. Arlott's love of cricket was further developed by his reading of Neville Cardus's book, *The Summer Game*, which afforded the first intimations that cricket might serve as a medium for descriptive genius.

He began his working career, however, as office boy to the Basingstoke town planning officer, and then became diet clerk at the local mental hospital. In 1934 he joined the police force, and, after a spell in the tough training school at Birmingham, went on the beat in Southampton. He watched Hampshire play whenever he could, and on one occasion his wildest fantasies were fulfilled when, in an emergency, he was asked to field (in borrowed flannels) for the county against Worcestershire.

During the Blitz he was appointed to the War Emergency Department, and then – having acquired a smattering of Norwegian and German to go with his French – he found himself translated into Detective Constable, Special Branch. In plain clothes, and out on inquiries, he formed the plan of producing a book of topographical verse, and tried unsuccessfully to engage John Betjeman as a co-editor. When John Masefield refused to allow one of his poems – on Worcestershire – to be used, Arlott stepped into the breach with his own

"Cricket at Worcester 1938", a poem which was published by Cyril Connolly in *Horizon.* The topographical anthology, *Landmarks*, was published in 1943; the following year a book of Arlott's own verse appeared, *Of Period and Place.*

He also became a member of the ENSA brains trust. Through this experience Michael Ayrton became a friend, and produced the lithographs for Arlott's sonnet sequence *Clausentium* (1945). Arlott's breakthrough came when Betjeman mentioned the phenomenon of the "policeman-poet" to Geoffrey Grigson, then a talks producer with the BBC at Bristol, who proceeded to commission a talk from the prodigy. Arlott huffily replied that he was not prepared to be exhibited as a freak, but agreed, nevertheless, to present himself for an audition. Grigson made no comment on Arlott's reading from Coleridge's *Biographia Literaria* but noted in his report: "This man is a natural broadcaster and should be encouraged."

Required to give further evidence of his abilities, Arlott wrote a piece entitled *The Hampshire Giants*, about Hambledon cricket club. Its broadcast constituted Arlott's debut alike as a broadcaster and as a cricket expert. Subsequently he was offered the chance to compere a programme of *Country Magazine*, and in 1945 he applied for and secured the job of literary programmes producer, Overseas Services, in London. Arlott was put in charge of two weekly programmes, one of poetry and one of prose. He produced the poetry programme *Book of Verse* for more than four years, working with many literary luminaries.

Then, in January 1946, Donald Stevenson, head of the BBC Eastern Service, asked Arlott to broadcast short (and unpaid) reports of the Indian touring team's first two matches. These transmissions were deemed so successful that Arlott was commissioned to persist with them throughout the summer. At the first Test match, at Lord's, some of his colleagues did not trouble to disguise their doubts about his cricketing knowledge. But by the end of the season Arlott was firmly established as a specialist broadcaster on the game. "I have listened to your broadcasts last summer," "Lobby" de Lotbiniere, head of outside broadcasts, told the new find, "and while I think you have a vulgar voice, I think you have a correspondingly interesting mind – would you like to broadcast on next summer's South African tour?"

The years after the Second World War were a vintage era for cricket, in particular 1947, when Compton and Edrich indulged in feasts of run-making, and 1948, the year of the all-conquering Australians, a summer that would live in Arlott's memory as *the* golden season.

After 1950 journalism went hand in hand with his BBC work, in turn with the London *Evening News*, the *News Chronicle*, the *Observer* and – most notably for his last 12 working years – as chief cricket correspondent for the *Guardian*. He also covered football for the *Guardian*, and had a lucky escape when he volunteered to cover Manchester United's game against Belgrade in February 1958. In the event the paper's main football correspondent decided to go himself, only to be killed at Munich on the return journey.

In 1980 Arlott retired to Alderney, together with his fine collection of wine. This hobby had taken wing after he had provided the editor of the *Evening News* with a sparkling Languedoc for a party. The wine was successfully passed off as champagne, and Arlott became the newspaper's wine correspondent. Thereafter the cellars in the Alresford home – a former pub – began to fill rapidly.

He learnt as he drank, and by no means confined himself to claret. Indeed he became an acknowledged expert on champagne and burgundy, on both of which he produced books – *Burgundy, Wines and Vines* (1976) and *Krug: House of Champagne* (1977). Doubtless, however, his purchase of a Nuits St Georges called Clos O'Arlot owed something to sentiment.

The cellarage at his home on Alderney was smaller than at Alresford, and a newspaper headline announced: "Arlott Declares at 4,000 Bottles". The head of Christie's wine department judged that he had never handled a finer collection, which included every first growth of the 1970 clarets. No wonder Arlott talked of being "gently hitched to idleness" on Alderney. Nevertheless, he produced a succession of books, bringing his total of cricket titles up to nearly 100, among which his biographies of Maurice Tate and Fred Trueman were particularly acclaimed. In addition no club or cricketer ever asked him in vain for a foreword. *English Cheeses of the South and West* (1956) bore witness to another enthusiasm.

Arlott was appointed OBE in 1970, and was made an honorary life member of MCC on his retirement. His first marriage, to Dawn Rees, was dissolved; they had two sons, the elder of whom was killed in a motor accident on New Year's Eve, 1965. He married secondly, in 1959, Valerie France, who died in 1976; they had a daughter (who died in infancy) and a son. He married thirdly, in 1977, Patricia Hoare.

E. W. Swanton writes: John Arlott was known as "the Voice of Cricket". It was a garland that no one begrudged him. His broadcasting had a flavour all its own, both in the imaginative, strictly individual way he painted the picture and the broad Hampshire tones in which he put it across.

In the early years after the war particularly – a boom time for cricket without parallel – his commentaries attracted the interest of a wide new public. In those days the BBC covered county cricket regularly and at length throughout the summer, giving the commentator ample scope to bring to life both the scene itself and the characters. To this end John cultivated from the first the friendship of the players. His work thus developed a warm humanity, well laced with humour, the whole effect enhanced by that rich, well-lubricated rumble.

Only a small minority perhaps minded that he sometimes went a bit astray on the technical and tactical side. In any case this mattered less when famous players joined the commentary team for talk between overs and summaries at intervals and close of play. Essentially Arlott was a reporter with a keen eye and a ripe vocabulary. A bowler with a stealthy, knees-bent run-up reminded him of "Groucho Marx chasing a pretty waitress". Streakers dashing across the field he took in their stride. Words never failed him. As a master of his craft he was in the class of Richard Dimbleby, Alistair Cooke and Howard Marshall.

December 16 1991

KITTY GODFREE

She was so very different from the powerful, temperamental and obsessive creatures who dominate women's tennis today. There, in a calf-length white frock and white stockings, was this tiny little figure with a wiry build. Her stance was erect and stately, her hair was invariably tied back with a blue silk bandeau. It seems to those who still remember her in action that she was playing a different game in a different world.

Kitty Godfree, who died aged 96, was the outstanding British woman player in a golden age of lawn tennis, when Wimbledon was still an amateur contest and winnings took the form of a five-guinea voucher from the London jewellers Mappin & Webb. Godfree collected the Wimbledon singles title twice, in 1924 and 1926. Earlier, at the 1920 Olympic Games in Antwerp, she and her partner, Winifred McNair, defeated the legendary Suzanne Lenglen and her partner to win a gold medal. In the same tournament Godfree, partnered by Max Woosnam, took the silver medal for the mixed doubles, as well as the bronze medal for the women's singles.

Self-taught as a player, she developed a powerful all-court game and a wide variety of strokes; she was one of the earliest women players to exploit the volley, frequently from the backhand. Quick-witted and fast on her feet, she was at her best in attack. Her determined temperament stood her in good stead against such opponents as Lenglen and, later, Helen Wills Moody.

However, Godfree did not confine herself to tennis. At 10 she won the National Skating Association bronze medal. In her late teens she became one of Britain's earliest women motorists. In the winter of 1919–20, after her Wimbledon debut, she took up badminton to such devastatingly good effect that she defeated Mrs R. C. Tragett to win the All-England Singles Championship in that same season, and retained the title for the next two years. After retiring from tournament tennis Godfree took up golf; but she found it too slow and went back to tennis, which she was still playing in her ninth decade, the bandeau replaced by a sprightly peaked cap.

Godfree had some forthright views about the modern incarnation of the game, which she regarded as a somewhat distasteful display of speed, money and gadgetry. "Today's players are professional entertainers. In my day I never saw a player march off court, it would have been unthinkable." And when asked about disputed line-calls, she said: "You always rather looked the other way quickly. You didn't want people to be embarrassed by the fact that they'd given the wrong decision. In my day the game was much more fun, not so serious. You didn't have to travel around getting points for the computer as they do now. The girls today don't look as if they're enjoying their tennis. None of us in my day was as dedicated, but I had a marvellous time. We were pure amateurs, we played for the fun of the game."

There was nothing like today's pressures on players. "If you remembered an appointment during a match you would just say, 'I'm awfully sorry, I have to leave, bye-bye'." However, she admired the fitness of contemporary players, and marvelled at their gruelling training programmes: "I didn't do anything like that. I used to skip quite a lot."

Born Kathleen McKane in West London on May 7, 1896, Godfree was the younger daughter of a prosperous pianoforte dealer. She and her sister Margaret were educated at home before going to St Paul's and later St Leonard's, where Godfree first learnt to play lawn tennis. She rose rapidly through the ranks at Kew Lawn Tennis Club, and made her Wimbledon debut in 1919 when the championships were still being played at Worple Road.

Between 1919 and 1934 she played 147 singles and doubles matches at Wimbledon, with a 38–11 record in the singles. In 1924 she beat Helen Wills in the final, 4–6, 6–4, 6–4 from 1–4 in the second set. It was the only defeat the American suffered in nine visits. Two years later it was the Spaniard, Lili de Alverez, whom she beat for her second title.

During the First World War she worked as a clerk, and then joined the Ford Motor Company as a War Office driver. She played tennis in her spare time at a local club at Kew, usually accompanied by her sister, a competent tournament player. Godfree came to public attention at her first tournament at Roehampton in 1919 when she forced an advantage set against Elizabeth Ryan, the powerful Californian player. That same year, in the quarter-final at Wimbledon she put up a strong fight against the slightly younger Suzanne Lenglen, who went on to win the title.

Godfree continued to improve her game with frequent knock-ups against distinguished male players on a hard court, and in May 1922 pursued Lenglen to a 10–8 first set in the semi-final of the World Hard Court Championships in Brussels. In 1923 she was chosen for the Lawn Tennis Association's first women's team tour of America. It was during that trip that Godfree first played against the 18-year-old Helen Wills at the inaugural International against the United States (now known as the Wightman Cup). Meanwhile she and her partner, Mrs Covell, became the first overseas winners of the US women's doubles championships.

She and Wills met again the next year at Wimbledon in the singles final, in which Godfree played perhaps the most characteristic match of her career. She lost the first set; then, with the score at 1–4 in the second set, went boldly on to the attack and not only saved the game but took the next five as well. In a close deciding set, she played another attacking game at the net to win 6–4.

At the Olympic Games in the same year (the last year in which tennis was an Olympic sport, before it was reinstated in 1988), Godfree took a bronze in the singles and a silver in the doubles. In the winter of 1925–26, on a tour with a mixed British team, captained by Leslie Godfree, she startled her team-mates and the press by announcing that they had married back in January. A lawyer by training, Leslie Godfree – who was to die 21 years before her – was Wimbledon doubles champion in 1923.

The newly-weds formed a formidable partnership on court, which brought Kitty Godfree's second mixed doubles success at Wimbledon in 1926, the only time the title has been won by a husband and wife team. In that same year she won the second of her Wimbledon singles titles, defeating the glamorous Spanish champion Senorita Lili de Alvarez within an hour.

Ill health dogged Godfree's career in the late 1920s, and in 1929 she withdrew from the game altogether to give birth to her first son. In the meantime she wrote her second book, *Lawn Tennis Simplified*, a successor to her earlier *Lawn Tennis: How to Improve Your Game* (1923), a huge volume in which she examined both the technical and psychological aspects of the game. She soon returned to play first-class tennis. He main successes over the next few years were in doubles. In the early Thirties, she found herself being overtaken by a younger generation of players, such as Peggy Scriven, Betty Nuttall and Eileen Bennett. Godfree had a second son in 1937, and spent the War years quietly in Devon. On her return to West London in the 1940s she retired from championship tennis, but played on in celebrity matches.

The first woman member to be appointed a vice-president by the All-England Club, Godfree played her last competitive match there four years before her death, at the age of 92. She and "Buzzer" Hadingham, then club chairman, played for the International Club of Great Britain, against a French pair who included Jean Borotra, then 93. In that same year Godfree, alert and sparkling as ever, was sent as a Wimbledon envoy to the Olympic Games at Seoul, where tennis was accepted back as a full-medal sport. She attended Wimbledon, as one friend said, "almost every minute of every year".

June 20 1992

REG HARRIS

REG HARRIS, one of Britain's most successful track cyclists, who died aged 72, was a sporting legend, twice voted the BBC's Sports Personality of the Year. Debonair and indomitable, Harris pursued his career over nearly half a century. In the immediate post-War years he was the fastest sprinter in the world. He took the amateur title in Paris in 1947, and won two silver medals in the 1948 Olympics before turning professional the next year, when he immediately won the first of his four professional championships in Copenhagen.

He stepped down from the saddle in 1957, eclipsed by Italy's Antonio Maspes. But 14 years later, Harris caused a sensation by announcing that he was returning to sprint racing at the age of 51. In 1971 he entered the British championship and reached the semi-final, which he lost to the Australian world champion "Gordie" Johnson, who was based in Britain. Undaunted, and by now convinced that age was no barrier to success, he took to intensive training, covering 120 miles a week.

He was sponsored by Drako Foam, a company for whom he worked as a consultant, and he also sought further help from his original sponsors, Raleigh. His age at first made Raleigh unwilling to back him again. However, when Harris pointed out that he was still beating the best Britain had – and that if they wanted the British title they should give him a bike – Raleigh agreed. And so in 1974, at the age of 54, he won his fifth British sprint championship, beating Trevor Bull on the steeply banked velodrome at Saffron Lane, Leicester. He was riding the original Raleigh frame, albeit slightly modified, that had brought him fame 25 years earlier.

Reginald Harris was born at Birtle, Lancashire, on March 1, 1920, and soon developed a love of bicycling. He began riding with the Bury section of the Cyclists' Touring Club. Young Reg's innate will to succeed quickly led him to competition. He moved first to the Lancashire Road Club and then in 1938 – after gentle persuasion from Jack Fletcher – he joined the Manchester Wheelers, the club with whom he remained throughout his competitive career.

During the Second World War, Harris served with the 10th Hussars ("the Shiners", nicknamed because their buttons were polished so brightly). As a tank driver in the Western Desert in North Africa in 1940, he was the only survivor when his tank was destroyed by enemy fire.

Harris was discharged as medically unfit, which he could not understand, as he had never felt better.

After the War he set his heart on competing in the 1948 Olympic Games in London. Already the world's fastest track rider, he considered himself capable of sweeping the board with gold medals in three events. It was not to be. Indeed, it seemed doubtful whether he would even be selected for the Olympics after a car accident which left him with his back broken in two places. He discharged himself from hospital in the spring of 1948 and four days later was in full training. However, a crash at Fallowfield Stadium, in Manchester, left him with a fractured radius.

Harris fought back to break the track kilometre record at Fallowfield (which he later acquired and renamed the Harris Stadium) of 1 minute 16.4 seconds. He was dismayed not to be selected for this, his favourite event in the Games. Nonetheless he won silver medals in the sprint race and, with Alan Bannister, in the tandem race. His memories of the 1948 Olympics were not happy, and he always regretted not winning a gold.

His five world records were all set as a professional. During his second incarnation it was typical of Harris not to retire without defending his title. Trevor Bull exacted his revenge in 1975. Though Harris then finally left the track, he continued to ride almost daily in the Cheshire lanes near his house in Lower Withington until he died. Reg Harris had a penchant for fast cars and cherished his stable of racing bicycles, as he did his wine cellar. Harris was appointed OBE in 1958. He is survived by his third wife, Jennifer.

June 23 1992

DAN MASKELL

DAN MASKELL, who died aged 84, had a magnificent record as a professional tennis player, but it was for his television coverage of Wimbledon that he became universally known, as integral a part of the tournament as strawberries and cream. His stock remarks – the enthusiastic "Oh, I say", the incredulous "quite extraordinary", the ecstatic "dream of a backhand" – became national catchphrases. They reflected not only Maskell's unfading appreciation of the game – viewed from "the best seat in the house" – but the warm-hearted nature of the man himself.

Arthur Ashe, the first black player to win the men's singles title at Wimbledon, summed up Maskell's appeal. Unable to attend the championships one year, he kept in touch through BBC Television, "and as soon as I heard Dan's voice I knew that all was well with the world".

An engineer's son, the seventh of eight children, Daniel Maskell was born on April 11, 1908, in Fulham, not far from Queen's Club, which would play a crucial part in his career. The boy's upbringing was humble but strict. Though his mother died when he was 14, his father maintained tight control, insisting that his children called him "Sir". At 11 Dan gained a place at the Upper Latymer School, Hammersmith. However, as the fees were beyond the family's means, he went instead to the local Everington Street School, where his athletic prowess soon became apparent. A centre-half, he captained the school football team.

Maskell's first brush with tennis was a job as a part-time ball-boy at Queen's Club during the school holidays. "It was a better way of earning pocket money than delivering bread," he said. At that epoch the club played host to many different games, including the Oxford and Cambridge football, rugby and athletic matches. Maskell never forgot seeing Harold Abrahams winning the 100 yards for Cambridge against Oxford's Rex Alston, later the BBC's chief cricket commentator; or Lord Burghley winning both the high and low hurdles for three years in succession.

Yet it was lawn tennis that became Maskell's passion. Every August, when many Queen's Club members were on holiday, there were tennis matches involving some of the club's younger members, the youngest club professionals and the best of the ball-boys. John Oliff, later a British Davis Cup player and tennis correspondent of *The Daily Telegraph*, immediately recognised Maskell as a special talent.

Maskell's ambition was to become a permanent Queen's Club ball-boy and then a teaching professional. In 1923 he achieved the first stage; and within a year was appointed a junior (teaching) professional. By 1926 he had a five-year contract to teach lawn tennis, real tennis, rackets and squash at Queen's. Maskell remembered being a ball-boy for the Duke of York (later King George VI), who partnered Wing-Cdr Louis Greig. The pair won the RAF doubles championship and competed at Wimbledon in 1926.

As the years went by Maskell found himself on court with many of the great players, from Jean Borotra, Henri Cochet, Suzanne Lenglen and Helen Wills in the 1920s to "Little Mo" Connolly and Doris Hart in the 1950s, and Angela Mortimer and Ann Jones in the 1960s. Maskell could not compete against these amateur players in tournaments. However, against fellow professionals, he excelled, winning the British Professional Championship 16 times by 1951. He also helped set up the World Professional Championships, and was the first winner of that now defunct tournament.

In 1929 Maskell became the first teaching professional at the All England Club. His duties at Wimbledon included assisting in the preparation of Britain's Davis Cup players, and he was coach to the team who, inspired by Fred Perry, not only won back the Davis Cup from France in Paris in 1933 but retained it on the Centre Court at Wimbledon for the next three years until Perry turned professional. During the Second World War – when Wimbledon variously housed civilian and military personnel, and the grounds were used for farming – Maskell served with the RAF as a rehabilitation officer, based first at the Palace Hotel, Torquay, and then at Loughborough.

His broadcasting career began in 1949, when he joined Max Robertson as a summariser in the wireless box at Wimbledon. Two years later he was invited, on trial, to join the late Freddie Grisewood in covering Wimbledon on television. He proved an instant success. When, a few months later, Grisewood became chairman for the launch of BBC Radio's *Any Questions?* Maskell took over his role at Wimbledon. He soon found his style. His golden rule, which he credited to the golfing legend Henry Longhurst, was that "a second's silence is worth a minute's talk". The long silent periods exasperated American television producers whenever BBC transmissions, complete with commentary, went directly to the States, though they elicited appreciative letters to the *New York Times*.

For 62 years – from 1929 until his retirement from the BBC at the end of 1991 – Maskell never missed a single day's play of the Wimbledon Championships. Indeed his association with the tournament went back even further, to the 1924 women's singles final, when he saw Kitty McKane (later Kitty Godfree) beat Helen Wills, the only match Wills lost in nine visits to the tournament.

In 1953 Maskell became the first professional to become an honorary member of the All England Club. Two years later, on his own insistence, he relinquished his role as Davis Cup coach. From then until his retirement in 1973 he devoted himself to transforming the coaching and development work of the Lawn Tennis Association. Not that this in any way diminished his support for domestic tennis. Hardly any national junior championships event passed without Maskell in attendance: he appraised each successive generation of players with the same meticulous devotion to detail which he applied to his research before every broadcast.

Maskell continued to be in great demand as a coach. He worked with Christine Truman (French champion at the age of 17 in 1959, and Wimbledon runner-up two years later) from the time she was 13. He coached Princess Alexandra, the Princess Royal (whom he considered had championship potential), Prince Charles and Prince Andrew.

Maskell wrote an engagingly modest autobiography, *From Where I Sit* (1988). He was also a keen skier and golfer. He was appointed CBE in 1982. He married, in 1936, Connie Cox, who died in a swimming accident in

Antigua in 1978. They had a son (a pilot killed in an accident in 1970) and a daughter. Maskell is survived by his second wife, Kay, whom he married in 1980.

December 11 1992

TED CROKER

EDGAR ALFRED "TED" CROKER did not know, when he became secretary of the Football Association in 1973, that he was facing the most violent and turbulent era in the game's history. It is a measure of the man that, had he known, he would certainly have still accepted the challenge. During his 16 years at Lancaster Gate, English professional football was almost forced to its knees by the tragedies of Heysel and Bradford, the exclusion from Europe of its clubs, the daily threat of hooliganism, poor playing standards and lax discipline on the pitch, declining gates, a crumbling economy within the game, and what he saw as political interference. That the game came through these dark years with its health and dignity more or less intact was due, in impressive degree, to Croker's firm but conciliatory approach to his job.

The FA's income from business enterprises and royalties when he took over was £24,000 a year. By the time he retired in 1989 the FA had, among other things, distributed £1.5 million on hard-play areas all over the country and had reserves of well over £3 million. It was his initiative, in his first year as FA secretary, which led to the annual FA Charity Shield match being moved to Wembley. Since 1974, it has raised more than £3 million for charity.

His diplomacy was not always faultless. He was frequently summoned to 10 Downing Street to account for hooliganism and on one visit, with a bold disregard for his own health, he suggested to Mrs Thatcher that "these people are society's problem and we don't want your hooligans in our sport". Neil Macfarlane, the Minister for Sport, said that later he felt like diving for shelter under the table, but the Prime Minister's reply was placatory. "Steady the Buffs," she said.

Croker, who was born in Kingston in February 1924, and whose father was a commercial traveller in confectionery, brought a personable image and new experience to the post of FA secretary. He was an RAF pilot who received the King's Commendation for Brave Conduct in the 1947 New Year's Honours List. This was after his plane had crashed in the Pennines and, with both ankles broken, he had crawled for help in freezing conditions. He was also a successful businessman who developed a snow-clearing vehicle. It was called the "Croker Sno-Blo", the first machine cost just under £1,000 and 300 of them were sold in six years. Later he moved into the field of concrete and motorways.

Croker learnt from a newspaper advertisement that the FA were looking for a secretary, and among the qualities which impressed the aldermen of Lancaster Gate was his experience as a professional footballer. He played eight First Division games for Charlton in 1950 as a resolute centre-half who later played good-quality non-League football. His elder brother, Peter, played for Charlton's winning side in the 1947 FA Cup Final. Ted Croker had an easy dignity and a warm, open manner which made him many friends. On the golf course and tennis court, however, he was a formidable competitor.

He leaves a wife, Kathy, a son, Andrew, and a daughter, Louise.

December 28 1992

ARTHUR ASHE

ARTHUR ASHE, the former Wimbledon tennis champion, who died in New York aged 49, was a true sporting hero, a paragon of grace, charm and dignity. In the Wimbledon quarter-finals of 1975 he beat Bjorn Borg, who had just won the French Open. He then engaged in a marathon struggle to beat Tony Roche, the Australian left-hander, 6–4 in the fifth set. Jimmy Connors, the defending champion and nine years Ashe's junior, was the clear favourite for the final. Ashe changed his entire style for that contest. The night before, with the help of friends, he had devised a brilliant tactical plan on a napkin over dinner, and he applied this on the day with exemplary craft and cunning, turning all Connors's ferocity against him.

Connors was then at his most intimidating, and during the change-overs would stare fiercely at his opponent; Ashe sat calmly, eyes closed. He stunned Connors by taking the opening two sets 6–1, and although "Jimbo" fought back to take the third 7–5, Ashe clinched victory in the fourth set 6–4. "The significance of my Wimbledon victory," Ashe later wrote, "began to dawn on me 48 hours later. I had to make an appearance for a sportswear company in Pittsburg, and 1,500 fans mobbed the store. Wimbledon is 'The Championship'. It represents the highest achievement in my craft."

Ashe became one of the most celebrated figures in America, widely tipped for an ambassadorship. However, he suffered from a congenital heart defect, and in 1979 had his first heart attack, which led to two multiple bypass operations. After the second of these, in 1983 – 18 months before the United States introduced routine blood screening – he was given two pints of blood tainted by the virus which later became known as HIV.

His athletic career at an end, Ashe devoted himself to various tennis activities, to broadcasting, writing and charity work. He was diagnosed as HIV positive in 1988, and in April 1992, when an American newspaper told him it was going to publish the fact of his illness, Ashe called a press conference to make his own announcement. The impact of this may be measured by the reaction of a notoriously foul-mouthed and cynical New York sports writer, who broke down and cried: "As a tennis player he was poetry in motion, sure – but that was a small thing. As a man he was the sweetest of the sweet."

Arthur Robert Ashe was born at Richmond, Virginia, on July 10, 1943. His mother died two years later, and he was brought up by his father, a special policeman in Richmond's recreational department. As he accompanied his father in delivering old clothes and food to poor families, young Arthur was imbued with the message that "you get nowhere by making enemies. You gain by helping others". It was an ethic he always subscribed to, though it was sometimes severely tested.

When he first wanted to play in junior tournaments in Richmond he was refused entry because he was black. He won a scholarship to the University of California at

Los Angeles, but when the tennis team were invited to play at fashionable country clubs Ashe was not included. As he wrote in *Off the Court* (1982): "There was a great deal of fuss about being the first black Junior Davis Cup player, the first black to win a tennis scholarship to UCLA ... the fact that this kind of accomplishment by a black player got so much attention was an indication that we still had so far to go." Later, as an established champion, Ashe made a point of visiting South Africa, where he was convinced that sport could help to overcome injustice. Many black South Africans opposed his visit, but when Nelson Mandela visited America, and was asked who he most wanted to meet, his first choice was Arthur Ashe.

In 1968 Ashe made his mark as an amateur with a brilliant victory in the US Open and turned professional. He also helped the United States to win back the Davis Cup from Australia for the first time in 10 years. In 1968 and 1969 Ashe reached the semi-finals at Wimbledon, losing on both occasions to Rod Laver. In the early 1970s he continued his tournament successes (including the Australian Open) and found an outlet for his political leanings in the newly formed Professional Players' Association. After winning Wimbledon Ashe continued to play for another four years, accumulating prize money of $1.58 million and winning 33 singles and 18 doubles titles.

He went on to become a tennis commentator on American television and a columnist on the *Washington Post*. In 1983 he began a five-year stint as captain of the US Davis Cup team, which entailed keeping such volatile personalities as Connors and John McEnroe in line. He supported a number of charities, and was a co-founder of the Black Tennis Association. He made a number of visits to Africa, where he discovered in Cameroon the 11-year-old Yannick Noah, who went on to win the French Open in 1983. Ashe won an Emmy for co-writing a television adaptation of his memoirs, *A Hard Road to Glory*. He was married and had a daughter.

February 8 1993

BOBBY MOORE

BOBBY MOORE was not only the greatest defender in British football history, but the most distinguished of all England captains. From the moment that he lifted the Jules Rimet Trophy after England's World Cup success at 5.15pm on July 30, 1966, he and his team-mates were guaranteed a place in English sporting folklore. Moore had achieved something no other player had managed as he steered England to the country's greatest sporting triumph with the 4–2 victory over West Germany. The pictures flashed around the world of Moore, lifted shoulder high by his team-mates, holding the World Cup aloft.

He and his team had fulfilled Sir Alf Ramsey's prophecy that this was to be "the biggest day of their lives". Ramsey, knighted the following year, told them: "You are going to win." Moore himself said: "It never crossed our minds we could lose. No, never. It didn't come into it." There were further honours for Moore, regarded by Pele as the world's best defender, when he was named the player of the tournament in 1966. He handled those accolades in the same even-handed way that he treated everything. More than just a great footballer, Moore was the perfect role model for the modern player.

It was again at Wembley that Moore, supported by his second wife Stephanie, and daughter Roberta, returned the week before his death for his final public appearance, as a commentator for Capital Gold Radio soon after announcing that cancer of the colon had spread to his liver. In spite of pain and the effects of chemotherapy Moore's insistence that he should be at the microphone for the World Cup game against San Marino illustrated the dignity and determination that was the hallmark of his life. He was a great ambassador for his country, recognised wherever he travelled with the England team, a shining example of all that was good in English football.

Born in Barking on April 12, 1941, Moore, like most footballers from the East End of London, began his professional career at West Ham United in the late 1950s. Others at the club, like Malcolm Allison, recognised that Moore had not only the talent but the temperament to become one of the world's outstanding performers. By the age of 17 Moore had captained England at youth level. He made eight under-23 appearances before making his full debut 11 days before the start of the 1962 World Cup in Chile.

His England career started against Peru in Lima on May 20, 1962. Until Peter Shilton overtook him in Denmark in 1989, he had won the most England caps. The last of his 108 games for his country was in the defeat by Italy at Wembley in November 1973. Until then no player had served his country so often, and few have served it with such distinction. Moore captained

England 90 times – a record that he shares with Billy Wright and which still stands – winning 57 matches and losing only 13. He was named the Football Writers' Association Footballer of the Year in 1964, and led West Ham to FA Cup success in 1964 and the European Cup-Winners' Cup a year later. He was awarded the OBE in 1967.

Even when he left Upton Park, his footballing home for almost 20 years, he helped Alan Mullery revive Fulham's fortunes, and in 1975 Moore was back at Wembley for the FA Cup Final, coincidentally against West Ham. There were darker periods, but with the exception of being falsely accused of stealing a bracelet in Bogota, Colombia, after a World Cup warm-up game in 1970, most came after his retirement.

With English football's typical failure to embrace those who have performed at the highest level – only Jack Charlton had a distinguished managerial career – Moore retired from football to concentrate on business interests in 1977. He was lured back into the game in 1979 as manager of non-League Oxford City, and in 1983 became manager and director of Southend. He left the club in 1986 and made his first venture into journalism, as sports editor of *Sunday Sport*. However, he was more comfortable as match analyser for Capital Radio. It offered Moore the chance to not only see London's leading sides, but also to travel again with the England football team. He said: "Analysing and commentating on these games is one of the great pleasures in my life."

On those trips players found Moore only too willing to pass on his experience. He was respected and held in high esteem by those who followed in his footsteps. Like all great sportsmen there was a humility about Moore that made him approachable not only to players and fans, but also to his fellow journalists who were searching for a valuable insight into the game he had graced.

He had been working hard in the winter before his death with his sports promotion company and was working on projects in the United States aimed at the 1994 World Cup finals.

Bryon Butler writes: Robert Frederick Chelsea Moore was undoubtedly created for the role and the moment. He and the World Cup looked so right together on that summer evening in 1966 when, for the first and only time, the country who gave football to the world also had the right to regard itself as the world's best at the game.

It was 5.15pm on the last Saturday on July; and as Moore, with his cropped and parted blond hair, open face and easy smile, held up the World Cup, a piece of gold about the height of a milk bottle, the boom of the Wembley crowd developed a subtle edge. It was like the purr of a cat. It was a moment of total fulfilment and Moore, at that moment, became someone very special in the history of a nation who care more for their sportsmen and entertainers than for their protectors and policy-makers. The victory was a moment which changed his life in many inevitable ways; but it did not change him. Indeed, it is a measure of Moore that the man will be remembered almost as much as the player. He had a natural dignity which persuaded many who did not know him that he was unemotional and even cold. He was, indeed, a private person, but he was also a good and caring friend with a dry sense of humour, a concern for others and, in the often unkind years which followed his playing career, he showed both patience and tolerance.

The style is the man and Moore as a player, as captain of England and West Ham, and a central character in more than 1,000 games, was always true to himself. He was a stylist who lent dignity to the simplest chore, never hurried, never emotional and able to work in a dimension of his own choosing.

He wore the No. 6 shirt in central defence, of course, a man who covered and provided depth with unobtrusive authority and when necessary carried the world on his shoulders. He was a tactician who frustrated rather than destroyed, an opponent who was at his best against the best. He seemed to dictate the pace of a game, to influence its mood and even to decide the areas in which the crucial battles were to be fought. Opposing managers and players were always looking for weaknesses in Moore's armoury. They discovered so many – lack of speed, poor heading ability, and lack of venom in the tackle – that it was a wonder he progressed beyond the local park. Poor chaps: they had missed the whole essence of Moore's game. His most important asset was the quickness of his mind, and the vision to assess a situation before others had noticed the situation existed. The simple truth is that Moore usually thought first and moved first. He had a natural relationship with every football. He was ahead of the game. And he attracted admiration and jealousy in equal parts.

Moore, however, was more than just a talented mugger. He could move forward with surprising quickness and then use the ball with stunning perception and accuracy. Everyone's final memory of the 1966 World Cup Final is of Geoff Hurst completing his hat-trick. Who remembers the 35-yard pass, delivered perfectly by

Moore, which sent Hurst thundering into the record books?

Moore at Wembley became an established sight in the mid-Sixties. Moore leading West Ham to victory in the 1964 FA Cup Final, Moore leading his club to triumph in the European Cup-Winners' Cup a year later and Moore, of course, as English football climbed its Everest, kissing that little winged seraphim known as the World Cup. However, never was Moore seen in a stronger light than in the 1970 World Cup in Mexico. Before the tournament began, he was outrageously accused by a shop girl of stealing an emerald and diamond bracelet from a small jewellery boutique in Bogota, where England were playing Colombia. He remained ice cool during four days of legal sword-play and global publicity, trained in between times and returned to Mexico to a hero's welcome and an outstanding World Cup. Pele described him simply as "the finest defender in the world".

Moore's career was not without its hiccups and warts. Ron Greenwood, his mentor at West Ham, remembered the young Moore as a first-class technician – but also as someone who was "heavy-legged, not a good runner and a poor header". Greenwood switched him from wing-half to central defence and, said Greenwood, Moore then made himself into a great player – "always asking questions, always picking people's brains and always listening very carefully".

There was also a dark occasion in 1971, when Moore, in the company of Jimmy Greaves and one or two other players, broke curfew on the night before an FA Cup tie at Blackpool. Greenwood wanted to sack them all, but was overruled by the West Ham directors. Moore, then, was more than a sporting icon: he was a stylish and dedicated man-about-town.

Moore, the man, adorned many of London's night-spots, but Moore, the player, also adorned every side he played for, and especially England. He won 108 caps and I remember talking to him near the end of his international career, in Turin in 1973, and he spoke as if the most important chapter in his life was closing. It was. Moore reached Wembley once more, in 1975, with the help of Alec Stock and Fulham, but life after football was not what it should have been. He never made it as a manager or as a businessman, but Moore, to the end, always knew his own worth. He was one of the few giants of our national game.

February 25 1993

JAMES HUNT

JAMES HUNT, who died aged 45, was one of the select band of English motor-racing world champions. He won the Formula One title in 1976 by one point, retired from the track after two more seasons, and later gained fresh fame on television for his authoritative counterpoint to the excitable Grand Prix commentating style of the much older Murray Walker.

Compared with the current crop of teetotal, non-smoking multi-millionaire world champions, Hunt seemed to belong to a different era. While in some ways personifying the devil-may-care relaxed approach of the gifted amateur, he could, as he proved in his championship-winning year, drive with the utmost skill and professionalism.

A stockbroker's son, James Simon Wallis Hunt was born in Surrey on August 29, 1947, and educated at Wellington College, where he was cross-country-running and rackets champion. From an early age he set his heart on a career in motor racing. When he left school he took various odd jobs, including hospital porter and ice-cream salesman, to save money for motor-racing instruction at Brands Hatch. He cut his racing teeth in Minis, graduating to Formula Three, a nursery for up-and-coming single-seat Grand Prix drivers. Never a natural driver in the Jim Clark mould, Hunt learnt the hard way in endless crashes, in the process earning himself the nickname "Hunt the Shunt". He seemed destined to be yet another eager young competitor who had struggled in the hard and unforgiving school of Formula Three, and begun the slog up the foothills of Formula One, the Everest of motor racing, when his luck changed.

Lord Hesketh, later Government Chief Whip in the House of Lords, but then a motor-racing enthusiast with money to spend, founded the Hesketh Grand Prix team to try and restore prestige to English motor racing. To preserve the essential public school spirit of the venture, which had a cuddly bear as its mascot, Hunt was the appointed driver. The main participants, Lord Hesketh ("*le patron*", or, as far as Hunt was concerned, "The Good Lord"), the manager "Bubbles" Horsley and to a lesser extent Hunt himself, deliberately fostered a Wodehousian image to confuse the foreign competition. Underneath, in perfidious English fashion, they were deadly serious. Hunt had, in fact, done surprisingly well in view of his accident-prone Formula Three record, in his Grand Prix debut season in 1973 with March Ford.

He announced himself as a newcomer to be reckoned with, scoring 14 points to finish a creditable eighth in the World Championship. He was sixth in the French Grand Prix; fourth at Silverstone; third in Holland; and ended the season a very close second in the United States Grand Prix at Watkins Glen. In the 1974 season, Hunt scored 15 World Championship points, again in eighth place, putting the new car on the front row of the starting grid in the American Grand Prix and finishing third.

Outright victory against heavily sponsored and fancied teams such as McLaren, Ferrari, Brabham and Lotus seemed like a pipedream, yet it was to be achieved in 1975, the Hesketh team's *annus mirabilis*. Hunt started the year on a high note, finishing second to the 1974 world champion, Emerson Fittipaldi's McLaren, in Argentina. On June 27, 1975, a day never to be forgotten by British motor-racing enthusiasts, the little Hesketh team won the Dutch Grand Prix, with Hunt beating Niki Lauda's Ferrari fair and square by one minute six seconds. This was to be the team's real moment of glory, though Hunt went on to achieve two more second places. He ended the year fourth in the Drivers' World Championship with 33 points, behind Lauda, Fittipaldi and Carlos Reutemann (Brabham-Ford).

He was to now receive that extra nudge of good luck that any driver needs. Fittipaldi, the double world champion, quixotically deserted McLaren to start his own Brazilian, and remarkably unsuccessful, Grand Prix team. An opportunity to drive for a Formula One team with a proven track record of winning world championships was too good to miss, and unexpectedly Hunt found himself as No. 1 driver with one of the Goliaths of the sport, instead of merely a promising David.

The 1976 season was to test his mettle to the utmost. Not only did he turn in some exceptionally fine driving performances, but the season was fraught with altercations and disputes over technicalities. It seemed as if far too many of the year's races were being decided in committee rooms on appeal. Even so, it was a titanic struggle throughout the year between Hunt and Lauda, conducted with fairness and mutual respect by both men, regardless of what was happening behind the scenes.

Lauda won the first two races in Brazil and South Africa, and Hunt won in Spain only to have the result contested and later reinstated. Lauda won in Monaco, but Hunt won in France. Lauda took the British Grand Prix and Hunt was victorious on that most daunting of all circuits, the Nurburgring, when Lauda was severely burnt when his Ferrari crashed. In Lauda's absence, Hunt won his second Dutch Grand Prix, as well as in Canada and America, so that when Lauda returned to racing within a few weeks of his crash, the World Championship was to be decided between the two men in the last race of the season, at the foot of Mount Fuji and in a deluge. Hunt had kept his nerve, and driven remarkably well, even though his critics maintained he had profited from Lauda's absence. However, he had also beaten Lauda fair and square and there was little to choose between either man, or the McLaren-Ford and the Ferrari.

Once again fortune favoured Hunt because Lauda was unable to see properly in the appalling conditions, and retired after two laps blinded by the spray from other cars. As car after car aquaplaned or spun off the track, Hunt, who had started on the front row alongside the eventual winner Mario Andretti (Lotus-Ford), drove the finest race of his career to finish third. In the process he gained four points, taking the Drivers' World Championship by one point from Lauda.

In 1979, Hunt stepped out of his car at the Monte Carlo Grand Prix and retired. He said later: "I was racing flat out, but after five laps I broke down. I felt enormous relief. I walked away from that car with a light step, well pleased. I have had no regrets." Excluding the Scots Jim Clark and Jackie Stewart, the Australians Sir Jack Brabham and Alan Jones, and the New Zealander Denny Hulme, Hunt belongs to the exclusive club of English world champions, Mike Hawthorn, Graham Hill, John Surtees and Nigel Mansell. His skilful and informative foil to Murray Walker in BBC Television Grand Prix reports, and his résumés in *The Daily Telegraph*'s sports pages gained him a new following in his later years.

With blond hair and a laconic personal style, Hunt had a glamorous and eventful private life, which kept him in the gossip columns as well as on the sports pages. Both his marriages ended in divorce. In 1974, he married former model Suzy Miller, who later married Richard Burton. His much-publicised six-year romance with model Jane Birbeck ended in 1981, soon after he returned with her, from tax exile in Marbella, to buy a house in Barons Court, West London, and a farm in Buckinghamshire. In 1983, he married Sarah Lomax, daughter of trainers Ian and Rosemary Lomax, and settled down in Wimbledon where he began breeding budgerigars. However, he and his wife parted in 1988, when their oldest son, Tom, was three and their youngest child, Freddie, was 15 months. In December 1990, receivers were called in when his business, the James Hunt Racing Centre, in

Milton Keynes, collapsed and in the same year his marriage was dissolved.

Murray Walker said: "What was extraordinary about James, as he pedalled around London on his bike in a T-shirt and shorts, was that he never showed any ill-feeling or self-pity about his predicament. He always talked about it with a laugh."

Timothy Collings writes: James Hunt was a warm, generous and independent man. He was a free spirit who enjoyed a full and colourful life, adding both a waspish humour and a serious understanding of the business to any sporting company. He was also a brilliant driver who won the world championship in 1976. Motor racing suffered a deep loss with his death. No Grand Prix paddock will seem quite the same again.

Always a maverick, James enjoyed a reputation for his eventful lifestyle, his sometimes light-hearted approach to conventions and his outspoken views as a television commentator with the BBC, and, of course, in his columns for *The Daily Telegraph*. During his racing years he had an image as a playboy with his blond hair, his sense of fun, his enjoyment of champagne and pretty girls. All this was true, as two broken marriages and several years of adventurous living, which led to financial difficulties, proved. However, none of it reflected the more relaxed and assured man he became in recent years, or threw sufficient praise on the talent which enabled him to become the first Englishman to win the world title since Graham Hill triumphed in 1968.

For much of his career, it seemed that James treated motor racing as a great pleasure, a "wheeze", something done for fun. "The only reason I walked up and down the pit road when I was a driver was to look at the crumpet," he admitted in later life. However, this was only a superficial view of an inconsistent, but sometimes dazzling driver who had an enormous impact on Formula One. James captured the imagination of a generation of racing fans with his stylish progress to the championship, won by just one point from Niki Lauda, when he finished third in the rain at Mount Fuji in Japan on October 24, 1976. He had been running fifth, with only a handful of laps remaining, but with typical competitive spirit fought his way through to take the title in utterly atrocious conditions.

"He was a bloody good driver, a very intelligent racer and so competitive that he would fight for every last fraction of an inch of the road," said John Watson. "He was very strong physically, and very athletic and he brought those qualities with him into his driving. It is ironic that, after driving those 92 Grands Prix in the 1970s, he should go in his middle forties. It's so hard to equate."

This same competitiveness remained with him in his attitude to all forms of sport. He lived his life the way he wanted, with his right foot down on the pedal, but he was fit and well, having given up drinking and smoking, and cycled several miles each day, before the heart attack while he slept at home in Wimbledon. His competitive sporting prowess showed early in his life and he competed in junior Wimbledon tennis, and was a squash player to county standard. However, it was cars not rackets which captured him and he chose to race first Minis and then, in 1968, Formula Ford before going on to break into Formula Three the following year. His outstanding performances earnt him the Grovewood

Award; his less outstanding ones the soubriquet "Hunt the Shunt".

In earlier days, particularly when he was driving for Lord Hesketh's charismatic, if small, team, James had earnt himself a reputation as a leader of riotous parties. He had grown up in the 1960s and not been short of disposable income. On one occasion, in Rio de Janeiro, it is said James relied upon his instant good humour and adroit sense of fun when he was caught riding up in a lift in the old-fashioned Copacabana Palace Hotel one night with a lady whose skin was many shades darker than his own. When faced by an angry desk clerk who informed him that ladies were not allowed in the guests' bedrooms, the instant reply was: "What do you mean? This is my sister."

Such adventures are just part of the folklore which went with Hunt from the earliest days of his career, when it was supposed he would become a doctor. Instead, he worked in a hospital as a porter, and later became an ice-cream salesman to help fund his motor-racing instruction. In recent times, however, James had devoted himself to his children whenever possible and on one recent occasion when I called him he told me he would ring me back because "I've got to nip out and buy fish and chips for their supper". Life was different but he seemed to enjoy the role of the middle-aged and responsible parent. James was the icon of his age in the 1970s and he will never be forgotten by that generation, who enjoyed his presence in the gossip columns as much as his speed on the track.

June 16 1993

DANNY BLANCHFLOWER

DANNY BLANCHFLOWER was a footballer who gave
the impression that the game was a higher art form which
would be so much better if only mud and wind, and
running and tackling and sweating, were not necessary.
The impression was misleading because Blanchflower
learnt to play between lamp-posts on the knee-scuffing
streets of his native Belfast; but he, perhaps more than
anyone, emphasised that men who kicked a ball for
a living could be intelligent, articulate, witty and
charming.

"The other team have their names on their track-
suits," observed the Duchess of Kent to Blanchflower as
she met Tottenham Hotspur's players before the 1961 FA
Cup Final against Leicester City. "Yes," replied the Spurs
captain, "but we know each other."

Robert Dennis Blanchflower, who died at the age of
67, was aware of his worth and was perfectly right for his
time, a time when the status of the professional footballer
was changing. He was one of a small number of men of
principle and courage who helped clear the path towards
the contractual and financial "freedom" of footballers in
the early 1960s.

Blanchflower played for Glentoran, Barnsley, Aston
Villa and Tottenham; captained Tottenham to the first
League and FA Cup Double of the 20th century in 1961,
and also to victory in the 1962 FA Cup and 1963
European Cup-Winners' Cup; was twice voted Footballer
of the Year; and led Northern Ireland to the quarter-
finals of the World Cup in 1958.

He managed Chelsea, briefly and ill-advisedly, and Northern Ireland, a little more successfully, and became a highly respected and outspoken journalist with the *Observer* and later the *Sunday Express*. "What do you think of this piece?" he would ask – and, without notes, recall every word, comma, and full stop of his latest article. He was once banned from the Arsenal press box, which gave him immense satisfaction.

Blanchflower, though, was much more than the sum of his milestones and medals. He was a realist but also a hopeless romantic; a winner but also a man of conscience; a rebel and a loner but a man who enjoyed the mateyness of the dressing-room. In some ways he was never young, in others he never quite grew up.

The style, above all, was the man. He was a wing-half who looked rather coltish when running, knee action high, shoulders squared, but his angular frame seemed to acquire new substance when there was business to be done. His balance and touch made ball control look the easiest thing in the world. His art was simplicity and he was, essentially, a correct player; but he was also an improviser who relished the unorthodox and who some-times treated himself – and the crowd – to little moments of self-indulgence. One foot would be brought down behind the other to clip a pass out to a wing.

Blanchflower's imagination and vision enabled him to change, subtly, the shape of a game or alter its balance of power. He probed for weaknesses like some-one stabbing a finger into an ample belly. In Dave Mackay he found a perfect counterpoint to his own ability and character. Together they were the fulcrum of Totten-ham's outstanding side of the early 1960s. Blanchflower on the right, Mackay of the left, Irish charm and Scottish steel, one thinking the game, the other carving it to pieces.

Bill Nicholson's Spurs were the stuff of dreams, efficient but brilliant, a team of collective excellence and individual brilliance, perfectly balanced, finely integrated. There was a perceptible air of superiority about them, almost a sense of destiny – and Blanchflower, as captain, had their total respect, which he guarded jealously.

In the 1958 World Cup, when Northern Ireland earnt the right, remarkably, to be regarded as one of the best eight sides in the world, it was Blanchflower as captain more than Peter Doherty, the manager, who gave the side their unorthodox character. It was he, for example, who rehearsed set-pieces, and some of his ideas were 20 years before their time. As manager of Northern Ireland, Blanchflower is remembered as a man who refused a contract and who had to be persuaded to claim his expenses. The game was always more to him than just a living.

He cherished his independence, a fact emphasised when he refused to be the subject of the television programme *This Is Your Life*. "I just didn't fancy the idea," he said simply. Blanchflower's private life was not always happy and was sometimes confused. He was married three times and, a few years ago, living in modest circumstances and in poor health, he was inordinately grateful for a testimonial which brought him £40,000. However, Blanchflower will be remembered as a man of charm and intelligence who chose the simple game of football as a way of expressing himself. He dignified and adorned his profession.

December 10 1993

SIR MATT BUSBY

SIR MATT BUSBY, who died aged 84, was a gentle Scot who became the father figure of English football and one of the greatest managers in its history. An illustrious career saw him achieve success first as a player, then as the far-seeing architect of three triumphant Manchester United teams of the Forties, Fifties and Sixties. The last of these came after the Munich air disaster had wiped out the "Busby Babes" – a team who, despite an average age of 21, contained a host of stars.

Eight players were among the 23 who died in the crash, which left Busby critically injured with fractured ribs and a punctured lung; he was twice given the last rites in a German hospital and the doctors issued a statement saying: "We do not have much hope of saving him."

Busby was haunted regularly by memories of the disaster, but he shrugged these off, found new and outstanding young players and within a season had fashioned a brilliant team of outstanding players who went on to become the first English side to win the European Cup. He described that as "the greatest and most memorable event of my life".

Busby was born on May 26, 1909, at Bellshill, in Lanarkshire, the eldest of four children who experienced a hard upbringing. When Busby was six his father was killed on the Somme. His mother had to take a job at the pit top to provide for her family. At grammar school Busby captained the football team, and in February 1928, then 17, he signed professional forms for Manchester City.

However, by the 1930 season he found himself without a place in the first or reserve teams. The turning point came when a player failed to appear for a first-team game. Busby, a forward, went into the half-back line and did so well that he never lost his position there. It was this experience that probably led to his reputation as a patient, kind manager. If a player was not doing well, Busby would usually persevere with him. He earnt an FA Cup runners-up medal with Manchester City in 1933, was in their winning side at Wembley 12 months later and shortly afterwards was capped by Scotland against Wales. In 1936 he was transferred to Liverpool and it was there that his playing career ended during the Second World War, when he joined the Army and became a physical training instructor.

His entry into management at Old Trafford on October 17, 1945, was scarcely auspicious. His first office was in a £30 Nissen hut at the bombed-out ground, but the modest, quietly spoken Scot quickly fashioned a successful team. By 1948 he was back at Wembley, as manager of United's first FA Cup-winning team since 1909. The team included such outstanding names as Aston, Carey, Cockburn, Delaney, Pearson, Rowley and Mitten; they beat Blackpool – Stanley Matthews and all – 4–2. Three years later United won their first League Championship for more than 40 years. Busby knew, though, he faced the difficult task of breaking up an ageing team and fashioning another.

By 1956 that job was well under way, with United again topping the First Division. This second team, the "Busby Babes", was probably the greatest of his three, with such names as Bryne, Edwards, Coleman, Taylor, Viollet and Pegg. They retained the championship in

1957, and failed to complete the Double largely because their goalkeeper was injured during the FA Cup Final against Aston Villa. No one can know how good the "Busby Babes" might have become.

On February 6, 1958, returning from a European Cup quarter-final in Belgrade, their BEA Elizabethan airliner twice tried to take off in the freezing snow of Munich airport, and each time it was aborted. On the third attempt the plane failed to gain sufficient speed, swerved towards the perimeter fence, struck a building and burst into flames.

The death of men he had regarded almost as sons was a dreadful blow to this most sensitive of men. Busby often saw their images as he gazed across the empty Old Trafford pitch. Years later, he still talked of them sadly and affectionately. He felt a certain guilt about the disaster. His team had gone to Belgrade to play in the European Cup against the wishes of the Football League, who, at that time, did not want to take attention away from domestic football. Busby often wondered whether he might have exerted influence on the pilot, Capt. James Thain, not to make a third attempt to get the chartered aircraft off the ground.

Months after the crash, when his own wounds had healed, he returned to his office at Old Trafford to begin rebuilding yet again. Football, and Manchester United, can thank his devoted wife, Jean, for his successful return to the sport. It was she who told him: "You know, Matt, the lads would have wanted you to carry on."

Immediately after the crash, the Manchester United team travelled to matches on the Continent by sea and train, nervous about taking to the air again. Busby admitted that facing flying again was particularly hard for him. He and the team cracked their fear only after he and the chairman, Mr Louis Edwards, went to the airport, drank "a lot of Scotches" and bought two day-return tickets to Rotterdam. "I've never had a problem with flying since," he said.

Those who escaped serious injury in the crash formed the nucleus of the new side: Bill Foulkes, Harry Gregg and Bobby Charlton. To these were added the likes of Denis Law, Pat Crerand, David Herd, Shay Brennan, Tony Dunne, and later George Best and Nobby Stiles. Arising from the ashes of Munich, the side won the FA Cup in 1963 and the League Championship in 1965 and 1967.

The greatest success was still to come. In May 1968, United beat Benfica in extra time in a passionate European Cup Final at Wembley, to become the first English holders of the elusive trophy. The following year, he became the first club manager in British football to be knighted.

Then, in January 1969, with the "reluctant" agreement of the directors, he announced that he would relinquish the team managership at the end of the season to take over the less taxing post of general manager. His achievements included four Cup Finals – two of them successful – and five League Championships and a further seven seasons when they were runners-up.

Busby became a highly respected elder statesman of English football as a United director, a vice-president of the League and an FA councillor. Following a heart attack in 1981, he resigned his League and FA positions in the summer of 1982. He also left the United board soon afterwards for health reasons, but continued to take an active interest in club affairs as president. He was rewarded with the CBE in 1958, soon after the Munich disaster, as well as the knighthood 10 years later. He was also made a freeman of the City of Manchester. The Pope awarded him a Knight Commander, Order of St Gregory the Great, for his work for charity and the Roman Catholic Church. Busby and his wife were married in 1931, and had five sons, four who predeceased him, and a daughter.

After Busby's long association with Manchester United had ended, it was pertinent to ask: "What made him the man he was?" There is no simple answer. However, it took courage, toughness, good humour, firmness, sensitivity, shrewdness, kindliness, bluntness, tolerance, a lifetime's dedication to the game he loved and, above all, great humanity to produce the Matt Busby whom all football revered.

A former United chairman, the late Harold Hardman, once explained how things were done at Old Trafford. "Matt," he said, "will seek the board's advice, ponder over it – then go away and do precisely what he wants." To the players, he was a father figure. "Mr Busby," one of his players once said, "talks to us quietly but never leaves us in doubt that he is the boss. Though a strict disciplinarian when he feels it is necessary, he always understands the players' point of view."

No one knew him better than Jimmy Murphy, the Welshman who was his assistant during most of the glorious years. "Patience," suggested Mr Murphy, "was his greatest asset. Our partnership was built on friendship, mutual trust and respect."

Bryon Butler writes: The spirit of Matt Busby will fill Old Trafford as long as it stands, and he would have hated the songs of praise which followed his death. Not because he was unaware of his achievements and monumental standing in the game – he always knew his own worth – but because he was, above all, a humble man. The greater the man, the greater the humility.

No club has given more to English football than Manchester United and no man gave more to United than Busby; but he was more than simply the most revered member of his profession – he was a symbol of sport on its highest plane. A true Olympian.

Busby was the son of a Lanarkshire miner who remained a man of the people, a singularly uncommon man who never lost the common touch. His achievements were mountainous but Busby was much more than the sum of his success. The style is the man and Busby stood alone. He was a family man and a spiritual man whose warmth was in his strong face, clear eyes and deep, warm voice. He had enormous self-respect but he had, too, enormous respect and compassion for others. Busby never forgot a Christian name and he was always impeccably dressed.

Busby was also a brave man, as well as a strong one. This was confirmed, above all, by the tragedy of Munich, but also by the way in which he led Manchester United into Europe while the rest of English football prevaricated shamelessly. It was just one more of the bridges he built. He had an eye for the grand design, but also for the smallest detail and he was, in most senses, ahead of his time.

Busby was the same after defeat as he was after victory. "Winning," he would say, "isn't the test of real achievement. There should be no conceit in victory and no despair in defeat." He never lost his conviction that football should be a thing of joy, an art as well as a science, and United, still, are proof that he was right.

He was always in charge, a man of immense charm but also iron-resolved: he was at his hardest when his voice was softest. He had the ability to reprimand without wounding. He commanded not only respect but also affection. He had his faults and, most of all, should have taken a much stronger line at times with certain players who let the club (and Busby) down; sometimes, though, he took severe action without making it public. The club always came first.

He was always a paternalist in a tough, unforgiving business. His pride in his players, his club and football knew no bounds, but he understood the frailty of the human condition. Busby grew with his club. His authority, the respect he commanded, the emphasis on team spirit and exemplary behaviour (compromised occasionally in his middle years but never for long) was a plant of slow growth, but he was always at his best when facing a crisis. He handled trouble intuitively, squarely and patiently, and his philosophy rarely let him down.

He was sometimes wrong but he always learnt from his mistakes and he said, often: "The time to judge me is when things are going wrong." He always found a bridge to cross troubled waters.

As time goes by, few will get near the real man. He was the most public, but also the most private, of men. Some will fail to separate reality and myth but Busby was essentially the most human of people, a man who always cared and always forgave. He was arguably the greatest manager of all; not the most successful, but if loyalty, respect, love and achievement in a broader sense

count for anything, then he stood apart. He breathed life
into Manchester United and joy into their football.

January 21 1994

JOHN CURRY

JOHN CURRY, who died aged 44 of an Aids-related
illness, was the first Briton to win an Olympic gold
medal for men's figure-skating. Before his performance at
the 1976 Olympics the men's events had been seen as
athletic exercises, judged purely on technique. Curry's
critics complained that he made the obligatory jumps
look "too easy"; one said he would never win top marks
as his skating was "not virile enough". However, he
persisted with his pioneering balletic style, and his graceful arabesques and elegant arm movements forced judges
to reappraise their methods of marking.

In his *annus mirabilis*, 1976, Curry won not only the
Olympic gold medal but also the European and World
titles. He then moved to America, where he formed his
own skating troupe and worked as a teacher and chore-
ographer in New York and San Francisco. He returned to
Britain in 1991, having developed Aids, and, though he
had previously been guarded about his personal life,
talked openly about the illness. "I think the more open
people are the easier it gets for everybody else, because it
demystifies it," he said. "I don't want other sufferers to
be frightened like I was."

John Curry was born in Solihull on September 9,
1949. His father owned a light-engineering firm in
Sutton Coldfield, and young John was brought up in the

Birmingham suburb of Acocks Green. To please his father, a sports enthusiast, he participated in track and field events at school. His real interest was ballet, which his father thought "not masculine", and persuaded him to try skating instead. "God knows why he thought figure-skating was OK," Curry said, "but he and my mother were marvellously encouraging."

John Curry immediately showed his talent as a skater. His athleticism made it easy for him to acquire the techniques of jumping and pirouetting, and he soon began to perfect his style. Early coaches were disconcerted by his gracefulness. "One coach used to grab my arm and push it back to my side if I finished with it in the air," he recalled. "It was natural to me but he hated it. It drove him crazy." The coach sent Curry to a doctor for "treatment" in an attempt to make him less elegant. Curry found a new coach, and by 1967 had become British junior champion.

He left school at 17, against his parents' wishes, and moved to Richmond to be near the ice-rink. He took a part-time job as a shelf-stacker at a local supermarket, and trained from 6 a.m. until noon every day. He spent the next three years in close competition with Haig Oundjian in Britain, finally beating him in 1970 to become British figure-skating champion.

In the early 1970s, after training with Carlo Fassi in Colorado, Curry quickly rose in international competition. From scraping a 12th place in the World Championships in 1971, he became silver medallist in the European Championships and bronze medallist in the World Championships of 1975. The next year he competed in the Winter Olympics. "My big worry during the Olympics," he recalled, "was that some fool would say, 'Curry skates like a gay and therefore has no right to a medal.'"

Curry's press conference was unique in that his team officials decided no reporters should attend. "I'm pretty frank," he remembered. "I think the officials were afraid that I'd say something that would blow it all." In the event Curry's sexuality proved to be of less interest than his talent on the ice. His combination of strength and elegance assured him the gold medal halfway through the event, though several of his major rivals had yet to skate.

Curry was appointed OBE in 1976. At the end of the year he gave up amateur status to start his troupe. He was not interested in the standard "ice spectaculars", which he described as "hundreds of skaters rushing about in a big white space". He favoured a carefully choreographed combination of skating and dancing. Curry was diagnosed HIV-positive in 1987, and left America for Britain four years later, having spent nearly all his savings on medical treatment. "New York is no place to be when you are ill," he said, "and I wanted to be around people I loved when things got really bad."

April 16 1994

AYRTON SENNA

AYRTON SENNA, who died after suffering head injuries in an accident during the San Marino Grand Prix, was widely regarded as the finest motor-racing driver of his generation and one of the greatest of all time. He was 34.

Born in São Paulo, Brazil, on March 21, 1960, Senna

started in 161 Grands Prix, winning 41 and claiming a record total of 65 pole positions. His final pole position was the one he took on the afternoon before his death during a final qualifying session at the tragedy-shrouded Autodromo Enzo e Dino Ferrari, where fellow competitor, Austrian Roland Ratzenberger, lost his life the previous day.

Senna's reputation as both a great driver and a man of deep feelings was demonstrated when he decided to travel by circuit car to see the scene of Ratzenberger's death for himself. Afterwards, he was unable to take any further part in the practice session.

Senna will be remembered for his brilliant talent as a racer, and also for his unprecedentedly high level of commitment to winning Grand Prix races. It was this which cost him his life. He had dedicated his adult life to succeeding in the business of Grand Prix racing after travelling from Brazil to enter the British Formula Ford 1600 Championship in 1981. Before this he had enjoyed a hugely successful karting career which had begun at the age of four, when he first climbed aboard a motorised vehicle. By the time he was 13 he was racing in go-karts. He went on to win the 1977 Pan American Championship and finished as runner-up in the karting world championships of 1979 and 1980.

He climbed the classic motor-racing career ladder by driving in the British Formula Ford series, winning the British and European Formula Ford 2000 Championship in 1982. The following year he won the British Formula Three championship with West Surrey Racing before entering Formula One for the first time in 1984 with the Toleman team. He made his debut in the 1984 Brazilian Grand Prix, and that season collected 13 points to finish ninth in the championship, his startling, brilliant and aggressive driving earning admiration from many, though also incurring the wrath of several of his senior fellow competitors. "Winning is like a drug," he once said. "I cannot justify in any circumstances coming second or third." Senna had the rare ability, and the courage, to go through gaps which others either could not see or felt they could not get through themselves.

The following season he transferred from Toleman to Lotus in a disputed move which led to accusations that he had broken his contract. However, for Senna, the only goal was success and in that season he claimed his first Grand Prix win in emphatic style in the rain at Estoril, Portugal. He finished fourth in the championship that year with 38 points. That first victory was the beginning of a dazzling collection as his career progressed from Lotus to the Marlboro-McLaren team, which he joined in 1988. In his first season with McLaren he collected 94 points and won the world championship, despite a season-long duel with his team-mate and arch-rival, Frenchman Alain Prost.

Senna remained with McLaren for six years, winning the world title three times before departing at the end of 1993. They were six glorious years for all those associated with the Woking-based team, as Senna established himself as the master of motor racing and arguably the greatest of his generation, with the possible exception of Prost. He made the decision to leave Mc-Laren at the end of 1993 because he wished to continue his single-minded pursuit of Formula One success with the team he felt best equipped to deliver it: Rothmans Williams-Renault.

However, Senna was unable to record a single race

victory with the Williams team, whose owner, Frank Williams, had given him his first test in a Formula One car a decade earlier, before he joined Toleman. Senna was an intelligent man, from a well-off family, and he accumulated great wealth of his own, commanding vast salaries for his work. Nothing, however, rewarded him so much as triumph on the track, something for which he will be remembered by everyone in Formula One.

He married, early in his racing career, his childhood sweetheart, but his young Brazilian wife found it impossible to cope in Europe and they later divorced. He had established a durable relationship with his girlfriend Adriane during the last 12 months of his life. He loved most sports, particularly water-skiing and jet-skiing, and was synonymous with everything Brazilian, taking every opportunity to promote his country, its culture, language, food and character.

An intensely religious man, Senna said: "To survive in Grand Prix racing you need to be afraid. Fear is a very important feeling to have. It helps you stay together. It helps you race longer and live longer."

May 2 1994

LEW HOAD

LEW HOAD, who died in Spain aged 59, was one of the greatest and most charismatic lawn tennis champions. With his striking blue eyes, blond hair and heroic build, Hoad was the heart-throb of the game, and on his day he was unbeatable. Apart from a fine serve and a potent volley, he developed a backhand return whereby he rolled his wrist at the moment of impact and sent the ball back like a bullet.

Such techniques compensated for the back pains he suffered in his early twenties. Hoad loved to tell the story of how, a few days before he won both the singles and doubles titles at Wimbledon in 1956, he saw an orthopaedic specialist about twinges in his back. He had already won the Australian, Italian and French titles that year, and was regarded as the fittest and strongest player that lawn tennis had seen. "I don't think the doctor who saw me knew who I was," he recalled, "because he told me, 'Young man, you must get more exercise.'"

A year later Hoad retained his Wimbledon crown by thrashing his fellow Australian, Ashley Cooper, 6–2, 6–1, 6–2 in 57 minutes: "Murder on the Centre Court", as one newspaper headline put it. It was Hoad's last match as an amateur. At the Lawn Tennis Association Ball, where his triumph was celebrated, he left everyone with the impression that he planned to defend his title again. However, it transpired that he did so only because he did not wish to spoil the occasion by announcing that he was about to turn professional. He had a wife, a small daughter, another child on the way and only £600 in the bank.

Along with such former champions as Sedgman, Gonzales and Segura, Hoad joined the Jack Kramer Circus, who toured the circuit until the rest of the world eventually bowed to pressure from the All England Club and the LTA that lawn tennis should be open to professionals. In 1968, with others who had been barred as professionals, Hoad returned to Wimbledon, where he won two rounds before losing to Bob Hewitt. He played again in 1970 and 1972, though beaten in the first round on both occasions. Though he maintained an air of nonchalance, his back pains were becoming unbearable.

After retiring as a player Hoad became a notable coach. For several years he was a member of the International Tennis Federation panel who nominated the men's world champion, and he was a favourite visitor to the world champion's dinner, held during the French Open. Earlier this year he was diagnosed as having leukaemia. He suffered a heart attack a few days before his death.

Lewis Alan Hoad was born in Glebe, near Sydney, on November 23, 1934, and as a teenager joined the exceptionally talented group of young players coached by Harry Hopman, who sustained the golden era of Australian tennis inaugurated by Frank Sedgman.

In the six years he played at Wimbledon as an amateur, Hoad's aggressive style made him as dominant as today's big servers and always carried him at least to the fourth round. It was in 1956, by which time he was already established on the world tennis scene, and as a doubles champion, that his game reached its peak. In that year he won the Australian, French and Wimbledon titles, and arrived at the US Open seemingly poised to become the first man since Don Budge to complete the Grand Slam. In the final at Forest Hills (where the US Open was then staged) Hoad found himself facing Ken Rosewall, whom he had beaten over four sets in both the Australian and Wimbledon finals in the previous months.

Hoad and Rosewall were born in the same month and had been junior rivals. They had gone on to astonish the lawn tennis world as senior doubles partners when, aged 17, they reached the semi-finals at all four major championships. A year later they won the doubles titles at three of them, and had taken Wimbledon in both 1953 and 1956. Hoad was tipped to beat Rosewall in New York and complete the Grand Slam, but his lightweight quondam partner proved sharper and took the match 4–6, 6–2, 6–3, 6–3.

In 1955 Hoad married Jenny Staley, then ranked No. 2 in Australia, at St Mary's, Wimbledon, on the day of the Queen's Club final, eight days before the Championships. After a one-day honeymoon they were ordered by their respective managers to their separate team headquarters. The Hoads, who had a son and two daughters, later settled in Spain, where they established the Lew Hoad Campo de Tennis, near Fuengirola, now run by their son.

Hoad proved an outstanding coach, both before and after the major back surgery he underwent in New York in 1977. Those he helped to win Grand Slam titles included Guillermo Vilas and Manual Orantes; there are many who believe that Hoad had a decisive influence in Spain's emergence as a tennis power.

John Parsons writes: Everyone in tennis loved Lew Hoad. Though humble about his achievements, he was a larger-than-life character, ready to help anyone at any time. He was a great sportsman with a heart of gold and an iron wrist. My lasting memory will be of how, after shaking hands with him, it always took an hour for my hand to recover.

July 5 1994

JEAN BOROTRA

JEAN BOROTRA, "the Bounding Basque", who died aged 95, won the Wimbledon singles title in 1924 and 1926, and was the leading member of the Four Muskateers – the others were René Lacoste, Henri Cochet and Jean "Toto" Brugnon – who kept the Davis Cup in France from 1927 to 1932.

An athletic volleyer and a shrewd tactician, Borotra also won the men's doubles at Wimbledon three times, with René Lacoste in 1925, and with Toto Brugnon in 1932 and 1933, as well as carrying off the mixed doubles with Suzanne Lenglen in 1925. He won the French Open singles in 1924 and 1931, and the doubles in 1925, 1928, 1929, 1934 and 1936. In 1928 he completed the hat-trick at the Australian Open, taking the singles, doubles and mixed doubles titles. His game was ideally suited to faster surfaces, as he showed by winning the British covered court singles 11 times between 1926 and 1949, and the equivalent French title 12 times between 1922 and 1947.

However, Borotra's appeal did not lie merely in records. His extravagantly explosive style and instinctive showmanship made him one of the most popular players to appear at Wimbledon. As Alan Little wrote in *Wimbledon Men* (1977): "He had only to don his black beret at the changeover, this being the signal for a major effort, to bring the Centre Court crowd applauding wildly. That he used his popularity to his advantage was obvious. He was less popular as an opponent. He was a great, if sometimes volatile, match player. From the start of his career to the end he engaged in a running battle with foot-fault judges. He was good theatre."

Yet Borotra was capable of the highest standards of sportsmanship. In the 1927 Wimbledon final he held six match points against Cochet, and on one of them he would have been declared the winner had he not drawn the umpire's attention to the fact that a ball which landed out had brushed him on the way past.

Borotra was always a favourite with women, who responded to his Gallic gallantry. He especially welcomed the chance to chase a wide shot for the opportunity it gave to land in a friendly lap. On one occasion at Wimbledon, when playing doubles with Brugnon, Borotra ran into two women while making a return, kissed the hands of both as Brugnon kept the rally going, and then raced back to win the point with another of his clinching volleys.

Borotra's career in the main Wimbledon tournament spanned 42 years, from 1922 to 1964. He played a total of 224 singles, doubles and mixed doubles matches, more than any other man in the history of the tournament; only Martina Navratilova and Billie Jean King have played more. He went on competing in Wimbledon veterans' events – and attracting large crowds – until 1977, 55 years after he first stepped on to a court at the All England Club. Uniquely, he played at Wimbledon in the 50th, 75th and 100th anniversary years of the tournament.

In Paris statues of the Four Mustakeers grace the square named after them at Roland Garros, and it became the custom for Borotra and Lacoste to present the men's singles trophy to the winner at the French Open.

Jean Robert Borotra was born into a well-to-do family

at Domaine de Pouy, near Biarritz, on August 13, 1898. At first his sporting enthusiasm focused on pelota and rugby, which have always been popular in that area. In 1912, however, he went to stay with a family called Wildy, who lived at Kemley, near Croydon, to polish his English (he had an English grandmother). "Do you think you could return a ball with this?" asked Mrs Wildy, thrusting a tennis racquet into his hand. Borotra, who was used to the smaller wicker racquet used in pelota, was quite certain he could; and justified his confidence by beating every rival that Kemley and the surrounding villages could offer.

The First World War intervened before he had time to hone his talent. His first attempt to volunteer was rejected because he was only 16, but in 1916 he was accepted into the 121st Horse Artillery Regiment. He went on to win the Croix de Guerre and was twice mentioned in despatches. After the Armistice, while serving with the French army of occupation in Germany, Borotra submitted to the one formal tennis lesson of his youth. On demobilisation, he entered the Ecole Polytechnic in Paris, where he developed his equally active business mind; later he became one of the richest men in France by selling motors for petrol pumps.

In 1922 Borotra played the first of 54 Davis Cup rubbers for France. He won 36 of them. He was still in the French Davis Cup team in 1947 at the age of 48, and four years later won a comfortable 6–3, 6–1 victory over the British Davis Cup player Tony Mottram, at Queen's Club.

During the Second World War Borotra had been Minister for Sport in the Vichy government. Later he was imprisoned by the Gestapo for more than two years after accusations that he had tried to flee Paris to join the Free French Army in North Africa. His Vichy service meant that he was on a black-list compiled by the British Foreign Office. He was not allowed to enter Wimbledon in 1946, and only returned to the tournament in 1948. Borotra always remained loyal to the memory of Marshall Pétain, whose trial, he said, had been a travesty, and he became a founder-member and vice-president of an association to defend the marshall's memory. Yet Borotra was also a devoted Anglophile, who enjoyed pointing out that the French had no word for "fair play".

A physical fitness fanatic – who allowed himself two glasses of good red wine every day – he was still following his first service into the net at the age of 75, and continued to play competitive tennis well beyond his 90th year, especially enjoying mixed doubles with Kitty Godfree, who as Kitty McKane had won the Wimbledon women's title in 1924, the year of his first triumph in the men's singles.

When tennis returned as an Olympic sport in Seoul in 1988, Borotra was determined to play on the Olympic courts, just as he had done in Paris in 1924, the last time tennis had been a full medal sport. However, his match against Otto Hauser, an old friend from Brazil, started nearly 90 minutes late because they were still debating controversial points in a match they had played against each other in the 1930s.

"Tennis keeps me in a good temper," Borotra held. At the age of 92, he paid for three lessons to help him develop a two-handed forehand which might prolong his career. The French Davis Cup victory in 1991 gave him much pleasure. "I don't know how much longer I could have waited," he told the victors.

Concerned by the domination of the serve in the modern game, Borotra believed that the men should be obliged to serve from a yard behind the baseline. But he knew what people would say: "It's Borotra's idea, and he never had a good serve anyway." He was also worried about the effect of professionalism on the spirit of the game; in 1968 he had suggested that professionals should play alongside amateurs only in 10 special tournaments each year.

In 1994 Borotra could not play in the match between the International Club of Paris and the IC of Great Britain. It was the first time he had missed the fixture since founding the IC of Paris in 1929, when he scored a rare victory over Bill Tilden in the event. "The only regret I have," he once said, "is the feeling that I will die without having played enough tennis."

Jean Borotra married first, in 1937, Mme Edouard Barachin, formerly Beatrice Mabel de Forest; they had a son. The marriage was dissolved. In 1988 Borotra married again; his wife, Janine, survives him.

July 18 1994

DAME MAREA HARTMAN

DAME MAREA HARTMAN, who died aged 74, was president of the Amateur Athletic Association and played a key role in raising the status of women athletes at both national and international levels. In the early 1950s only five events were recognised in women's athletics: the 100 yards, 220 yards, 440 yards, the high jump and the shot. "And you had to do the shot with both arms because of a doctor's ruling," Hartman recalled. "There was this tremendous fear that women would drop dead." Hartman made it her business to persuade the authorities to extend the range of events to the 20 disciplines open to women by the time of her death.

One of her many innovations was to ban padded brassieres. "Falsies," she declared, "can mean unfair victory in photo-finishes." She also introduced head-to-toe medical checks, a procedure adopted by the men's team in 1972.

In 1969, anxious for a sharp competition against the East Germans, Hartman announced her celebrated "big girls' scheme". She recalled: "I went on TV and made an appeal for intelligent girls who were big and strong and prepared to train for six evenings a week. We started off with over 850 and ended up with four when they found out what the training was. You need speed, you see, and lots of bulk, and no one likes to think of herself as a big girl."

As manager of various national teams Hartman kept a close eye on her "girls" during overseas competitions. She was swift to pounce on sweet-suckers or late-night radio listeners, took particular pride in the fact that she never had to impose a curfew and always insisted on accompanying the team on their nights out. During a long career devoted to nurturing female athletic talent, her greatest coup was at the 1964 Tokyo Olympics, when the British women's team walked off with two gold medals, a silver and a bronze.

Gladys Marea Hartman was born in South London on June 22, 1920. Both her parents worked in the hotel trade, but young Marea was more interested in keep-fit than catering. She was a regular runner at her local track, where she was spotted by Teddy Knowles, the founder of the Spartan Athletic Club, who invited her to join his club. She was soon drinking orange squash with the boys and "training like a footballer". She won a gold medal as a sprinter for Surrey, and in 1950 was appointed honorary treasurer of the Women's AAA, a post she held for 10 years.

Hartman was the first female athlete to be sponsored by a commercial company, and in the 1950s she secured sponsorship deals with such companies as Bovril, Kraft and Sunsilk, all keen to help promote women's championships. "The WAAA were always able to get sponsors," Hartman declared, "because the girls were so pretty." It was a forward-thinking move, and the number of women's athletics events grew steadily.

Hartman was appointed manager of the British women's team in 1956 (the year of the Melbourne Olympics), and remained in that post until 1978. During those years she was involved in another five Olympic Games, as well as the European Championships and the Commonwealth Games. The 1964 Olympic Games were the high point of her career: Mary Rand took the gold in the long jump, silver in the pentathlon and bronze in the 4x100 metre relay; Ann Packer won the gold in the 800 metres.

While attending the Mexico Olympics in 1968, Hartman was appointed chairman of the Women's Commission of the International Amateur Athletic Federation, a post she retained until 1981. One of her stars in Mexico was the 400-metre runner Lillian Board, who died of cancer two years later. Hartman established a trophy in her memory, which was presented annually at the WAAA Championships.

Hartman's career was by no means trouble-free. In 1975 she lost her long fight to keep the national women's championships a separate event, and after disastrous performances by the British team in the 1976 Montreal Olympics, Hartman – along with Sir Arthur Gold, her colleague on the British Amateur Athletic Board – was criticised for being out of touch, though she survived a vote of no confidence.

It was Hartman's expertise as chairman of the then British Amateur Athletic Board that brought about the creation in 1991 of a new administrative body, the British Athletic Federation. The same year she was unanimously elected president of the AAA. She was honorary secretary of the Women's AAA for 30 years, and served on the executive committee of the Central Council of Physical Recreation from 1972, becoming deputy chairman and honorary treasurer.

In the late 1970s Hartman had been involved in the development of athletics for women in Japan, in recognition of which she was given the Prince Chichibu Award. Hartman was appointed MBE in 1967, CBE in 1978 and DBE in the 1994 New Year's Honours List. She was unmarried.

September 2 1994

BILLY WRIGHT

BILLY WRIGHT, who died aged 70, was the first golden boy of post-War English football. Star of Wolverhampton Wanderers in the club's heyday in the 1940s and 1950s, Wright was a fine reader of the game, remarkable for his courage and timing. He specialised in what would today be called the long-ball game, but was then called "kick and rush". In the course of 13 seasons he made 490 League appearances, and Wolves won the FA Cup in 1949, and the First Division Championship in 1954, 1958 and 1959.

Wright was also the first Englishman to win 100 caps, with a final tally of 105. He was first capped at Wembley in 1947, playing against Scotland. Appointed captain the following year, he went on to lead the team 90 times. Wright had some triumphant moments with England – particularly against Scotland – though more than his share of disasters. In the 1950 World Cup, at Belo Horizonte in Brazil, he led England to a 1–0 defeat against the United States.

Three years later he captained England against Hungary, when the Hungarians became the first foreign side to win at Wembley, and added insult to injury by winning 6–3. Badly wrong-footed by Ferenc Puskas, who went on to score a classic goal, Wright was described by one commentator as "like a fire-engine rushing at full speed to the wrong fire". A few months later he took England to a return match in Budapest, where the team were humiliated still further by a 7–1 defeat. "Without doubt the Hungarians were the best team I came across in my career," Wright declared. "They did so many things with the ball that we had never seen before – a truly great side." Wright had some consolation for these debacles when he led Wolves to victory at Molineux in a friendly against Honved, the Hungarian champions.

Having retired at 35 after taking Wolves to their third championship, he went on to coach the England

Youth and Under-23 teams and then became manager of Arsenal in 1962; it was said at the time that he would have been given the England team had he not gone to Highbury. Wright's tenure there was not a success, though. Victories were few, attendances declined dramatically, and crowds stood outside the ground chanting, "Wright must go!" and "We want a manager!" After four seasons he was sacked. "I was too emotional a person to be a manager," Wright recalled. "I was too involved. I used to be physically sick during a game. Managing was much harder than playing."

It is as a player that Billy Wright will be remembered. At 5ft 8in he was short for a centre-field player, but he more than made up for that in enthusiasm and spirit. Blond, handsome, amiable and polite, he was never sent off or even booked.

As a captain he led by example: "I do shout occasionally when it's needed," he explained, "but I'd rather do my work. If the players see the captain bawling all the while and not doing anything to help the team, they've got good cause to grieve."

William Ambrose Wright was born at Ironbridge, Shropshire, on February 6, 1924. As a schoolboy he played centre-forward and once scored 10 goals in a match. Rejected at first by Major Frank Buckley, "the Martinet of Molineux", for being too small, Wright joined the groundstaff at Wolves at 14. In 1941 he turned professional as an inside-forward, later switching to right-half and then to centre-half.

After his dismissal from Arsenal he became head of sport at ATV, the now defunct Midlands television company, where he helped to pioneer sports coverage; he retired in 1989. The next year Sir Jack Hayward appointed Wright to the board of Wolves, and named a new stand after him at Molineux. Wright was Footballer of the Year in 1952, and to mark his 100th cap in April 1959 he was made an honorary life member of the FA. He was appointed CBE in 1959. He married, in 1958, Joy Beverley, eldest of the Beverley Sisters singers; they had two daughters and a stepson.

September 5 1994

P. B. H. MAY

PETER MAY, the cricketer, who died aged 64, was a successful England captain and one of the finest batsmen since the Second World War. From 1951 when, as a Cambridge undergraduate, he despatched his first ball in a Test match for four, and went on to make a hundred, until his retirement from the game in 1962, May's batting for Surrey and England was beyond reproach. With the exemplary technique and unwavering application which characterised all the best English batsmen of his time, May was an outstanding performer in the classical amateur tradition.

Six foot in height, broad in the shoulders and long in the leg, May always played with a perfectly straight bat. His trademark as a batsman was his superb style and strength when driving off the front foot through mid-on; but he had all the strokes. May was a great admirer of Sir Leonard Hutton, whom he succeeded as captain of England in 1955. Like Hutton, he was a thoughtful and sound, rather than exciting, leader, and was at all times conspicuously considerate towards the members of his team.

When May joined the side, England's fortunes were already on the turn. From 1951 to 1958 the team contested 11 successive rubbers without defeat, winning eight and drawing three. Of these Brown won one, Hutton three and May four. It was not all one-way traffic, though, and under May's leadership England lost twice to Australia.

Batting in the first half of his Test career at No. 3, and in the latter half at No 4, May was the picture of unruffled composure, taking crises in his stride. In his 66 Tests, of which he was captain for 41, he made 13 hundreds and scored more than 50 (four times in the nineties) in another 22 innings. He made 4,537 Test runs, averaging 46. Over the course of his first-class career he accumulated 27,592 runs, at an average of 51, including 85 hundreds. The figures are remarkable considering that he played for fewer than 12 seasons.

As it turned out, May missed by a year the counties' adoption of one-day cricket. Though he was admirably equipped for any variation in the game, calling on May to play limited-over cricket would, in J. J. Warr's words, have been "like asking Sir Thomas Beecham to conduct the Rolling Stones".

Peter Barker Howard May was born at Reading on December 31, 1929. He was educated at Charterhouse, where he enjoyed four highly productive years in the First XI. His first mentor was George Geary, a fine bowler between the wars, and the cricket coach at Charterhouse. In his autobiography May quotes the Geary gospel, which he aimed always to follow: "Keep your head still. Stand still as long as you can. When you move your feet move quickly, but the longer you stand still the later you'll play the shot."

May did his National Service as a writer in the Royal Navy, whom he represented at cricket, before going up in 1949 to Pembroke College, Cambridge, where he read history and economics. In his first year he picked up a football Blue (later becoming captain), before playing against Oxford at Lord's for three successive summers.

From the outset May was a heavy run-maker for both Cambridge and Surrey; during his second university year, in 1951, he scored a chanceless 138 on his Test debut, against South Africa at Headingley. Strangely, however, he failed to come off in the University Match. Perhaps as a consequence David Sheppard, later Bishop of Liverpool, was preferred to him as captain in 1952.

It took May a while to make his mark against the touring Australians in 1953. After failing in his only innings in the first Test he was dropped, for the first and last time in his life. Brought back for the final Test at the Oval, May played an effective part in the victory that won the Ashes, which Australia had held for nearly 20 years. Thereafter he gave heart and sinew to England's sometimes fragile batting for 52 successive Tests, and played in several more after his career was twice interrupted by illness. In 1955, in his first series as captain, England narrowly beat South Africa, with May averaging 72.

In 1956 May's side retained the Ashes, and his average was 90. In 1957, when England beat the West Indies 3–0, it was 97. As England captain he won 20 Tests (an unsurpassed record), lost 10 and drew 11. At Edgbaston in the 1957 series May and Colin Cowdrey built the largest fourth-wicket stand in Test history (and the highest by England for any wicket): 288 runs behind after the first innings and forced to follow on, the English pair put on an astonishing 411. Unsure of picking Ramadhin's spin, May and Cowdrey pushed forward for hour after hour, using the front pad as a second line of defence. As an exercise in stamina and concentration the partnership was peerless. May, who occupied the crease for just short of 10 hours, was 285 not out, the highest score of his career. Cowdrey's share of the runs was 154.

May may have set another record in 1957. Not by nature a convivial person, he nevertheless attended and spoke at 75 dinners in the course of the year. As captain of Surrey and England May regarded it as part of his job to be an ambassador for the game. He was always guided by a strong sense of duty, and so was especially wounded by the crude media criticism of his conduct as chairman of selectors.

His three overseas tours to South Africa, Australia and the West Indies were less happy for May than the home series of the 1950s. On the South African tour he amassed 1,270 runs, but only once made it past 50; after much stodgy cricket all round, the rubber was drawn. In Australia, in the winter of 1958, England faced several bowlers whose suspect actions went unpenalised. May held the batting together with Cowdrey, and bore the frustration with characteristic silence. However, the team's morale suffered and Australia regained the Ashes with ease.

May missed half the 1959 season through illness, and his health again failed in the West Indies that winter, though not before England had handsomely won the only completed Test of the series. Unfit for all of 1960, May was persuaded to lead England against Australia once

more in 1961. After his powerful first innings of 95 had
put England in a commanding position in the fourth
Test at Old Trafford, England collapsed on the final day,
missing a golden opportunity to recapture the Ashes.

On the county scene May led Surrey to the last two
of their seven successive championships in 1957 and
1958; he remained as captain until his retirement at the
end of 1962. May then pursued a business career as an
insurance broker and underwriter at Lloyds, and from
1990 as a consultant to William Corroon Ltd. But he
also played a full part at Lord's, first as a member of the
England selection committee for four years and then,
from 1982 to 1988, as chairman. He also chaired,
at different times, the TCCB and MCC cricket sub-
committees.

From 1980 to 1981 May was a charming yet firm
and decisive president of MCC. In 1985 he published his
memoirs, *A Game Enjoyed*. An active member of the
Surrey committee, May would have been president of the
club in 1995, the 150th anniversary year. He was
appointed CBE in 1981. May married, in 1959, Virginia,
daughter of the Sussex and England captain A. H. H.
Gilligan; they had four daughters, all talented horse-
women.

December 28 1994

HAROLD STEVENSON

HAROLD "TIGER" STEVENSON, who died aged 87,
was a leading figure in the early days of dirt-track
motorcycling. Dirt-track racing, or speedway racing, as it

was later known, was popularised by Australian motor-cycle riders in the late 1920s. Stevenson, a protégé of the great American rider Lloyd "Sprouts" Elder, was one of the first Englishmen to challenge the supremacy of the Australian speedway stars. His dare-devil style, which included spectacular leg-trailing, soon earnt him the soubriquet "Tiger".

On one occasion the Prince of Wales, later Edward VIII, approached Stevenson at the old Crystal Palace track, and said he hoped he would always uphold the prestige of the Old Country. "By God, sir," Stevenson replied, "I'll try."

A garage manager's son, Harold Montague Stevenson was born at Sunbury-on-Thames on November 1, 1907. While working for his father – "the strictest teacher I ever had" – he took evening classes and gained a degree in mechanical engineering. In 1929 he was made captain of the old east London track at West Ham, and during the next decade he led his team to scores of successes, as well as notching up many individual triumphs. In 1933 he won the British Individual Championship, the equiv-alent of the present world championship.

Stevenson was appointed captain of England, whom he led both in Britain and in Test matches in Australia. He represented his country 27 times, and was particularly effective in the 1933–34 season in Australia, when he won 48 of his 53 races. Though it was the height of the Bodyline bowling controversy, "The Tiger" was a great favourite with the Australian public; in 1934 he was granted the Freedom of Sydney. Stevenson rode speedway all over the world; in the huge winter stadiums of Russia he proved himself a master of speedway on ice. Back in England he raced at Brooklands, where he caught his hand in the machine's primary chain, losing a fingertip but winning the race.

In the late 1930s he learnt to fly, and on the outbreak of the Second World War was commissioned into the RAF as a pilot. After seeing action over France he was transferred to the Royal Electrical and Mechanical Engineers and promoted major. He used his engineering skills to help to perfect the double Duplex floating tanks, which eventually "swam" on to the Normandy beaches on D-Day.

After the War many of Stevenson's former colleagues were climbing back into the saddle and riding to renewed glory. However, he chose otherwise. "The time has come," he said, "for the old-timers to hang up their leathers and train the boys who are to carry on the tradition we established." He dedicated himself to promoting speedway racing, and in 1946 founded novices' schools which laid the foundations for the new third division of the speedway leagues. He went on to manage Stoke, and for a time renewed his association with West Ham, as clerk of the course. Stevenson married first, in 1936, Mary De Sales Boyle, whom he met in Australia. He married secondly, in 1983, Molly Lawson.

January 17 1995

FRED PERRY

FRED PERRY, who died aged 85 in Melbourne, was the greatest player in the history of British lawn tennis, and the last British player to win the men's singles title at Wimbledon. Indeed he won the title in three successive years from 1934 to 1936. Perry was the first player to win all four Grand Slam championships: Wimbledon, the United States, France and Australia. He also played a key part in Britain's four Davis Cup triumphs between 1933 and 1936.

Especially memorable was the decisive final rubber against France, in Paris in 1933. Perry, who had taken five sets to beat Henri Cochet on the opening day, recovered from losing the first set and being two set points down in the second set to beat Andre Merlin 4–6, 8–6, 6–2, 7–5. It was Britain's first success since 1912, and ended six years of French domination. When the team arrived back at Dover, they received a telegram of congratulation from King George V. A crowd of 10,000 greeted the train when it reached Victoria. Perry competed in a total of 20 Davis Cup matches, winning 34 of his 38 rubbers in singles, and 11 out of 14 in doubles.

At 20 Perry had been world table-tennis champion, and he brought to the court the speed of reaction – and some of the shots – that he had developed on the table. His speciality on the tennis court was a running forehand, taken early and often at great risk; other British players imitated him at their peril. Perry, though, had a wonderful eye and an abnormally strong wrist. He favoured the Continental grip with no change of hand position between backhand and forehand.

His brilliant shot-making was matched by his competitive steel; and he trained far more zealously than most of his rivals. Twice, on his way to becoming Wimbledon champion for the first time, he was stretched to five sets. He was under less pressure in the next two years, dropping only three sets in 1935 and one in 1936, when, in the final, he beat the injured Baron Gottfried von Cramm

6–1, 6–1, 6–0. In addition to his three successes in the men's singles at Wimbledon, in 1935 and 1936 he also won the mixed doubles with Dorothy Round.

Yet though Perry claimed that, from the first time he saw the Centre Court as a paying spectator in 1928, he "always had a love affair with Wimbledon", his relationships with the All England Club were often prickly. As he wrote in his autobiography in 1984: "It shows how we have all mellowed over the years from the days when some elements in the All England Club and the Lawn Tennis Association looked down on me as a hot-headed, outspoken tearaway rebel, not quite the class of the chap they *really* wanted to see winning Wimbledon, even if he *was* English.

"I've mellowed, too. I think I'm very much a leopard who has changed his spots. Looking back, I have to concede that I was sometimes a little brash and aggressive about what I regarded as the class-ridden set-up there. But at the time, a young man with my background was bound to feel that snobbery very keenly, and I still get angry about the shabby way I was treated when I won Wimbledon in 1934, the first Englishman to do it for 20 years."

Before the Second World War there were no on-court presentation ceremonies at Wimbledon. The chairman would seek out the champion, congratulate him and present him with the club tie, as confirmation of his being made an honorary member. Perry often told how, taking a long soak in the bath after beating the defending champion, Jack Crawford, in the final, he had overheard a member of the All England Club committee tell the Australian: "Congratulations. This was one day when the best man didn't win." Crawford was also presented with a bottle of champagne. All Perry received was the club tie draped over his chair, and a £25 voucher redeemable at Mappin & Webb. No congratulations were offered.

"Instead of Fred J. Perry, the champ," he recalled, "I felt like Fred J. Muggs, the chimp. I've never been so angry in my whole life. It really hurt. All my paranoia about the old-school brigade surfaced with a vengeance." It is only fair to observe that Perry's attitude as a player was never calculated to please. He did not believe in congratulating an opponent on a good shot, nor in correcting a bad call in his favour. "I didn't aspire to be a good sport," he said. "Champion was good enough for me."

In 1936, when he turned professional after his third Wimbledon success, his membership of the All England Club was automatically rescinded, as he knew it would be. The very mention of the word "professional" remained anathema there until 1968, when amateurs and professionals were at last allowed to compete in the same events.

Frederick John Perry was born at Stockport on May 18, 1909, the son of a cotton spinner who became secretary of the Co-operative Party and Labour MP for Kettering. When Fred was a boy he lived briefly at Bolton and then at Liverpool, where he was one of 45 children in a class at Wallasey Grammar School. Towards the end of the First World War the family moved to London, and it was while living at the village of Brentham, near Ealing, that Fred's sporting talents began to blossom.

He played football and cricket, though his great passion was table tennis. It was not until he was 14 that he started playing lawn tennis, inspired by watching the game at Devonshire Park while on holiday at Eastbourne. Success came swiftly in table tennis, and he played for England in the same team as Adrian Haydon, the father of Ann Haydon Jones, who would also be a world table-tennis and a Wimbledon champion. Perry won the world table-tennis singles championship at Budapest in 1929.

However, his father was unimpressed. "You play at night-time in a smoky room," he complained, "you look like death warmed up – why not concentrate on tennis?" So at 20 Fred Perry gave up table tennis for the open-air game, undeterred by the memory of how, at the Wimbledon junior championships, his only racquet had broken and he was beaten in the fourth round.

In county competitions Middlesex claimed his loyalty. In 1929, a few days after playing for Chiswick Park in the Middlesex club competition, he qualified for Wimbledon for the first time and won two matches before losing in four sets to John Oliff. A year later, while Perry was beating Umberto do Morpurgo, an Italian baron and First World War air ace, an LTA committee chose him to join a four-man team to tour the United States. "My tennis career began on that day," he later said. The tour introduced him to a new way of life. In Hollywood he met, and made friends with, Mary Pickford, Marlene Dietrich, Douglas Fairbanks, Randolph Scott, David Niven, Errol Flynn and Bebe Daniels. To Perry, an entertainer at heart, the appeal was irresistible.

He won the United States National Championships (now the US Open) in 1933, 1934 and 1936; the Australian singles and doubles in 1934; and the French Open in 1935. Earlier in Paris he had won the mixed doubles with Betty Nuthall and the men's doubles with Pat Hughes.

Perry continued to flourish as a professional, acquitting himself well against such players as Ellsworth Vines, Bill Tilden and Don Budge. With Vines he bought a major interest in the Beverly Hills Tennis Club, then a haven for showbusiness personalities. He became an American citizen, and served with the United States Air Force in the Second World War. Afterwards, he held coaching posts in Jamaica and Florida.

In 1947, at the instigation of Slazenger, he returned to Britain and toured the country with Dan Maskell, playing a series of exhibition matches, which helped to raise funds for clubs to repair their facilities, and to resurrect interest in British tennis. Perry always regretted that he was not asked by the British tennis authorities to help more in this respect, as he was by Israel and the USSR. He did, though, work briefly with British Davis Cup teams in the mid-1950s.

In 1950 he founded Fred Perry Sportswear with Theodore Wegner, and worked hard to turn it into one of the world's best-known sportswear brand names. From 1948 he was a member of the BBC's radio commentary team at Wimbledon, and from 1977 a founder-member of the panel of former champions established by the International Tennis Federation to nominate the men's world champion. To the end he remained a pungent critic of the game, both as writer and broadcaster.

Every year he would travel from his home at Boca Raton, Florida, to tournaments all over the world. From 1947 until 1983, when he blacked out in his car while driving home from Wimbledon, Perry did not miss a single day's play at the tournament. Just as he was about to be discharged from hospital, he suffered a major heart attack, which he survived only because medical aid was at hand. He was back in 1984, and continued to attend every day until the end of 1994, working for BBC Radio and writing for *The Daily Telegraph*.

He never tired of watching, analysing and discussing matches, especially the technical and tactical merits of a player's game. His skill and accuracy were unrivalled, and Bjorn Borg and John McEnroe were among the many who appreciated his comments. In 1984, to commemorate the 50th anniversary of his first singles triumph at Wimbledon, the All England Club commissioned a statue of Perry, which stands in a rose garden opposite the Members' Enclosure of the club. They also renamed the Somerset Road entrance to the grounds as the Fred Perry Gates.

Undaunted by major heart surgery in 1992, Perry continued his exhausting world tours. However, the lack of guile in the modern game bothered him; in his day, he held, "you could use your noggin a little bit more than you can now". Perry married four times. His last wife, Bobby, whom he married in 1952, was his constant travelling companion. They had a daughter and adopted a son.

February 3 1995

JUAN MANUEL FANGIO

JUAN MANUEL FANGIO, the Argentinian racing driver who died aged 84, was to his sport what Pele was to football and Bradman to cricket. Though Fangio did not compete in the world championship until he was almost 39 – at which age Grand Prix drivers are now regarded as over the hill – he won five championships between 1951 and 1957, and from only 51 starts wrested a remarkable 24 Grand Prix victories, 23 fastest laps and 22 second places.

Cool and seemingly fearless, Fangio had superb control over his car, and never drove faster than was necessary, though he could keep his foot slammed down longer than any of his opponents dared. His remarkable stamina had been built up in the marathon road races of South America in the late 1930s and 1940s, when he crossed and re-crossed 6,000 miles of bad roads in unsuitable motor-cars, acting as his own mechanic. "The man who wants to be world champion must cover himself in grease from head to foot," said Fangio. "He must work on his car with his hand and his heart. Before becoming a driver he must become a mechanic – almost a manufacturer . . ."

He drove for all the top teams of his day: Alfa-Romeo, Ferrari, Mercedes and Maserati. Fangio's brilliance was exemplified by his mastery of the old Nurburgring track. Racing on this, he said, was like "getting to know a woman". "You can't memorise 176 curves over more than 14 miles," he observed, "just as you can't memorise 176 feminine wiles after a short acquaintance."

At Nurburgring in 1957 he notched up his last – and greatest – victory. After a lengthy pit-stop he had to make up more than a minute on the leading Ferraris of Mike Hawthorn and Peter Collins. Breaking the lap record 10 times in his Maserati, he screamed past both his rivals. They applauded his victory as ecstatically as the crowd.

An immigrant Italian stonemason's son, Juan Manual

Fangio was born at Balcarce, 200 miles from Buenos Aires, on June 24, 1911. As a boy he was apprenticed to a blacksmith but soon found a job in a garage. Mechanics and football quickly became his passions, and it was his task to drive the team to away matches over the muddy tracks that passed for roads. Before long, he set up his own garage, and entered his first races to win publicity for the business. In 1940 he became national road-racing champion.

In 1942 all motor racing ceased, and when it resumed, in 1947, European-style racing on purpose-built tracks was introduced to Argentina. For the first time Argentinian drivers competed against Europeans. In 1949 Fangio enjoyed his first full European season, and caused a sensation by winning nine races. He returned to Argentina to find that the Tango Fangio had been composed in his honour. Such was his enduring popularity in South America and Europe that years later a dock strike was lifted at Genoa to allow Fangio's car to be loaded.

Some 30 drivers were killed during his seasons in Europe, and Fangio was vociferous in his complaints about the lack of safety precautions on the track. However, such was his skill – and luck – that his only serious accident, which cost him much of the 1952 season, was a result of exhaustion.

His good nature was exemplified by a bizarre incident in Havana in 1958, when he was kidnapped before a race by anti-Batista insurgents. Fangio later said that he had endured awful problems during practice with the car he was due to drive in the minor event, and was sure the kidnappers had done him a good turn. He said he had been well treated and even interceded on behalf of a kidnapper who was captured. On his retirement Fangio became an ambassador for motorsport as well as president of Mercedes-Benz (Argentina). His appearance was guaranteed to create a stir at any motoring event: even in old age he was a charismatic and dignified figure with piercing grey eyes.

For all his wide gifts – his friends said that if he had gone into the Church he would have become a cardinal – Fangio never mastered English. He made George VI laugh when he was presented at Silverstone in 1950. "No spik English – spik Italian, spik Spanish," stammered Fangio to the King, who looked a little embarrassed. Fangio turned to the interpreter at his side. "Please tell His Majesty," he said, "that I don't have to speak English to be able to drive."

Fangio had a long and mysterious relationship with a woman who was always with him at circuits and was mistakenly thought to be his wife; but he never married.

July 18 1995

HAROLD LARWOOD

HAROLD LARWOOD, who died in Sydney aged 90, was the most feared and celebrated fast bowler of his time. "Lol" Larwood had long been the sole survivor of the first Tests in which he played, the memorable series of 1926 when England won back the Ashes. Among modern England cricketers only R. E. S. Wyatt, who died two months earlier, approached him in playing seniority: Wyatt's first Tests were in South Africa in 1927–28. Larwood's international career would certainly have been longer but for the MCC tour to Australia of 1932–33, in which he and his captain, D. R. Jardine, were the central figures in the most bitter and protracted confrontation to darken the game. Jardine was the tactical brain, and Larwood and his county colleague, the left-arm Bill Voce, were the chief executors of a new type of bowling labelled Bodyline. This was an apt description because both bowlers aimed to pitch the ball short, in the neighbourhood of the batsman's ribs, to induce a catch in one of the five or even six close fielders on the leg side as the batsman aimed to escape being hit on the body.

The method adopted by Jardine owed something to prior discussion with A. W. Carr, the Nottinghamshire captain, who at times in previous seasons had encouraged his two fast bowlers to fire away short at the body to a strong leg-side field. On the faster Australian pitches Larwood's extreme accuracy had immediate effect, and soon aroused Australian protest. By the third Test at Adelaide, Australian resentment and the reactions of the crowd had reached such a pitch that the Australian Board sent the first of a lengthy exchange of cables to MCC: "Bodyline bowling has assumed such proportions as to menace the best interests of the game. This is causing intensely bitter feeling between the players, as well as injury. In our opinion, it is unsportsmanlike." At the insistence of MCC, the board subsequently withdrew the charge of "unsportsmanlike" behaviour.

After two batsmen, Bill Woodfull and Bertie Oldfield, had been painfully struck, mounted troops were assembled behind the pavilion lest Bradman, the popular hero, should be laid low and spectators rush the field in revenge. The tactics had been devised in an effort to prevent Bradman's batting from monopolising an

England–Australia rubber, as it had done in England two years earlier. By speed of footwork and swift reaction Bradman avoided being hit and emerged from the series at the head of the averages with 56; such was his reputation that this figure was rated a failure.

The cost, though, was a row that shook Anglo-Australian relations to the roots, and took all the savour out of victory. When, belatedly, the true nature of the English attack was appreciated at Lord's, MCC made such a method illegal. Though short, fast bowling with intimidatory intent is a perennial issue, there have been no subsequent attempts at a repetition of the 1932–33 tactics, with the crescent of close leg-side fielders.

In the Bodyline series Larwood took 33 wickets at 19 runs apiece, and so had the major share in bringing home the Ashes. However, it was an expensive success for Larwood as well as for English cricket because, in the fifth Test, the constant pounding of his left foot on the hard pitches resulted in a fracture in the big toe which ended his career as a truly fast bowler. The next summer he could play for Nottinghamshire only as a batsman; he had five more English seasons before retiring at the age of 33, bowling usually at a sharp medium pace with an occasional fast ball.

Whether or not in this guise Larwood would have again been chosen for England (as Voce was), the possibility was discounted by certain inflammatory writing ghosted under his name in the popular press, which put him out of court with the authorities. He was, in short, manipulated, in a way much more common nowadays than it was then.

A cricketer of the old breed from the coalfields of Nottinghamshire and Derbyshire, Harold Larwood was born at Nuncargate, Notts, on November 14, 1904. He left the pits for Trent Bridge in 1924, and two years later, a slim but finely proportioned young man of medium height, made his first appearances for England. For the next seven years he was, without argument, the fastest bowler in world cricket. Indeed those who saw him at the closest quarters during the tour of 1932–33 maintained that his speed has never been equalled. Such estimates, of course, are impossible to prove, though it cannot be doubted that the general intimidatory effect was unparalleled.

As far as personal relations were concerned, the end of the story redeems much. When in 1949 MCC decided to offer honorary membership to celebrated old professionals Larwood's name was on the first list. A year later, at the instigation of J. H. Fingleton and John Arlott, he moved with his family to Sydney, where he was warmly welcomed. In later years English visitors found him alert and lively of mind, though his eyesight deteriorated and in the end he was almost blind. He was appointed MBE in 1993. Larwood married in 1928, and had five daughters.

E. W. Swanton writes: Harold Larwood's mastery in English cricket is illustrated by his having, for five seasons, headed the bowling averages. He took 1,427 wickets at 17 runs each, 78 of them in 21 Tests at 28. Though it was seldom that many runs were needed from him, he made 7,290, averaging a shade under 20.

One could not imagine a more admirable action for a fast bowler than that of Larwood, from the start of his controlled run of some 20 yards to the rhythmic, perfectly balanced delivery stride, wherein the right arm described so long an arc that the knuckles in the follow-through sometimes actually brushed the pitch.

He was a dangerous bat of the hard-hitting sort. When, greatly to his displeasure after a hard day in the field, he was sent in overnight in his last Test match, at Sydney, he went on the next morning to make 98. He was a high-class, all-round fielder and a safe close-catcher, with, as might be expected, a magnificent throw.

July 24 1995

MICKEY MANTLE

MICKEY MANTLE, who died of cancer aged 63, was one of the great baseball players of the century. With his mammoth swing and spectacular drive, Mantle was hailed in the early 1950s as a prodigy. Joe DiMaggio, who helped train him, described Mantle as the best rookie he had seen. Like DiMaggio, Mantle played centre field for the New York Yankees: he was the mainstay of the team for several seasons, helping them win 12 American League championships and seven World Series.

Mantle hit 536 home runs, including a record 18 in the World Series. In 1953 he hit a home run estimated to have travelled 565ft, one of the longest in history. He was the American League's Most Valuable Player three times. Blond and fresh-faced, with an easy smile, a gentle twang and great physical grace, "The Mick" seemed every bit the clean-living country boy. He became a symbol of post-War optimism and a national idol.

However, a year before his death he shattered his wholesome image by confessing to a long-term addiction to alcohol. As a baseball player, he said, he drank heavily, and often would start the day with a large glass of Kahlua, brandy and cream. When he retired from the game in 1968 he was overwhelmed by feelings of "loneliness and emptiness", and turned to the bottle in earnest. Sometimes he would forget "what day is was, what month it was, what city I was in". Shortly before his death he received a liver transplant, which attracted so much publicity that tens of thousands of Americans applied for organ donor cards.

Mickey Charles Mantle was born at Spavinaw, Oklahoma, on October 20, 1931; the family moved to Commerce, Oklahoma, in 1935. As a boy he would play baseball for more than 12 hours a day. His father, "Mutt" Mantle, was a miner and a right-handed semi-professional baseball pitcher; his grandfather had pitched left-handed for a mining team. The two men trained young Mickey to be a "switch-hitter", able to bat both with his left hand (against his father's pitching) and with his right (against his grandfather).

At Commerce High School, where he played for the football, basketball and baseball teams, Mickey was dubbed "The Commerce Comet". A week after graduating he was spotted by a New York Yankee scout, and after two seasons with "bush league" teams, he leapfrogged to the Major League as a Yankee regular in 1951. He recalled that at one point he told his father he was considering leaving the game. "I thought I raised a man," said Mutt Mantle, "not a coward."

Mickey Mantle was rejected for military service three times because of a chronic bone infection he had developed as a teenager. And a fourth time after spraining his right knee. However, his injuries did not keep him from the baseball field. His father died at 41 from Hodgkin's disease, and Mickey Mantle expected to follow him to an early grave. "If I had known I would live this long," he said in later life, "I might have taken better care of myself." He married, in 1951, Merlyn Louise Johnson, his high-school sweetheart; they had four sons.

August 14 1995

MOLLY HIDE

MOLLY HIDE, who died aged 81, was captain of the England women's cricket team from 1937 to 1954, an era when home Test matches commanded crowds of up to 15,000. A talented all-rounder, Hide made her Test debut in 1934 on the first women's tour of Australia and New Zealand. She established herself in the team with a career-best 189 against New Zealand, which included a second-wicket partnership of 235 with Betty Snowball, amassed in only 142 minutes.

Hide was appointed captain for Australia's return visit, and her astute leadership and tactical awareness won her many admirers, including Sir Neville Cardus. She was never one to rest on her laurels and always led from the front. On a further tour to Australia in 1949 she followed a first-innings 63 at Sydney with an undefeated 124 in the second innings. Her achievements in the Test were recognised when a portrait of her was hung in the pavilion at Sydney.

Molly Hide was born in Shanghai on October 24, 1913, where her father ran a business, and returned to England at the age of four. At her local school at

Haslemere, Surrey, a games mistress instilled an enthusiasm for cricket. She went on to Wycombe Abbey and then studied agriculture at Reading University. Hide defied her parents to go on the first tour to Australia; when she planned to return for the 1939 tour, they insisted that she should not "go gallivanting" again. In the event, the tour was aborted when War broke out, and she spent four years working on her father's farm.

As a captain, Hide never contemplated playing for a draw when there was the slightest sniff of victory. She was as demanding of her players as she was of herself, and could be particularly ruthless with her bowlers. On one occasion an England "quickie" was toiling without reward, since she was failing to bowl to the field her captain had set. Hide encouraged her, saying: "Bowl one on middle and leg and you should get one to pop up." "I've been trying to do that for the last six overs," retorted the disheartened bowler. "Oh," replied Hide, and immediately relieved her of her duties.

Something of a pioneer, Hide was delighted with the attention that women's cricket received during her years as captain. Looking back on the 1949 tour to Australia, she recalled how thrilled she had been to play on such grounds as Sydney, the Adelaide Oval and the WACA in Perth. The third Test in Sydney in 1949 was especially memorable; not only because of her glut of runs, but because it was the first time that women were permitted to use the men's dressing-rooms in the main pavilion. At the farewell party after the game, Hide observed that long evening dresses had never before hung from the hooks on the walls.

As well as captaining England for 17 years, Hide also turned out regularly for her local club at Mitcham Green in Surrey and attracted large crowds whenever she played. Her Test batting average was a respectable 36.33. Though she was a genuine all-rounder she failed to appreciate her own spin bowling, and probably did not bowl herself enough. She took her career-best figures of five for 20 against Australia in the second Test in Blackpool in 1937, a match England won by 25 runs. Hide became president of the Women's Cricket Association in 1973 and continued to be a devoted member of Surrey.

September 13 1995

BOBBY RIGGS

BOBBY RIGGS, the American tennis player who died aged 77, was the last man to achieve the triple crown at Wimbledon; he won the singles, doubles and mixed doubles in 1939, a few weeks before the outbreak of the Second World War. Thirty-four years later, in 1973, "The Hustler" (as Riggs was known because of his passion for gambling) devised two "Battle of the Sexes" matches. The first was against Margaret Court, the top women's player; the second against Billie Jean King, as extrovert a player as Riggs, and the most outspoken feminist in the game.

Riggs, then 55 and a self-proclaimed "king of male chauvinist pigs", had declared that feminism, which was starting to become a major issue in tennis, was a farce, and that the best of the female tennis professionals would not be able to beat even "an old man with one foot in the grave like me". He challenged Court to a winner-take-all challenge match on Mother's Day, at a Californian resort he was helping to launch. She proved a sucker for his skilful junk shots and trick shots. Her resistance quickly crumbled and Riggs won 6–2, 6–1.

The match against Billie Jean King, staged in the Houston Astrodome, was preceded by a tremendous brou-haha. The media descended in force, as did a crowd of 30,472 – the largest to have attended a tennis match – who paid up to $100 a ticket. Riggs claimed to have trained for the match by consuming 415 pills each day. In the event King, as one report put it, made Riggs "look like Humpty Dumpty". Her resounding victory was watched on television in 50 million homes, and was front-page news throughout the world. The occasion raised £1.5 million for the organisers, who included Riggs. It also made him more of a household name than he had been as a Wimbledon champion. However, his pride was badly dented by his defeat.

Riggs was an incorrigible gambler. In his auto-biography, *Tennis Is My Racket*, he related how as a professional he would deliberately begin to lose a match, while his brother went around the stands taking bets. Once there was enough money on a Riggs defeat, his brother would give a signal, and Bobby would mount a spectacular comeback. Indeed, when he went down 6–0, 6–1 to the unfancied Baron von Cramm in the 1939 final of the London Grass Court Championships at Queen's Club (forerunner of the Stella Artois Champion-ships) there were a few dark hints that Riggs had not exactly minded losing. In those days it was expected that the winner of that competition would go on to take the Wimbledon title, and after Riggs's defeat at Queen's the odds against him winning Wimbledon increased considerably. The story goes that "The Hustler" backed himself to win with a clutch of bookmakers, and ended up £25,000 to the good.

Robert Larrimore Riggs was born in Los Angeles on February 25, 1918, and began playing tennis when he was 12. Though slightly built, especially by comparison with his main rivals, Don Budge and Jack Kramer, Riggs, a right-hander, quickly showed himself one of the smartest, most resourceful and calculating players of his time. He was renowned not only for a wonderfully equable temperament – the occasional shake of the head was the only clue to any frustration – but also as a superb strategist. He had the brains to quell much harder-hitting opponents, usually with his brilliant execution of the now neglected drop shot, from both forehand and backhand, and the lob.

Riggs was United States champion in 1939 and 1941, and decided to join the growing ranks of professionals in America. He never returned to the All England Club as a player, and remains the only player to have competed in all three events and remain unbeaten. He won the 1939 men's doubles title with his fellow American Ellswood Cooke and the mixed doubles with Alice Marble, who also won the triple crown that year.

Riggs served with the American Navy during the War, and then enjoyed a successful career as a touring professional in the United States, where he and Budge had a rivalry as intense as that between McEnroe and Borg in the 1970s. In 1947, when Kramer won Wimbledon and turned professional, his match with Riggs drew a crowd of 15,114 to Madison Square Garden, even though most of New York was under nearly two feet of snow that night. In the 1950s Riggs briefly tried his hand as a promoter when "Gorgeous Gussie" Moran made her debut as a professional. Otherwise, apart from the matches against Court and King in 1973, he faded into the background, though he was still eager to gamble, not only in the casinos of Las Vegas, but also on various business ventures which came his way. Riggs was twice divorced and had six children.

October 27 1995

BOB PAISLEY

BOB PAISLEY, who died aged 77, was the most success-ful club manager in British football history. He took over at Liverpool in 1974 and led the club to 13 major trophies in nine years, including three European Cups and six League Championships. Paisley himself won the Manager of the Year award on a record six occasions.

In typical Liverpool fashion, Paisley emerged from the "boot room" – he had served the club as a player, reserve coach and trainer. He ascended to the top job after the retirement of the great Bill Shankly. Famed for his remark that "Football isn't a matter of life and death, it's more important than that", Shankly was not easy to follow, but Paisley quickly established winning ways – the League and the UEFA Cup in 1976 – and ensured the loyalty of players and fans.

A shy man, Paisley did not court the media. "When I took over," he wrote, "I said I hoped the team would do the talking for me. It did." Although he was a friendly and paternal figure at Anfield, he was also a ruthless disciplinarian, on and off the pitch. Indeed, discipline was the hallmark of his intelligent, quick-passing teams, though with players such as Kevin Keegan, Kenny Dalglish, Alan Hansen and Graeme Souness, he also had an abundance of talent at his disposal.

Paisley did not gloat over his victories and – on the rare occasions when he had to be – he was a sporting loser. With a self-effacing manner, he preferred to heap glory on to his players rather than himself, though he was aware that he had made some impact at Liverpool. "In all modesty," he said, "I think I can claim to have played a part in the story of the club's success."

The son of a miner, Bob Paisley was born at Hetton-le-Hole, County Durham, on January 23, 1919, and was educated at Eppleton Senior Mixed School before becoming an apprentice bricklayer. He began his playing career as an amateur with Bishop Auckland in 1938. His services were soon sought by Liverpool, but he delayed his departure from the North-East to play in the Amateur Cup Final – and collect a winner's medal.

He arrived at Liverpool as a wing-half on May 8, 1939 and received a signing-on fee of £10 and a weekly salary of £5. His debut was put back by the Second World War. He served from 1939 to 1946 with the Royal Artillery in Egypt and Italy. After Liverpool's European Cup victory in Rome over Borussia Munchengladbach in 1977 he said: "The last time I came here was in a Churchill tank."

On his return to Liverpool, Paisley won a League Championship medal in 1947 and made 252 appearances for the club, scoring 10 times. He hung up his boots in 1954 and intended to return to bricklaying, but was persuaded to stay on at Anfield as a trainer, then physiotherapist, then as assistant to Bill Shankly.

Though he never craved the limelight, he was persuaded to take the manager's job for the good of the club and to carry on the work of his illustrious predecessor. Few expected, or even hoped, that his achievements would so comfortably eclipse Shankly's. On his retirement from the manager's job in 1983, he wrote his autobiography, and in the same year became a member of the Liverpool board and served in this capacity until 1992 when ill-health forced him finally to retire after more than half a century's devotion to the club.

Football was the dominant force in Paisley's life, though he maintained an intense interest in all types of sport, especially cricket, horseracing and boxing. He was appointed OBE in 1977 and became a freeman of the City of Liverpool in 1983. Though many considered Liverpool FC to be his family, Paisley did have his own. He married, in 1946, Jessie Chandler; they had two sons and a daughter.

February 15 1996

PAT SMYTHE

PAT SMYTHE, the show-jumping champion who died aged 67, broke into a sport that had previously been dominated by men to become the best-known woman rider in the world, and the first woman to ride in the Olympic Games. This was in Stockholm in 1956, when she was a member of the British team who won a bronze medal.

From 1947 until 1963 Pat Smythe won Grands Prix not only in Britain but at all the top shows, in Europe,

North and South America, and Australia. The secret of her success lay in her remarkable rapport with her horses, which was both deep and instant; she was a formidable competitor even on horses she had just borrowed.

Her first big triumph came in 1949 when, riding Finality at Harringay, she became the Leading Show Jumper of the Year. In 1950 she broke the European Women's High Jump record with a height of 6ft 10⅞in, only to beat this the next year on Prince Hal with 7ft 3in. Prince Hal, a chestnut gelding, was Pat Smythe's favourite horse. She and her mother bought him in 1950 when he was put up for sale as a broken-down steeple-chaser. With Prince Hal – and later on with other horses, including Tosca, Flanagan and Scorchin – she became the regular star of the Horse of the Year Show. When women were finally allowed to ride in the Nations Cup teams, in 1952, Pat Smythe and Tosca, a grey mare, were chosen for the British team who won at the White City.

Her greatest regret was that Prince Hal was over-looked for the Olympic team in 1960. However, she won the European Championship four times, between 1957 and 1961, and in 1962 triumphed in the British Jumping Derby at Hickstead. Pat Smythe remained at the pinnacle of her sport for two decades. Her astonishing run of success was earnt, not bought, by a mixture of innate talent and total dedication. In contrast to the rich sponsorship and huge prize money available today, her triumphs never sufficed to support her.

Patricia Rosemary Smythe was born at East Sheen, Surrey, on November 22, 1928, the daughter of a former soldier who had become an engineer after winning the MC and Bar in the First World War. A scion of the Irish Ascendancy, she counted among her ancestors William

Smyth, who built Barbavilla, County Westmeath, in the 1730s. The house was named after his wife Barbara, the daughter of Sir George Ingoldsby, whose wife Elizabeth Cromwell was a first cousin of the Lord Protector.

Pat Smythe's love of horses was instilled at an early age by her mother, herself a horsewoman of no mean ability, who gave Pat and her brother Ronald their early riding lessons in Richmond Park, where she schooled polo ponies. Young Pat's first pony, Pixie, was, like all her subsequent champion horses, bought cheaply, for the very good reason that she could never afford anything expensive. Only later, when she had proved her ability, did owners send her horses to ride.

Nevertheless, at the Richmond Royal Show of 1939 she and Pixie, in the under-13.2-hands high-jumping class, tied for first place with Fred Winter (later to become a great National Hunt jockey) and Douglas Bunn, founder and owner of Britain's top show-jumping arena, at Hickstead.

Thanks to the generosity of relatives, Pat Smythe attended a number of private schools, including Downe House, Seaford, and Fern House and Fonthill Abbey in Wiltshire. In 1940 the family moved to Crickley Lodge, near Cheltenham, where Pat went to the grammar school; the Smythes took in paying guests to help make ends meet – an expedient that would continue for many years. At weekends Pat Smythe would harness Pixie to a trap in which home-grown vegetables were taken to Cheltenham and sold to hotels. She also rode him in local gymkhanas, where the entry fee of 2s 6d held out the prospect of winning the first prize of £1. In her school holidays she worked on local farms for 5d an hour, milking cows and mucking out sheds.

One day her mother hacked the nine miles to Cheltenham station to lead home Finality, the offspring of a thoroughbred stallion and Kitty, a milkcart pony. At first Finality did not impress, but mother and daughter persevered until she became the first outstanding horse in Pat's career.

Eric Smythe, her father, who for many years had been crippled by rheumatoid arthritis, died of heart failure early in 1945. Pat and her mother had to move again, to two rooms over a pub near Bath racecourse. At this point Finality decided to jump out of her field, only to get tangled in barbed wire and was so badly hurt it seemed that she might have to be put down. However, later that summer, after the mare had been nursed back to health, Pat won the Open Jumping at the Melksham Show, beating Brian Butler and Tankard, winners of the King George V Gold Cup.

Finality, as unlucky as she was tough, caught strangles in the winter of 1945–46. After recovering she was entered for the Victory Show at the White City, the precursor of the Royal International Horse Show. Just before this event, though, Finality was kicked on the head by a loose horse at a local show. Pat Smythe went to the White City as a spectator, and found her determination to compete at the highest level redoubled. This was the beginning of the golden age of show jumping in Britain, masterminded by Colonel (later Sir) Mike Ansell.

When Pat Smythe and Finality did make it to the White City, they performed so well that they were invited to join the British team for international shows in Belgium. It was only the second time in her life that Pat Smythe had been abroad. Pat Smythe and Finality had the only British clear round in the Grand Prix. Pat

Smythe was then knocked unconscious when about to win the speed competition; Finality had turned a somersault, as a result of being blinded by the setting sun. The Smythe family funds remained slender, and they were forced to sell Finality. But by then the young rider's ability had been noted, and she was being asked to ride other people's horses.

Meanwhile Pat Smythe and her mother had moved into a house at Miserden, in Gloucestershire, where they made ends meet by taking in students from the Royal Agricultural College at Cirencester. At the end of 1952, while driving two of the students to Stroud station, Frances Smythe was killed when her Jeep slid on the icy road. One of the first telephone calls that Pat Smythe received after the accident was from her mother's bank manager, demanding the repayment of her mother's overdraft. But by this time her career was well established.

Pat Smythe wrote several autobiographies, including *Jump for Joy* (1954), and a number of children's books, featuring the adventures of the Three Jays, their ponies and their farm animals. The success of her books enabled her to buy Sudgrove House, in Gloucestershire. Pat Smythe retired from show jumping in 1963, when she married Sam Koechlin, a Swiss lawyer and businessman; subsequently she was based in Switzerland. She travelled with him all over the world, pursuing her interest in conservation and the preservation of rare animals.

After Koechlin's death in 1985 Pat Smythe returned to Sudgrove. Latterly she suffered, like her father before her, from osteo-arthritis, and had both hips replaced. In the mid-1980s she was found to be suffering from congenital heart disease. But she continued to work for the World Wildlife Fund, and from 1986 to 1989 was president of the British Show Jumping Association. Pat Smythe was appointed OBE in 1956. She had two daughters.

February 29 1996

JOHN SNAGGE

JOHN SNAGGE, the broadcaster who died aged 91, was one of the best-loved voices of the BBC. He was most familiar for his annual commentaries on the Boat Race, which he covered from 1931 to 1980. He would time the strokes with a throaty chant of "in, out". In 1935 the *Manchester Guardian* commented that the lead which Cambridge soon established in that year's race allowed small chance for an exciting commentary. However, Snagge was an Oxford man and his "scrupulous determination not to give Oxford more than their share of his attention or praise adds a pleasant and amusing note to his broadcast".

In 1938 his sound commentary accompanied the first televising of the race. In 1949 he was heard to say: "Oxford are ahead. No, Cambridge are ahead. I don't know who's ahead – it's either Oxford or Cambridge." At the end of his last Boat Race commentary, on Easter Saturday 1980, he presented the trophy.

It had been Snagge's idea to present a sovereign minted in 1829, the year of the first race, for the presidents to toss. "Someone had the brilliant idea that it should be kept by the losing president," he recalled, "so that the race was being run to *lose* money – you can't get more amateur than that."

John Snagge

In a career lasting from 1924 to 1965, Snagge's imperturbable tones were broadcast from almost every kind of public event. In 1938 he made the first broadcast from within a diver's suit. In the same year he also spoke to the nation from a bucket 120 feet down a shaft in the Derwent hills, from a bare-back circus ride and from mid-air as he jumped through a window into a sheet in a firefighting exercise.

During the Second World War he announced the attack on Pearl Harbor, the capture of Rome and D-Day. He prepared for months for VE Day. "When it finally happened," he recollected, "May 7 and 8 almost merged into one. Churchill was expected to speak at 6 p.m. then cancelled it. Great anti-climax; except that at midnight the chap in charge of the various transmitters came into the duty room and said, 'I wouldn't bother sleeping much if I were you'.

"Word of VE Day came early from No. 10. I just thought, 'Thank God it's over.' At nine I announced the King, then we did messages from Eisenhower, Alexander, Mountbatten and Montgomery. At 10.45 p.m., when broadcasting ended, I was summoned by Sir William Haley, the Director-General, to his office for a glass of sherry." He suddenly remembered it was his 41st birthday.

When working with outside broadcast in the 1930s he had to circumvent a ban by the Football Association on transmission of the Cup Final at Wembley. "We had to pay our way through the turnstiles, and then leave at intervals to report on the match by microphone at a house rented nearby." In 1936 he made successful broadcasts from the *Queen Mary* during her maiden voyage, speaking on air from 28 microphones set up in the first-class dining-room, the swimming pool and the crow's nest.

After the Coronation in 1953 he received an apology from the Archbishop of Canterbury. "He said he turned over two pages at once," Snagge remembered, "and that I must have had a heart attack when, instead of introducing 'All people who on Earth do dwell', he said, 'Let us pray'. I told him that nobody in the Abbey was praying half as hard as I was."

Snagge's voice was once described as rumbling up "from lungs surely bred on inhaling only the best of tobacco or having sniffed the best of port". Snagge himself recalled that his own "Voice of doom" was reserved for especially portentous announcements.

John Merrick Mordaunt Snagge was born on May 8, 1904, the second son of Judge Sir Mordaunt Snagge. He was educated at Winchester and Pembroke College, Oxford, where by his own admission he did not excel academically. Nor did he row for the university.

He joined the BBC in 1924 straight from Oxford as assistant station director at Stoke-on-Trent. His voice and aptitude led in 1928 to promotion as announcer at Savoy Hill. The Corporation was not always an easy place in which to work. As a young announcer, Snagge was paid £350 a year. One day Lord Reith, the Director-General, summoned him and his colleagues to tell them that a maximum of £500 would in future be fixed for an announcer's salary. "I told him I could not accept a fixed ceiling and the meeting ended frigidly," Snagge recalled. "Half an hour later he sent for me again and asked what I had meant. I told him I could not accept a ceiling for a job in which I might remain for life. He agreed, but he warned me never again to argue with him in public."

Snagge was, however, intensely loyal to the BBC and applied his public school code of honour to all he did. He was a good mixer in the pubs and clubs around Savoy Hill (and, later, Broadcasting House) but made no secret of his preference for integrity above personal gain. Though more at home at the microphone than at a desk, he filled a succession of administrative jobs, eventually becoming Head of Presentation (Sound).

In retirement Snagge bought a small lake near his home at Stoke Poges, Buckinghamshire, on which to row as exercise. An early member of the Lord's Taverners, he was thrice chairman, and was their president in 1952 and 1964. He was appointed OBE in 1944. He married first, in 1936, Eileen Joscelyne, who died in 1980. He married secondly, in 1983, Joan Wilson, who died in 1992.

When Snagge commented on his last Boat Race, the *Radio Times* carried some verses by Roger Woddis:

> *Yours is the kind of soldier-scholar face*
> *That seems designed for a saluting-base.*
> *Youth goes; the voice has mercifully remained,*
> *God's gift, you say, and Corporation-trained.*

March 27 1996

CISSIE CHARLTON

CISSIE CHARLTON, who died aged 83, passed on her enthusiasm for football to her sons, and was rewarded in 1966 when Bobby and Jack became the only brothers to play on the winning side in a World Cup Final. It is a testimony to her motherly influence that her elder sons became two of Britain's best-known and most loved sportsmen.

Jack Charlton's rugged playing style secured him a regular place in the England team. He went on to manage Ireland with extraordinary success. The Irish President told him that the only thing preventing his canonisation was "the technicality that he was still breathing". Bobby Charlton holds England's goalscoring record, and in his playing days was considered to be one of the most accomplished and complete footballers in Europe. For fans around the world he epitomised the time-honoured English virtues of modesty and fair play.

Thrust into the limelight after her sons' successes, Cissie revelled in the attention. Journalists who called at her home rarely left without a good story and a hot meal. She was immensely proud of her Variety Club award as "Northern Personality of the Year", and of being the first to receive one of Esther Rantzen's "Hearts of Gold".

She was born Elizabeth Milburn on November 11, 1912, into a footballing family at Ashington, a mining town in Northumberland. Four of her brothers played professionally – Jack, George and Jim for Leeds and Stan for Leicester. Her cousin was the great Jackie Milburn, so loved in Newcastle that he is still known simply as "Wor Jackie". One of Cissie Charlton's last public appearances was at the unveiling of his statue in 1995.

She grew up in poverty in Ashington's yellow-brick terraces. Even though she won a scholarship to a local high school, she was unable to accept the place because her parents could not afford the bus fares. Sport was a means of escape as much as a recreation, and Ashington had more than its fair share of cricketers, footballers and athletes.

Cissie herself did not approve of women's football. "It's a physical game," she said, "and it's the physical side that I like to see. Women just have too many bits to get hurt." Yet she also insisted: "I never had a doll in my life – I just wanted to play football with the lads. It is in my blood."

She married Bon Charlton, whose main interest was boxing. After winning £1 in a booth bout, he spent 17s 6d on a ring for her, which she wore until she died. The couple had four sons – Jack, Bobby, Gordon and Tommy – and she soon instilled in them a love for football. "I took them to Ashington's home games from a very early age," she said. "Bobby, just a babe in his pram, would jump with fright at the roar whenever a goal was scored. He was a quiet lad even then. But Jack was just the opposite and has never changed. Jack was always a live wire, always getting into scrapes and leading other kids into trouble."

Jack signed for Leeds and Bobby went to Old Trafford. How directly Cissie Charlton developed their talents is unclear. But the enduring image is that of the bright-eyed young mother, pinnie on under her cardigan, demonstrating trapping and turning techniques in the cobbled alley at the back of her terraced house.

After her husband died, she moved from the house Jack had bought her in the Dales and back to her home town, where, aged 73, she was soon coaching the local school football team. No tears was the first rule she taught them. "Anybody who cries is back in the classroom." As her sons found out, "You'll never play football if you're soft."

March 28 1996

WILLIE GUNN

WILLIE GUNN, the fisherman who died aged 86, gave his name to one of the deadliest salmon flies that has ever been tied. The fly is an essential part of many a salmon fisherman's equipment and is especially productive in cold water conditions, at the beginning or end of the season. "To be Willie Gunnless on any Highland stream was to be improperly dressed," wrote Bruce Sandison, in *Trout & Salmon*.

It was Rob Wilson, who had a tackle shop in Brora, Sutherland, who tied the original Willie Gunn fly. It was one of about 20 experimental patterns, and Wilson asked Gunn to select one. Gunn's experienced eye fell upon one which was intended to be a hair-wing variation of another noted salmon fly, the Thunder & Lightning. "By gum," said Gunn, "that one looks bonny. That's the fly I would use." "Well," said Wilson, "you must have it and we will name the fly the Willie Gunn."

Gunn's instant judgement was rapidly vindicated. That very day he caught six fish with the black, orange and yellow fly, and four the day after. Word spread and everyone on the River Brora began to use the Willie Gunn. Now it is known throughout the salmon fishing world. According to one story, the Queen Mother, a skilled and enthusiastic salmon fisher, knew the fly, though not the man himself. It is said that she turned to her ghillie on an unproductive day and asked why they had not tried the Willie Gunn. "Ma'am," he said, "I am Willie Gunn."

Lord Strathnaver, the son of the Countess of Sutherland, for whose family Gunn acted as chauffeur and ghillie, said of him: "Willie was an extremely amusing gentleman and, of course, famous as both fisherman and ghillie.

"He loved to help people to catch their first salmon. He always knew where fish were likely to be caught whatever the river level, and he was an absolute master of short casting. He could not see the need for long casting, preferring to keep everything as simple as possible."

Willie Gunn was born on January 1, 1910 at Skerray on the wild north coast of Sutherland. He spent his early years in what he was later to describe as very poor conditions. His parents were crofters at Skerray; his father fished to make ends meet. Skerray is a community originally created by the Highland Clearances in the 19th century when thousands of people were driven from their homes to make more room for sheep. Some emigrated; others clung to the coast.

Gunn arrived on the Sutherland Estate aged about 18, after spells with the Forestry Commission and in farming, and soon fell in love with it. He began by working with the gundogs and he learnt quickly, He mastered the art of stalking deer by watching the experienced stalkers working their guests into perfect position for a shot at the stage. A football injury put an end to his stalking. The job could mean walking many miles a day in rough terrain, and Gunn was no longer capable of that.

His life with rod and line began as a hobby. He began as a trout fisherman, but his horizons widened when he caught his first (16lb) salmon on the River Mallart. The largest fish he caught was a 28-pounder taken from the Bengie pool on his beloved Brora. Gunn was promoted in the early 1950s to Uppat, the

Sutherland family home. He retired when he was 70. Willie Gunn married, in 1946, Euphemia (Phemmie) Mackintosh.

April 10 1996

BERYL BURTON

BERYL BURTON, who died aged 58, gained seven world cycling titles between 1959 and 1967 and dominated women's racing in Britain for a quarter of a century. Most of her records still stand, including the British 12-hour time trial figure of 277.25 miles which, when it was set in 1967, was the greatest distance achieved by any rider, male or female.

She won the world 3,000 metres pursuit title on the track five times between 1959 and 1966, and was the women's world road race champion in 1960 and 1967. She won 13 national pursuit titles and 12 in bunched road racing, but by far her biggest tally came in road time trials where, in addition to her 25 British best all-rounder titles (1959–1983), she won the national 25-mile championship 24 times and the 100-mile title 18 times. Burton broke the women's national 25-mile record 11 times from 1959, and her best time of 53min 21sec set in 1976 still stands, as does her 50-mile figure of 1hr 51min 30sec set in the same year. Though she held the national 100-mile title as recently as 1981, neither Burton nor anybody else has improved on her British record of 3hr 55min 5sec set in 1968.

She was born Beryl Charnock on May 12, 1937 in Leeds and educated at Stainbeck Secondary School; her competitive nature first became evident in swimming. She became interested in cycling when she met her future husband, Charlie, at the Burton clothing factory where they worked. She began riding competitively in 1955, taking only a short break for the birth of her daughter, Denise, in January 1956. Her first season of serious competition at national level was in 1957, when she finished second in the national 100-mile championship and fifth in the British best all-rounder competition.

The other notable rider of the day was the late Millie Robinson, of Manx Viking Wheelers, who won the national 25-mile title in 1955, 1956 and 1957; but by 1958 Burton had beaten Robinson to take the first of her seven consecutive national titles at that distance.

In her autobiography, *Personal Best* (1986), Burton recalled the day in 1967 when she beat Mike McNamara, the British men's best all-rounder in that year, to set her all-comers' 12-hour record of 277.25 miles. When she caught McNamara, who had started two minutes ahead, "Mac raised his head slightly and looked at me," Burton recalled. "Goodness knows what was going on in his mind, but I thought some gesture was required on my part. I was carrying a bag of Liquorice Allsorts in the pocket of my jersey and on impulse I groped into the bag and pulled one out. I can still remember that it was one of those Swiss-roll shaped ones, white with a coating of black liquorice. 'Liquorice Allsort, Mac?' I shouted, and held it towards him. He gave a wan smile. 'Ta, love,' he said, popping the sweet into his mouth. I put my head down and drew away." McNamara, who went on to clock a British men's record of 276.52 miles, harboured no ill-feeling.

Beryl Burton was appointed MBE in 1964 and OBE

in 1968. She married, in 1955, Charlie Burton; they had one daughter, Denise, who won the women's national road race title in 1976.

May 7 1996

HENRY JOHNS

HENRY JOHNS, who died aged 85, was the world's senior real tennis professional, and a veteran of the golden age of tennis — the age of the leisured patron, the elegant amateur and, above all, the cultivation of style. As head professional at Lord's for 21 years, Johns coached several generations of top players. He was the archetypal professional of the old school: deferential, but never sub-servient, he demanded from his pupils exemplary manners both on and off the court.

His own skill at the game was consummate. His service showed effortless skill, subtle change of pace and great variety; his anticipation of return was faultless; and his strokes were smooth and accurate, using the mini-mum force required for each type of shot. All these qualities are reflected in the play of the past and present champions he taught.

Before going to Lord's, Johns worked at the old Prince's Club, in Knightsbridge, where he played real tennis against Sir Edwin Lutyens, whose reflexes, he recalled, were "nearly non-existent"; and against the Maharajah of Alwar, whose service, he was instructed, was not to be returned. Tumultuous applause from the Maharajah's retinue in the dedans greeted every winning point. Before he played, the court was always searched by one of his servants, because a soothsayer had predicted that he would die by the bite of a mad dog. But it was tennis that got the Maharajah in the end: he fell down the steps of a French court and broke his neck.

Henry Johns was born in Fulham on July 21, 1910, and grew up close to Queen's Club, where he occasionally earned sixpence an evening as a ball-boy. He was offered a job in the tennis professional's shop just before his 14th birthday, working a six-and-a-half-day week for four shillings, sewing balls and stringing racquets. Two years later he was tempted away by Prince's Club for a shilling a week more, working with five other ball-boys under W. H. Webb.

Johns recalled the panic to find a suitable opponent for the Duke of Windsor – a squash player with more enthusiasm than skill – during the Army's Squash and Rackets Tournament. A Captain Smith-Bingham was found, with the guarantee that even His Royal Highness would be able to defeat him. The Duke duly won his first game.

During August, when the clubs closed, young Henry would be taken by Lord Revelstoke on a "poor boy's holiday" to stay in his Lutyens castle on Lambay Island. There he played on the eccentric, roofless Irish court, where the main hazards were rainwater in wet weather and seagull droppings in dry.

Johns left Prince's in 1935 to work as the private professional to the Cazalets, at Fairlawns, which had (and still has, though no longer used for play) its own real tennis court. The next year he first went to work at Lord's.

In August 1939 Johns enlisted in the Army, and went on to serve throughout the Second World War, attaining the rank of sergeant. After the War he returned to Lord's and, as Lord Aberdare has recorded, saved the American game (known as "court tennis") by taking on an order to supply 3,000 balls. The balls were handmade with strips of cloth torn (in the era of clothes rationing) from old coats and flannel trousers. The cloth had to be torn into ⅜-inch strips, which took hours, before the actual making of the ball could begin. Fellow professionals George Beton and George Ferguson made up the kernel, about one inch in diameter; then Johns built them up to the required size and correct weight and tied them; finally his wife Mona and Mrs Beton covered them with Melton cloth. The task took five years to complete.

Johns took over from Jack Groom as head professional at Lord's in 1954. He remained there until 1975, when he went into semi-retirement and was accorded honorary full membership of MCC, only the third employee of the club to receive this accolade. Jim Dear, world rackets champion and Johns's fellow ball-boy at Prince's in 1927, called him "the champion of the world at Lord's".

One of Johns's best friends was Sir Ralph Richardson, an accomplished squash player in his youth, but less skilful at real tennis which he took up when he was nearing 50. Even after his 80th birthday, Richardson would play with Johns every Friday that he was free, roaring up to Lord's on his motorcycle. After their game, he and Johns would sit chatting in the dedans. Two days before Richardson died, he turned up as usual, but as he didn't feel well enough to play they just talked. Some years later Johns was asked how good Ralph Richardson was. "As good as the day he started," Johns replied, adding, with a twinkle in his eye, "Blooming awful, really."

No expert was more modest than Johns, and no

professional better loved. His 80th birthday luncheon at Queen's Club attracted elderly and middle-aged players from every corner of Britain. It is a great tribute to the younger generations – the fit, fiercely competitive (and often Australian) athletes who have developed real tennis skills to a level never before seen – that they are seen to practise the true courtesies with club members and among themselves which came so naturally to Johns. Henry Johns was survived by his wife, Mona. They had two sons and two daughters.

June 1 1996

KEITH BOYCE

KEITH BOYCE, the cricketer, who died in his native Barbados aged 53, promised excitement whenever he played. Lithe of movement, lean of build, he was not, as a bowler, quite so robust or dangerously fast as Andy Roberts or Michael Holding. Nevertheless he was an opponent to fear, capable of turning a match with ball or bat.

Boyce would have played more than his 21 Tests but for a proneness to injury which had something to do with his wholehearted service to Essex between 1966 and 1977. Although he took his 852 first-class wickets at only 25 runs each, and scored four centuries in a career which earnt him 8,800 runs, he was often at his thrilling best in limited-overs cricket. The family crowds who filled Essex grounds on Sundays paid special attention whenever he strode to the wicket: entertainment was guaranteed and any spectator might be in danger.

Keith Boyce was born at St Peter, Barbados, on October 11, 1943, and educated locally. He played cricket for the Wanderers in Bridgetown. His fielding was joyous and brilliant, though, as with the rest of his game, it could be undisciplined. Once in a Test at the Kennington Oval an England batsman gained seven from one shot as Boyce hurled his throw from the boundary far over the wicketkeeper's head. He approached life much as he did his cricket; following his instinct for adventure and fun. There were evenings when he did no harm to the Barbadian rum industry.

Boyce's greatest match was for Essex against Leicestershire at Chelmsford in 1975 when he took 12 for 73 and scored a century in 58 minutes. In Test cricket his outstanding performance was at the Oval in 1973 when he took 11 for 147 and hit 72 at No. 9. His 19 wickets in that three-Test series cost him only 15 runs each. Against Australia at Adelaide in 1976, he saved a West Indian follow-on by scoring 95 not out from 104 balls against Lillee and Thomson and then made 69 in the second innings.

Apart from the tour to Australia, when his bowling was hampered by injuries, he also toured England twice, and toured India and Pakistan. In all Tests he scored 657 runs at an average of 24 and took 60 wickets at 30. Appropriately, he was prominent in the West Indian victory over Australia in the first World Cup Final at Lord's in 1975.

Trevor Bailey writes: While I was captaining the Rothman Cavaliers on a tour to the West Indies in 1965, we played a couple of matches in Barbados. The first was against Barbados, and then most of their team departed to Jamaica for the first Test against Australia, which meant that our second game was against what was almost their Second XI, though considerably stronger than any county side.

I shall never forget that match because it was the first time I saw and met Keith Boyce. He bowled fast, hit the ball with exceptional power, and was able to throw the ball full-toss to the 'keeper with a flat trajectory from the boundary. I instinctively knew that here was a potential Test cricketer. I have always believed that if you bring into county cricket an overseas player who is not already an international star, he must be a spectacular performer, so I wanted Keith. My next job was to find out what he was like as a person, because the last thing Essex could afford was someone who could not fit into an essentially happy club. The reports I received were excellent. Before I left the island I had signed Keith on.

Interestingly, the tour manager was Les Ames, and he arranged for the other Bajan cricketer I fancied, John Shepherd, to join Kent. A few months later I met Keith at Heathrow, having fixed up accommodation for him with help from our coach, Frank Rist, who had to look after him for that first summer as at that time some residential qualification was required for overseas players. As a result, Keith played for Essex Second XI, Essex Club and Ground, and Walthamstow Cricket Club, with great success both on and off the field.

Keith epitomised all the best of Caribbean cricket and brought to this country not just ability, but also entertainment, laughter, and a love of the game.

October 15 1996

NEVILLE CRUMP

NEVILLE CRUMP, who died aged 86, trained the winners of three Grand Nationals. He was known for his booming voice and Chaucerian humour. At Liverpool once Crump was asked about the suitability of a stand-in steward. "Oh, he'd be perfect," he said. "He's deaf, he's blind, and he knows sod-all about racing."

Crump eschewed political correctness. He once told a car-load of Japanese tourists who had lost their way and strayed on to his gallops: "You found your way to Pearl Harbor easily enough, you should be able to find your way to Leyburn."

At Middleham, in Yorkshire, where he trained for 40 years, the Captain, as he was known, would be seen riding out on winter mornings clad in a black Army overcoat, trousers kept up with binder-twine and a flat cap pulled down over his ears. He would rouse his lads with tuneless songs and the occasional blast on the hunting horn. Beneath the bluster, though, he was the kindest and most loyal of men, an exceptional judge of horses and a genius at training staying steeplechasers.

Neville Franklin Crump was born at Beckenham on December 27, 1910. His father, a cheese manufacturer, was a Master of Foxhounds and a superb horseman (he had been a rancher in Australia), and young Neville learnt to ride almost as soon as he could walk. Crump was educated at Marlborough and Balliol, where he scraped a pass. In later life, when he met Edward Heath, Crump mentioned that they had both been at Balliol. "Who was your tutor?" inquired the Prime Minister.

"Christ, I can't remember," Crump replied. "Oh," said Heath and turned away.

Crump was commissioned in the 4th Hussars, only to resign in 1935. By this stage he was already making a name for himself as a jockey at point-to-points, and he soon started riding as an amateur under Rules. He spent two years as a paying assistant to Sonny Hall near Lambourn, before taking out a licence to train a small string at Upavon on Salisbury Plain. He won his first race, an optional seller worth £58, at Torquay in 1938.

During the Second World War, Crump served as a captain in the North Somerset Yeomanry in Palestine, and then as a tank trainer at Barnard Castle, where his friends included John Le Mesurier. On demobilisation, Crump returned to training and soon moved to Middleham. He sent out the first of his Aintree Grand National winners in 1948. Sheila's Cottage, under his stable jockey Arthur Thompson, came home at 50–1.

A year earlier, the same mare – a moody, reckless animal given to biting and kicking – had been first past the post, but riderless. Next, she had attempted the Scottish Grand National, then held at Bogside on the Ayrshire coast. Again, she unseated Thompson, this time proceeding to gallop into the Firth of Clyde and swim across an inlet. She was eventually retrieved by Crump from Irvine police station at midnight. Crump would later describe Sheila's Cottage as "a good game plodder, but rather an ornery old cow".

Following the 1948 Grand National, Crump was much in demand and his string quickly expanded. He built a new yard and eventually found room for 66 horses. Over the next 15 National Hunt seasons, he was among the top six trainers 10 times and headed the list twice.

Crump consolidated his reputation by winning the 1949 Scottish National with Wot No Sun and the Welsh National with Skyreholme (ridden by Dick Francis) in 1951.

The next year he had his second Aintree winner with Teal, at odds of 40–1. The victory paid rich dividends for its owner, a hard-betting builder named Harry Lane. Crump had earlier told Lane that Teal was a "good thing" for the National, though the horse first had to run in a preliminary race at Kelso. Lane had not yet had his bet, however, and not wishing to see Teal's odds shorten unduly for the National, he telephoned Crump and, to the trainer's horror, threatened to remove his horse from the stable unless he was "stopped" in the Kelso race. When the race started, Teal set off at a gallop, and was a jump ahead of the rest of the field by halfway, at which point Arthur Thompson dismounted, ostensibly to look for a stone in the horse's hoof, then remounted and finished second. It was the nearest Crump came to saddling a non-trier, and on several occasions in later years he threw out good horses whose owners wanted them to be given "an easy race".

Crump's third and most convincing Grand National winner was Merryman II, who overcame an interrupted preparation to romp home by 15 lengths in 1960, the first year that the race was televised, and the last to feature the old-style fences at their most forbidding. Merryman was ridden by Thompson's successor as stable jockey, Gerry Scott, who kept the ride despite suffering three breaks to his collarbones in the fortnight before the race. It was an indication of the fierce loyalty Crump always showed his jockeys.

On an earlier occasion, an owner suggested, wrongly,

that Scott – at that time an apprentice jockey claiming 7lb – had stopped his horse. Scott was full of trepidation, but Crump told him not to worry, telephoned the owner and demanded that he remove the horse from his yard immediately. Crump generally preferred to have a professional jockey on board. After watching an amateur lose by a short head on one of his horses, he was heard to remark: "Oh sure, very artistic. Just like a duck f-ing a bag of nails."

Other big-race wins included three Whitbread Gold Cups, with Much Obliged, Hoodwinked and Dormant. In 1962 he saddled the first two home in the Hennessy Gold Cup at Newbury: Springbok and Rough Tweed. He also won the Topham Trophy two years running and the Grand Sefton Chase, both over the big Liverpool fences, the Massey-Ferguson Gold Cup and the Mackeson Gold Cup. In the early 1980s, Narvik won the Welsh National, and Salkend and Canton won the Scottish National. Crump eventually retired in 1989.

A large florid man, Crump possessed a short fuse, but his bark was worse than his bite. Quarrels were quickly forgotten and he never bore grudges. He took pleasure in the good fortune of others, and was quick to congratulate. He became a great friend of many of his owners, especially Lord Cadogan and the late Lord Lovat. Crump enjoyed hunting – he was Master of the Aldershot Draghounds before the War – but regretted that he had never learnt to shoot: his father had told him that "shooting is just for shits".

He hated wearing jackets, finding them too tight under the armpits, and would refuse dinner invitations unless allowed to wear a sweater. He was also reluctant to go out if *Emmerdale Farm* was on the television. Crump married, in 1937, Sylvia "Brownie" Bird, the grand-daughter of the custard magnate, Sir Alfred Bird. She predeceased him. They had a daughter.

January 22 1997

WILFRED WOOLLER

WILFRED WOOLLER, who died aged 84, was a games player of astonishing versatility: a renowned Welsh rugby international; captain of the Glamorgan side who won the County Cricket Championship in 1948; a footballer good enough to play (albeit once) for Cardiff City; a squash player for Wales; an outstanding sprinter and long-jumper; and an accomplished performer at water polo.

At rugby, Wilf Wooller was one of the greatest centre three-quarters of all time. *The Daily Telegraph*'s Howard Marshall wrote of his tremendous pace and his siege-gun kicking, and his ability to win a game on his own by some gargantuan thrust. Wooller was tall and strongly built (even as a schoolboy he weighed 13 stone), and when he was in full flight for the line seemed to "eat up the earth as if he were covering it with seven-league boots".

Particularly memorable was his performance for Wales against the All Blacks in December 1935. The All Blacks were in the lead when, just after half-time, Wooller received the ball in his own half at full stride. "And what a stride it was," Howard Marshall reported. "A strange loping stride, with those long legs going like pistons, carrying him bang through the shallow defence, while 50,000 screamed. 'He's away – he's away!' they shouted – 10, 20, 30 yards – the powerful Gilbert coming in to tackle – Wooller punting over his head, racing after the bouncing ball, over-running it on the line, and there was Rees-Jones dashing in from the wing to touch down for a most glorious try."

Three minutes from time Wooller and Rees-Jones combined in much the same manner to score another try, and Wales had won a famous victory by 13–12. In celebration, Wooller required little assistance in heaving a piano over the bannisters of the team's hotel into the foyer below. He would play for Wales 18 times and captained the side in 1938–39.

As a cricketer Wooller was one of the last true amateurs, a fast-medium bowler, robust hitter and intrepid close fielder. He made 13,856 runs, averaging 22, and took 956 wickets at 26 each. He also took 409 catches. However, it was as a captain that he excelled. He first led the Glamorgan side in 1947, and the next year inspired them to a wholly unexpected triumph in the County Championship. Nine of the team had been born in Wales, and the spirit that Wooller engendered – expressed in aggressive fielding and brilliant catching around the bat (with the captain to the fore at short leg) – carried off the championship. "It was two seasons before Jim Swanton would believe it," he recalled with relish.

Wilfred Wooller was born at Colwyn Bay on November 20, 1912, the son of a builder. He was educated at Rydal School, and won his first rugby cap for Wales at the age of 20, in 1933. Later that year he went up to Christ's College, Cambridge, where he became a double Blue for rugby and cricket.

During his three years in the Cambridge XV he

formed a remarkable partnership with the fly-half Cliff Jones. In his first University Match, 1933, Cambridge lost 5–3, but the next year they scored a crushing 29–4 victory against an Oxford side who contained eight present or future internationals. In that game Wooller scored a gigantic drop goal from within his own half; as he recalled it, the ball (of heavy leather not the modern plastic) landed in Twickenham's North Stand. In 1935 the match was a scoreless draw.

Wooller went on to play club rugby for Sale and Cardiff. In the summer he won a place in the Glamorgan side under Maurice Turnbull, another great Welsh games-player of Cambridge pedigree. In 1939 he made 111 and took six wickets as Glamorgan defeated the West Indies by 73 runs. At the outbreak of the Second World War Wooller was commissioned into the Royal Artillery. Captured by the Japanese in Java in 1942 he spent the rest of the War in a PoW camp. Though he was not subjected to the worst excesses of the Japanese, imprisonment was a trial to someone of his personality: he hardly suffered fools at all, let alone gladly.

His years at Glamorgan (he retired as a player in 1960 but continued as secretary until 1977) were peppered with controversy; on one occasion he provoked the resignation of half the committee. Wooller's views were right-wing and authoritarian. He had been brought up, he said, "as a God-fearing man with a respect for the Establishment". He held that "leadership qualities improve with the right training. Often that came from the right schooling."

He was never averse to a row. When the South African rugby team toured Britain in 1969–70 he was subjected to protests from the anti-apartheid lobby.

Wooller told the Archbishop of Wales that support for the demonstrators was "disgraceful", an example of the "usual un-Christian attitude" to be found in the Church. Ninety-nine per cent of the trouble, he suggested, was caused by "Lefties, weirdies, and odd bods". He described Denis Howell, Labour's Sports Minister, as "not unlike a 50p piece – double-faced, many-sided and not worth a great deal". Howell's successor, the Conservative Eldon Griffiths, was dismissed as a politician playing at sport.

Wooller was a Test selector from 1955 to 1961, and in 1961 served on Col R. S. Rait Kerr's committee on the future of cricket. From 1961 to 1988 he wrote about rugby and cricket for *The Sunday Telegraph*. His views were trenchant, and he did not warm to the training methods and technical dedication of modern rugby players. Wilfred Wooller married first, in 1941 (dissolved 1947), Lady Gillian Windsor-Clive, eldest daughter of the 2nd Earl of Plymouth. He married secondly, in 1948, Enid James; they had three sons and two daughters.

March 12 1997

WILLIAM VANS AGNEW

BILL VANS AGNEW, who died aged 71, helped the British hockey team win a gold medal at the Seoul Olympic Games of 1988 with his tactical approach. The realisation that in hockey, as in football, control of the midfield held the key to success came to Vans Agnew when he was captaining the successful London club side Beckenham in 1960. He therefore challenged conventional thinking by introducing the 4–2–3–1–1 formation. Most of the principal hockey-playing countries adopted the system or a variation of it. It has become the basis of today's game in both men's and women's hockey.

William Vans Agnew was born on August 14, 1925 in Manila, where his father was working as chief accountant for Shell. After spending his early years in India, young Bill was educated at Loretto School in Edinburgh. He went on to read Medicine at Cambridge, where he won a hockey Blue. After qualifying at Guy's Hospital he was commissioned into the RAMC and captained the all-international Army hockey team, who included such players as Conroy, Bedford, Nuttall and Green. At international level he played for Scotland between 1947 and 1955, captaining the side from 1951. In many internationals he played alongside his brother Mike.

Bill Vans Agnew was well known for his determination. In 1953, as captain of Scotland when the English team was thought all-powerful, he found his side 3–1 down at half-time. He was under explicit instructions not to make any positional changes, but within a minute of the restart, though on the programme as right-half, he had instructed the centre-half to change places with him. Then, playing like a man possessed, he helped Scotland score two goals to draw level. England was lucky to hang on for the draw in the closing minutes.

When his playing days were over, Vans Agnew's competitive urge took him back into international hockey as a coach and manager. After he had successfully managed the Kent side to two championship victories in 1966 and 1967, his achievements demanded recognition, and in 1970 he was invited to take the England team on a European tour. At that time British hockey was in the international wilderness, but during the tour Vans Agnew helped restore pride by notable victories over some of the leading Continental sides.

On the strength of his success he was appointed manager of the British team, and in winter 1971 took them to the final of the renowned Nehru Tournament in Delhi. Under his leadership the team had become competitive and technically aware, and went on to a creditable sixth place in the 1972 Munich Olympics.

Vans Agnew was highly regarded as a general practitioner. He practised at Chelsfield, in Kent, from 1955 to 1986, and was consultant dermatologist in the Bromley area. He was chairman of the Bromley Health Committee and of the local St John's Ambulance.

In golf, Bill Vans Agnew was captain of the Knole Park Club in Sevenoaks, a member of Rye, the Royal & Ancient and the Seniors. With his brother Mike he had been a popular annual competitor in the Halford Hewitt competition. He married, in 1953, Peggy Davies; they had a son and two daughters.

April 22 1997

DENIS COMPTON

DENIS COMPTON, who died aged 78, was one of the greatest and most dashing of all English batsmen. He was at his zenith after the Second World War, when in four summers and two overseas tours – to Australia in 1946–47 and to South Africa in 1948–49 – he scored 14,641 runs and made 60 centuries. Statistics, though, tell little of a player whose genius was born of daring and improvisation.

Compton used a light (2lb 2oz) bat – though a tendency to leave his equipment behind meant that he was sometimes obliged to pick up whatever he could find – and he wielded it as a rapier rather than a bludgeon. His trademark was the sweep, of which he deployed several different varieties and which he did not hesitate to play off balls that would have hit the middle stump. He relished the opportunity to hook bumpers. On one occasion, having slipped and fallen flat on his back in mid-stroke, he managed to execute a one-handed late cut that sent the ball winging to the boundary.

In the late 1940s Compton became a national idol, his Brylcreemed form staring down from posters all over the land. Sir Neville Cardus perfectly caught the manner in which he irradiated a drab post-War Britain. "Never have I been so deeply touched on a cricket ground," Cardus wrote, "as I was in this heavenly summer of 1947 when I went to Lord's to see a pale-faced crowd, existing on rations, the rocket-bomb still in the ears of most folks – and see this worn, dowdy crowd raptly watching Compton. The strain of long years of anxiety and affliction passed from all heads and shoulders at the sight of Compton in full sail, sending the ball here, there, and everywhere, each stroke a flick of delight, a propulsion of happy, sane, healthy life. There were no rations in an innings by Compton."

The Corinthian image created when playing for Middlesex and England in the summer was fortified in the winter, when Compton turned his attention to football. He was good enough to hold his place in the great Arsenal sides before and after the War, collecting both a League and a Cup medal. He also won 14 War-time international caps for England. By 1950, when he appeared in the Cup Final against Liverpool, he was already into his thirties, inclined to run out of puff, and troubled by a notorious knee injury. In the first half, in his own words, he "played a stinker"; in the second, fuelled by a mammoth slug of whisky, administered by Alex James, he put in a dazzling performance.

His excised knee cap, incidentally, is now kept at Lord's. "It's a revolting thing," Compton observed. "Looks as if rats have been nipping at it. I can't imagine why *anyone* would want to look at it."

As a professional, Compton necessarily played games to win; chiefly, though, he played them for fun. The attention he gave to events on the field was often divided with his concern for the fortunes of the horses he had backed that afternoon.

He lives in the minds of all who saw him, and of many who did not, as the cavalier of cricket. He was appointed CBE in 1958, had a stand named after him at Lord's (over mid-on, looking out from the pavilion, on the left of the sight-screen), and was for his last seven years president of Middlesex. Yet the old champion did not entirely approve of the modern game. He hated the helmets, the visors and the chest protectors. Above all, he hated the grimness that afflicts English cricketers. "I would dearly love the boys to go out there like play-boys," he remarked in 1993, "play off the back foot, and enjoy it."

Denis Charles Scott Compton was born on May 23, 1918, the son of Jessie and Harry Compton who ran a painting and decorating business in Hendon. There was a sister, and an elder brother, Leslie, who played centre-half for Arsenal and England, and wicketkeeper for Middlesex. Denis was educated at Bell Lane School, and learnt his cricket up against the lamp-post in Alexandra Road, Hendon. His father captained Bell Lane School's old boys' team and used to take his sons along to matches. The day came when the team was one short, and the 12-year-old Denis was drafted in – to the derision of the opposition who protested that they could not bowl properly to one so small. They were told to bowl as fast as they liked, and did so, only to find the ball conjured to all parts of the ground.

Denis Compton already knew that the No. 13 bus went from Hendon to Lord's. At 14 he made his first appearance at the ground, captaining the Elementary Schools and duly making a century. The innings caught the eye of Sir Pelham Warner, and the next summer Compton was recruited to the MCC groundstaff at Lord's. He started at the foot of the ladder as one of the "Nippers" or "Roller boys" who were put to various ground duties and received net practice and tuition. His salary was 25 shillings a week, the same amount as he was paid in the winter by Arsenal.

Compton had little need of formal tuition, as the basic principles of batting came naturally to him. At 15 he scored a century for the MCC against Suffolk at Felixstowe; two years later he shared a century partnership with E. W. Swanton for Middlesex 2nd XI against Kent at Folkstone. Later in the week, a few days after his 18th birthday, he was promoted to the full county side for the Whitsuntide match against Sussex at Lord's. Sussex made only a modest 185 in their first innings, but when Compton came in to bat, at No. 11, Middlesex still required 24 for the lead.

"Whatever you do, play forward," instructed Gubby Allen, his partner at the wicket. Compton played back to the first ball and saw it whistle over his stumps. Emphatically rebuked by Allen, he stayed at the crease to make 14 and secure the first-innings lead. Three weeks later he scored his maiden first-class century, at Northampton. By the end of 1936 he had passed the 1,000 mark, won his county cap, and only narrowly missed being selected for the England tour of Australia. Emphatically, he was on his way.

E. W. Swanton writes: What marked Denis Compton's batting from the first was a sense of enjoyment in it all, of risks taken and bowlers teased, that at once communicated itself to the crowd. Yet, while it was the liberties he sometimes took which were written and talked about, when the need arose his defence could be as orthodox as anyone's.

He was only 20 when, in 1938, with all the poise and coolness of an old hand, he saved England from probable defeat against Australia at Lord's in an innings of 76 not out. A fortnight earlier, in his first Test against Australia at Trent Bridge, on a perfect wicket, he had made the fourth hundred of the innings, following those of Barnet, Hutton and Paynter. But it was in the Lord's game, on a pitch made awkward by rain, before that most discriminating of crowds, that he buckled down to the job and showed both the full range of his skill and the temperament to go with it.

He had been chosen first for England in the third and last Test of the 1937 summer against New Zealand, making 65 before, as the non-striker, being run out from an accidental diversion by the bowler. That was pure ill-luck, but prophetic in that the one flaw in his batting was running between the wickets. His great friend and partner, W. J. Edrich, is credited with the remark that Denis's initial call was no more than a basis for nego-tiation, and this happy-go-lucky approach – banished only at the crease when things really mattered – occasion-ally tested the patience of his captain. Hence J. J. Warr's remark that Compton took 415 catches in the course of his career "when he was looking".

As might be expected, Compton did not thrive on leadership, either as vice-captain to F. R. Brown on the Australia tour of 1950–51, or with Middlesex when he and Edrich shared the captaincy in 1951 and 1952. He was too pressed in organising himself to relish the responsibility of looking after 10 others.

His personality was otherwise expressed. Good-looking and debonair, Compton was the idol of spectators every-where, in Australia, South Africa and the West Indies, as well as at home. To a War-weary nation, aching for entertainment, he was the national "pin-up", a hero dangerously exalted who was yet never spoilt. Compton was one of the first sportsmen for whom an agent was an urgent necessity, to cope not only with commercial approaches but cascading fan-mail.

His *annus mirabilis* was 1947 when he made 3,816 runs (easily topping Tom Hayward's record 3,518, made in 1906). His 18 hundreds that year exceeded the record 16 of Sir Jack Hobbs, made in 1925; his average was 90. It was a gloriously hot, dry summer during which the South Africans suffered most from his bat, to the tune of six hundreds, four of them in Tests. Compton, however, was never an accumulator for the sake of it; and it was only Middlesex's need for plenty of quick runs in their successful chase of the County Championship that sustained his appetite.

Perhaps his two greatest innings were those against Bradman's all-conquering Australians in 1948: 184 at Trent Bridge in an eerie, yellow light with Lindwall and Miller at their fastest, and 145 not out at Old Trafford. This was the time when, within a few minutes of going in, he was obliged to retire for stitches to a cut eyebrow, sustained in hooking at a no-ball from Lindwall. We saw now, in the words of Neville Cardus, the Ironside breastplate as well as the Cavalier plume. Bandaged but indomitable, he returned to play an innings which laid the foundation of what would likely have been an England victory had the weather not interfered.

At this point, he had made eight hundreds in the last 10 Tests, a sequence which only Bradman had achieved. But now, at his peak, an old football injury to Compton's right knee began to give out danger signals. For a while the surgeons and "physios" contrived to keep him on the field, and in the spring of 1950, in his last game of football, with the knee heavily bandaged, he helped Arsenal to victory in the Cup Final. Within a few weeks he was hobbling off the field at Lord's, and W. E. Tucker, the famous orthopaedic surgeon, was performing the first of numerous operations, which culminated in 1955 with the removal of his knee cap.

In the tour of Australia in 1950–51, with English batting at their weakest, Compton had an utter failure, his only one in a Test series. He never touched again the brilliance of his golden period. Nevertheless, handicapped in mobility as he was, he was still an automatic choice for England, and in the following three rubbers against Australia was batting at the moment of victory. The Ashes were regained in 1953 and retained in 1954–55.

In 1956, at the Oval, shortly after a rigorous surgical

manipulation, and still with a limp, Compton faced the old enemy for the last time. Showing many glimpses of his best, he made 94, the highest score of the match, and 35 not out. Sir Donald Bradman described his 94 as the best innings of the series.

The following winter Compton made his last MCC tour, to South Africa, and then announced that 1957 would be his final season. He made 1,554 runs that summer at an average of 34, and in the last match at Lord's showed his flair for the occasion by hitting the Worcestershire bowlers for a sparkling 143.

Though scarcely an all-rounder in the Test sense, Compton, bowling slow left-arm, sometimes in the classical style, sometimes with wrist-spin, had days of high success. At the Oval in 1947 against Surrey he took 12 for 174 in addition to making 137 not out. In three successive summers he bowled 2,000 overs and took 208 wickets, besides scoring 36 hundreds. Against Australia in the fateful Test at Headingley in 1948, he would surely have won the day for England on a dusty pitch if Bradman (twice), and Morris had not been missed off his bowling early in their innings. As it was, they respectively made 173 not out and 182 out of 404 for three, which brought victory, and the rubber, to Australia.

When one considers the loss of six War-time summers from the age of 21 onwards, and the later physical handicap, Compton's achievements, numerically speaking, are marvellous indeed. His 38,942 runs, including 123 hundreds, were made at an average of 51.85; his 5,807 Test runs, including 17 hundreds, at 50. His slow left-arm bowling yielded 622 rather expensive wickets.

Retiring before his 40th birthday, Compton made successful careers in advertising and journalism with the *Sunday Express*, for whom he wrote about cricket (generally not unaided) from 1950 to 1988. He also commentated over many years on television, often with unexpected force.

Denis Compton, who died on St George's Day after a long illness, had a son by his first wife, Doris Rich, a dancer, and two sons by his second, Valerie Platt. He married, thirdly, in 1975, Christine Franklin Tobias; they had two daughters.

April 24 1997

EDDIE THOMAS

EDDIE THOMAS, who died aged 70, held the British, European and Empire welterweight titles, and later became one of boxing's most successful managers. A miner's son, Edward Thomas was born at Merthyr Tydfil on July 27, 1926, and left school at 14 to join his father in the pits. His grandfather had died in a mining accident.

By 1946 Thomas was the Amateur Boxing Association's lightweight champion. He soon turned professional, though he did not stop working as a miner. It was not unknown for him to work from 7 a.m. to 2.15 p.m. on the day before a fight and then go underground again from 10.30 p.m. to 5.30 a.m. before travelling to his contest.

He was soon recognised as one of Britain's most dangerous boxers, fighting with a speed and ferocity which belied his innocent looks. The press christened him "the choirboy boxer". He fought 48 times between

1947 and 1954, winning 40 fights, against two draws and six losses.

In 1949 Thomas outpointed Henry Hall over 15 rounds at Harringay Arena to become Wales's first British welterweight champion for 34 years. He returned to Merthyr to find the streets lined with well-wishers. Typically he took advantage of the opportunity to organise a public concert for the blind and elderly, the first of many acts of charity.

In January 1951 Thomas knocked out a South African, Pat Patrick, in Johannesburg to take the Empire title. He then became a triple champion by outpointing the holder of the European title, a tough Italian called Michele Palermo, at the Market Hall, Carmarthen. Later that year he was booked to meet Sugar Ray Robinson, but the world champion decided to move up to middle-weight. A broken hand destroyed Thomas's chances of challenging for the world welterweight championship; increasingly, too, the effort to meet the welterweight limit drained his energies in the ring. In June 1951 Thomas lost his European title, taking a bad beating from Charles Humez of France. And that October he surrendered his British and Empire titles to Wally Thom over 15 rounds.

Thomas invested his ring earnings in an open-cast mine outside Merthyr Tydfil, and became a boxing trainer and manager with such success that he was the first Briton to manage two boxers to world championships. He steered his fellow Merthyr fighter Howard Winstone to the vacant world featherweight title in London in 1968. Two years later another protégé, the Scot Ken Buchanan, took the world lightweight title. When Buchanan defended his title against Ismael Laguna at Madison

Square Garden in 1971, Thomas proved brilliantly resourceful in draining the blood from a dangerous swelling above Buchanan's eye. He also managed the Swansea welterweight Colin Jones, who won the British and European titles. Jones came close to winning the world title, boxing a draw with Milton McCrory in 1983.

In 1966 Thomas was one of the first to arrive at the scene of the Aberfan school disaster, and used his mining expertise to help free children smothered by the landslip. He had no time for intrusions of the media, telling reporters covering the tragedy to go away as they were hindering efforts to save lives.

A hugely popular figure in Merthyr Tydfil, Eddie Thomas was elected to the council in 1990, and four years later became Mayor. The town had made him a freeman in 1992. He was appointed MBE in 1984. He was married twice, and is survived by his widow, Kay, and by five children.

June 6 1997

LADY HEATHCOAT AMORY

LADY HEATHCOAT AMORY, formerly Joyce Wethered, who died aged 96, was arguably the greatest woman golfer of all time. Indeed, when Bobby Jones was asked if there had been a better woman player, he replied: "I am very doubtful if there has even been a better player, man or woman." He had come to this conclusion after playing Joyce Wethered at St Andrews in 1931, the year after he had won the professional and amateur Opens of both Britain and the United States. They drove from the same tees, and Joyce Wethered was two up with three to play. Though she lost the last three holes she was still round in 71. But for his greater strength, Jones acknowledged, he was "utterly outclassed".

Joyce Wethered was born at Brook, Surrey, on November 17, 1901, and educated privately, having been judged too frail to go to school. She first hit a golf ball at the seaside town of Bude, in Cornwall; 80 years later she still remembered the outrage she felt when a small boy scuttled his ball along the ground past her shot. She received only one lesson, from Tom Lyle, the professional at Bude, though she occasionally caught glimpses of such great champions as Harry Vardon and J. H. Taylor. In the holidays she played at Dornoch with her brother Roger, who won the British Amateur Championship in 1923.

Her swing was a model of balance and grace. Ideally, she used to say, nothing on earth could dislodge her from her right foot at the top of the back swing, or from her left at the finish of her follow-through. The most remarkable feature of her game was her accuracy with iron shots. Yet Joyce Wethered never thought of playing championship golf until 1920, when Molly Griffith, a leading Surrey player, suggested she should come with her to the English Women's Golf Championship at Sheringham, in Norfolk.

Joyce Wethered proceeded to play her way to the final, in which she encountered the formidable "Cecil" Leitch. She found herself six down with only 16 holes to play. Wrapping herself into a cocoon of concentration – she always played the course rather than the opponent –

she managed to retrieve the situation and win 2 and 1 on the 17th green. Had she not been disturbed, she was asked afterwards, by the train that whistled as she was bending over her winning putt? "What train?" she returned. The victory was the more remarkable as she was going down with whooping cough which kept her in bed for weeks afterwards.

In 1925 Joyce Wethered retired from competition, but was tempted back to play in the Ladies' Open of 1929, on the Old Course at St Andrews, her favourite. The final, in which she took on the American champion Glenna Collett, was a memorable contest. Joyce Wethered was five down after nine holes (her opponent going out in 34), but clawed her way back to win 2 and 1. Once more Joyce Wethered retired from championship play, though in 1931 she captained the British women's team to conclusive victory against the French. They lost to the Americans the next year, but Joyce Wethered inflicted another defeat on Glenna Collett.

Her family were now on their uppers, and the next year she took a job advising customers about golf equipment at Fortnum & Mason. In 1935 she undertook a tour of America, to publicise Wanamaker's golf supplies with a series of exhibition matches. At first things did not go well, at least by her standards. "The change from amateur to professional has affected my game in a way I really cannot describe," she mused. "Perhaps it is a feeling of obligation to the public instead of the old idea of simply hitting the ball." But, she told reporters, she would do better when she became acquainted with American greens and with the coarser sand in the bunkers ("I fancy a heavier niblick might help"). Five months later, she had played 53 matches in all parts of America, and established

36 records, notwithstanding the vast distances travelled and her lack of knowledge of local conditions. She also made herself a tidy £4,000 – perhaps £100,000 in today's money.

In 1931 Joyce Wethered had been engaged to the Scottish golfer Major Cecil Hutchinson, though the match never came off. In 1937 she married Sir John Heathcoat Amory, 3rd Bt. He was the elder brother of Derick Heathcoat Amory, who was Chancellor of the Exchequer from 1958 to 1960 and created Viscount Amory. It is said that Sir John had refused to propose to Joyce Wethered until he had beaten her at golf, a rash undertaking even for a fine games-player with a handicap of two.

From 1921 Joyce Wethered had invariably been the star of the annual mixed foursomes at Worplesdon. Even in 1930, when she was partnered by Lord Charles Hope, who fired the ball in all directions and into every obstacle, she only lost 2 and 1. In the next three years she was partnered successively by Michael Scott, R. H. Oppenheimer and Bernard Darwin, and won every time. "Why bother to hold the meeting?" asked Darwin in 1933, after Joyce Wethered had announced her intention of playing with Oppenheimer again the next year. She triumphed eight times in the tournament between 1922 and 1936, with seven different partners. But she never managed to win at Worplesdon with her husband, despite reaching the final in 1948. As a pair, they seemed less happy on the golf course than off it, and in the 1950s they abandoned the event.

With Sir John Heathcoat Amory suffering from arthritis, they increasingly concentrated their energies on their garden at Knightshayes House, near Tiverton. It became celebrated for its alpines, rhododendrons and azaleas; and Lady Heathcoat Amory was awarded the Royal Horticultural Society's Victoria Medal of Honour.

Sir John Heathcoat Amory died in 1972. His widow continued to live at Knightshayes House, which was now run by the National Trust. The remarkable collection of pictures which her husband and she had acquired (including Poussin's *The Mystic Marriage of St Catherine*) went to various national galleries, subject to Lady Heathcoat Amory's life interest.

Joyce Heathcoat Amory took a detached view of the gothic glories of Knightshayes, built in the 1870s in a queasy mixture of red Hensley and yellowish Ham stone. "Perhaps it would be as well to admit at once that the Amorys were unable, from early days, to appreciate Victorian architecture," she told a visitor. "Each generation has played its part in dismantling the house's most eccentric features." Nevertheless, she looked on with fortitude as the National Trust restored the lost workmanship of William Burges and J. D. Crace.

She retained her interest in golf, though no longer as a player. In 1951 she had become the first president of the English Women's Golf Association. She was admitted into America's Hall of Fame. Always a perfect sportswoman herself, and never given to complaints about bad luck, she did not like everything about the modern game. She considered that Nick Faldo would do well to stop fiddling with his swing and practising morning, noon and night. Her preference was for more romantic players such as Seve Ballesteros, or chivalrous competitors such as Nick Price.

In 1994, under the auspices of *The Daily Telegraph*, the Joyce Wethered Award was established to be presented annually to an outstanding and upstanding woman golfer under the age of 25.

November 20 1997

BIG DADDY

BIG DADDY, the fighting name of Shirley Crabtree, who died aged 64, was the star attraction of the professional wrestling circuit during its televised heyday in the Seventies and Eighties. Weighing in at 28 stone and clad in spangled top hat and overburdened leotard, Big Daddy was a portly avenging angel in the comic-book world of heroes in white trunks and villains in black masks.

At its peak, wrestling drew Saturday afternoon audiences of 10 million, attracted not so much by the finer points of the hammerlock and Boston crab as by its unvarying rituals. These began with the commentator Kent Walton's welcome – "Greetings, grapple fans" – and climaxed with the entry of Big Daddy into the ring, usually to save a small wrestler from the attentions of his *bête noire*, Giant Haystacks. His arrival was accompanied by chants of "Ea-sy, ea-sy" from the stout matrons in the crowd, in manner the spiritual descendants of the *tricoteuses* who sat by the guillotine. Big Daddy's vast belly easily held opponents at bay before he despatched them with his speciality – the "splashdown". This was a manoeuvre in which he mounted the ropes, leapt on top of his stupefied opponent, and squashed him flat to the canvas.

These antics brought Big Daddy notable fans, among them the Queen, whose interest in the sport was first recorded in Richard Crossman's diaries, and Margaret Thatcher, who found the wrestler a useful topic of conversation in Africa, where he was a household name.

The persona of Big Daddy was the creation of Shirley Crabtree's brother, Max, and only came relatively late in the wrestler's career. The name was taken from that of the character played by Burl Ives in the film of *Cat On A Hot Tin Roof*. Max Crabtree was one of the sport's main promoters, and the revelation in the mid-Eighties that the result of many of the bouts was predetermined, while no surprise to those who had seen the unathletic carriage of Big Daddy, dented its popularity. Some in the profession blamed the Crabtree brothers for making the sport too predictable, and its image was further damaged when Mal Kirk, a similarly large wrestler, died of a heart attack in 1987 while fighting Big Daddy. A year later ITV stopped showing wrestling, deeming audience taste to have changed; the sport has never recovered its lustre.

Shirley Crabtree was born in Halifax in 1933, though as he strove to prolong his career his real age became as uncertain as the true colour of the blond hair he sported. He was named after his father, who had in turn been called after the eponymous heroine of Charlotte Brontë's novel by his mother, a 22-stone music-hall actress. She admired the character so much that she chose her baby's name before knowing its sex.

Shirley Snr became a rugby league player for Halifax and later worked as a circus strongman. He believed that poverty could only be resisted by the tough, and taught his three boys to wrestle from an early age. This came in useful in the playground of Battinson Road Primary School where such skills were needed to fend off jokes about Shirley Temple.

When young Shirley was seven, his father left their mother, who subsequently brought up the boys, working in a brickyard for the half-wages paid to women. Shirley particularly disliked Christmas, as the presents dispensed to him by well-meaning charities were invariably dolls and girls' annuals. He left school at 14 and worked as a doffer in a cotton mill, replacing empty bobbins with full ones. Two years later he left to join Bradford Northern rugby league club, but his aggressiveness led to numerous suspensions for foul play and he became a lifeguard at Blackpool instead. Crabtree began his wrestling career as a middleweight, weighing in at a mere 16 stone and fighting as "The Blond Adonis" and "Mr Universe". His two brothers often appeared on the same bill, until Max, who had the best technique, became a promoter, and Brian, after breaking his leg, turned to refereeing.

By the early 1960s Shirley Crabtree had realised that it was the larger wrestlers who gained the biggest following, and he began to boost his weight with a concentrated diet of steak, eggs and cream cakes. His size made him a considerable attraction on the circuit, but he was still cast in the mould of villain, most notably as "The Battling Guardsman", a role created for him by his brother. Crabtree had briefly served in the Coldstream Guards, and would enter the ring wearing a bearskin, to the sound of Joseph Locke singing "The Soldier's Dream". It was not until 1975 that the Big Daddy character was created, with his first leotard being made from the chintz covers of his wife's sofa. He was twice married and had six children.

December 3 1997

HELEN WILLS MOODY

HELEN WILLS MOODY, who died in California aged 91, was the tennis champion known as the "Queen of the Courts" for her domination of the women's game in the 1920s and 1930s; she transformed the reputation of women's tennis as a competitive sport. She won eight Wimbledon and seven American singles titles, and she was French champion from 1927 to 1930. She played the steadiest and most determined game of any of her contemporaries, refusing to concede defeat until the last point had been contested.

Early on, she decided that steadiness rather than brilliance was the quality to aim for, and that every stroke should tell. "There is no game like the direct attack," she once said. "Fancy strokes, while effective to watch, do not bring the results a fast driving game does." She also resolutely played her own game. Despite barracking from spectators during the 1924 Paris Olympics, she refused to take chances against the French finalist Didi Vlasto, and won.

Helen Newington Wills was born at Centreville, California, on October 6, 1906, the younger child of Clarence A. Wills, a surgeon. Before long the family moved to Berkeley, and as a teenager she attended a boarding school in Vermont, going on to the University of California. She had begun to play tennis only to please her adored elder brother, but then her father began to coach her. She proved a natural player, winning the Pacific Coast Junior Championships in her first season, and being invited to represent the state the next year at the National Junior Championships at Forest Hills, where she defeated an 18-year-old opponent.

At 17, Helen Wills entered international tennis. She was selected for the American team in the first Wightman Cup contest (Mrs George Wightman herself being captain) and defeated the then Kitty McKane (later Godfree), the English champion. At about this time, she also set the fashion for the "Californian eyeshade", which had not previously been seen outside the home state.

During her last year at university – where she developed a gift for painting and drawing – she was selected for the Olympics team and for Wimbledon, where she appeared in her old school uniform of white shirt and skirt. She had by now been nicknamed "Miss Poker Face" by the press. At Wimbledon, she reached the final, but was defeated by Kitty Godfree. After taking the first set 6–4 and leading 4–1 in the second, she missed several chances to consolidate her lead, partly due to her opponent's greater experience and "feel" for the Centre Court atmosphere. It was Helen Wills's most keenly felt defeat, and the only occasion on which she wept after a match. From then on, she considered Kitty Godfree the best player she met, apart from Suzanne Lenglen.

In 1926, she played against Suzanne Lenglen in the Monte Carlo championships. The rivalry between the two women was magnified by the French press, and there was heavy betting on the match, with all the money on Suzanne Lenglen. Helen Wills took the first set, but Suzanne Lenglen triumphed. Later that year, Helen Wills missed both the French Championships and Wimbledon following an emergency operation for appendicitis. While recuperating, she was commissioned by *The Sketch* to make drawings for Wimbledon, and she did some advertising work for the White Star Line. Later in the season, she played a demonstration match at Fulham Palace, partnering the Bishop of London, A. F. Winnington Ingram (then aged almost 70), who became her devoted admirer.

In 1927 she was back at Wimbledon as top seed, meeting Lili d'Alvarez in the final. She described Lili d'Alvarez as the hardest hitter she met. After Helen Wills took the first set 6–2, the score stood at 2–4 in Lili d'Alvarez's favour in the second set. The great game of the match then got under way, with the Spaniard attacking Helen Wills's backhand, driving across and deep, and the ball crossing the net 40 times in the final rally, until at last Lili d'Alvarez failed to return it. Both women showed obvious strain, but it was Helen Wills who recovered to take her opponent's service in a love game, and went on to win the set and the match. Spectators described it as the finest women's tennis they had seen.

The next season she defeated the British player Eileen Bennett at Wimbledon and in the French Championships, and won her fifth US national title, defeating the rising young player Helen Jacobs 6–2, 6–1. She was to defeat Helen Jacobs again the next summer at Wimbledon by much the same margin – despite the distractions of her art and her busy social life, which earnt her the nickname "Queen Helen". She showed her paintings at the Cooling Galleries, and was painted by Augustus John; she was presented at Court, and spent weekends at Cliveden. At the end of 1928 she married Frederick S. Moody, Jnr, a stockbroker, and thereafter competed as Mrs Wills Moody.

The next year she was back at Wimbledon, beating Joan Ryan 6–2, 6–2 for the women's title. In France, she again defeated Helen Jacobs, 6–1, 6–1. She also exhibited her paintings at the Grand Central Art Gallery in New York, and wrote, and illustrated, a series of articles for the American press on Japan, when she went there to play exhibition matches. Her husband suffered badly in the 1929 stockbroker crash, and her professional journalism proved a useful standby in the Depression years.

In Paris for the French Championships in 1932, she also wrote articles for syndication in America, interviewing the aviator Amelia Earhart on the very day of the final, which Helen Wills then went on to win. She also covered the Paris fashion shows, and the funeral of the assassinated President Doumer, before moving on to Wimbledon, where she again decisively vanquished Helen Jacobs.

Early in 1933 she damaged her back while gardening, but still played at Wimbledon that summer. She met the English player Dorothy Round in the final, taking the first set 6–4 after some long rallies. The second set went to Miss Round (usually described in the English press as a "Sunday school teacher") at 9–7, after a lengthy and acrimonious dispute over a line decision. It was one of the few occasions on which Helen Wills lost a set at Wimbledon. She went on to win the third set 6–3, though almost immobilised by her back and by blistered feet. Subsequently, a serious spinal injury was diagnosed, and in 1934 she played no tennis.

By 1935, she felt fit enough to attempt Wimbledon again. Meeting Helen Jacobs in the final, she took the first set, but was feeling the strain badly at the start of the second. But she recovered her concentration, and in a battle lasting an hour and 40 minutes took the set in the 12th game when, with the score at deuce, she forced

Helen Jacobs to hit out of court three times in succession. Looking back, Helen Wills reflected that this match drew on the sum of her whole career's experience.

She and her husband had been drifting apart, and in 1937 they divorced. When she returned to Wimbledon in 1938, her two seasons' absence had in no way diminished her game. She defeated Helen Jacobs 6–4, 6–0 in the final, which was her farewell to the Centre Court. After the final, she retired from tournament play, and in 1939 married Aidan Roark, settling at Berkeley. Her later years were passed in some seclusion, and she invariably declined invitations from the All England Club to attend their championships.

January 3 1998

ROGER CLARK

ROGER CLARK, who died aged 58, was for many years the undisputed king of British rally drivers. In 1972 he interrupted the Scandinavian dominance of the sport by winning the RAC Rally in a Ford Escort, with Tony Mason as co-driver, and he repeated this success in 1976 with Stuart Pegg, bringing his total of victories in national and international rallies to 46. He won the British Championship four times and the Scottish Rally six times.

In his heyday with the Ford team, whom he joined in 1966, Clark spent up to eight months a year out of the country, rallying on all manner of surfaces, in all kinds of conditions. A notable triumph was his victory in the tough Acropolis Rally of 1968. Later that year, though, he suffered a great disappointment in the London to Sydney marathon. After 10,000 bone-shaking miles and within five hours of the finishing flag, Clark, in a Ford Cortina, was in the lead, only to be foiled by a snapped rear axle. Even then he managed to finish, after persuading a fisherman to sell him a second-hand axle.

A superb mechanic as well as a magnificent driver, Clark was exceptionally skilled at nursing his cars through the roughest conditions. However, his greatest asset was his ability to remain calm under pressure. While his co-driver was at the wheel he found no difficulty in sleeping; when he was in charge only a slightly raised chin denoted that he was making a special effort. No man was less likely to ruin his chances with a hasty, tense decision.

"He was sensible enough to know that you've got to finish to win," remembered Jim Porter, his co-driver in the early days. "You win as slowly as you can. You don't need to win by 30 miles. You just drive to stay in front."

Yet Clark's equable temperament did not preclude flamboyant driving. His speciality, celebrated in the title of his autobiography, *Sideways to Victory* (1976), was entering corners sideways and steering with the back wheels; he found this gave more balance and more control in emergencies. But there was no merit, he added, in coming *out* of corners sideways.

The crowds loved Clark, a handsome man with the square build and thick arms of a rugby forward (indeed at school he had been an excellent player). Most of all, though, he was respected by his peers. "He's the easiest guy to work with," one of his mechanics said in 1980. "He's got the fame. But he's not too grand for the mechanics or for the fans. He has not become part of the Campari-and-soda set like the others."

Roger Albert Clark was born on August 5, 1939 at Narborough, Leicestershire, where his father was a garage owner, and educated at Hinckley Grammar School. Outside school he spent most of his boyhood in and under cars, and passed his driving test within two days of his 17th birthday. Soon he was rallying at amateur events, at first in an old Thames van "borrowed" from his father.

In 1961, in a Mini Cooper, he carried off his first important title, the East Midland Championship. He went on to drive a Reliant in the Liege–Sofia–Liege rally, and then joined first Triumph and then Rover, with whom he came fifth in the Monte Carlo Rally of 1965. The next year he gained a place with the Ford works team.

In 1980 Clark moved to British Leyland, for whom he drove Triumph TR7s. He later competed privately in various cars – a Metro, a Ford Escort and a Subaru. He showed no enthusiasm for retirement. "If someone provides me with a motor car, I'll drive it," he said. "Why not? The excitement is as good as ever it was. It's still, basically, being paid for going berserk in a car."

However, Clark drove with the spirit of an amateur. "When I went rallying," he recalled only months before his death, "you'd just open the door, get in and press the pedals. Now the guys are full professionals, as fit as Olympic athletes. I was never fit. Walking to the pub was the only exercise I took." Once there, he was always the life and soul of the party.

Clark's idea of relaxation was racing powerboats, or flying his Cessna. For years he ran the family company with his younger brother Stanley; by 1980 they had four garages and employed some 150 people. But his side of the business did not prosper after he split with his brother in the late 1980s. Nor did he recoup his fortunes with Roger Clark Motor Sport, who built cars for rally driving.

In 1997 the television programme *Top Gear* ran a feature about the Ford Escort in which Clark won the RAC Rally in 1972. The car had been perfectly reconstructed, and he showed himself to be as skilled as ever in its handling. He was appointed MBE in 1979. He is survived by his wife, Judith, and by two sons, both of whom are rally drivers.

January 14 1998

LORD HOWELL

LORD HOWELL, formerly Denis Howell, the Labour politician who died aged 74, became Britain's first Minister for sport in 1964. His official title was Joint Parliamentary Under-Secretary of Education and Science. Though promoted minister of state and moved to Housing and Local Government in 1969, he remained responsible for sport until Labour lost office in 1970.

When Labour regained power in 1974, Howell returned to the DES, where for five more years he was responsible for a portfolio that included the environment and water resources as well as sport. In 1976 Howell appeared as a miraculous rain-maker when, two days after being put in charge of emergency measures against the drought, the heavens opened and torrential rains fell for most of the month. He was no less successful in delivering the country from snow in the winter of 1977–78.

Though Howell never reached the Cabinet, he made his mark as Minister for Sport. His appointment had originally been criticised as a Wilsonian gimmick, but over his 10 years in the post his boundless energy, enthusiasm and expertise made the office an enduring feature of British government. Even the touchiest sports administrators were unable to resent Howell's obvious good intentions.

It helped, too, that Howell had been the first Football Association referee to become an MP. "All politicians should be sportsmen," he would reply to those who expressed surprise that he continued refereeing after arriving at Westminster. However, he gave up refereeing in 1965 after his standing as minister had been impugned by noisy crowd reaction to his performance during a match between Cardiff and Bury.

Howell's most important move as minister came in 1965; he set up and became first chairman of the Sports Council, aimed at promoting sport and improving facilities. As for politics in sport, he took a strong line with South Africa over apartheid. In 1968 he held fast to principle in the case of the cricketer Basil d'Oliveira, a Cape coloured who was selected for the England team to tour South Africa. The South African Government refused to accept d'Oliveira as a player and eventually cancelled the tour.

In general Howell opposed fixtures with segregated teams, without going so far as to ban them. Thus it was on grounds of the threat to public order that the Labour Government, with Jim Callaghan to the fore, obliged the MCC to cancel the South African cricket tour of 1970. Four years later Howell would clearly have liked to cancel the British Lions' rugby tour of South Africa, and it was only after much agonising that, at the end of the tour, he attended a "welcome home" breakfast for Willie John McBride's victorious side. He then banned a tour of England by a Rhodesian team because of that country's "illegal" regime. The Rhodesians, though, made the trip as private individuals.

Though an uninspiring speaker, Howell excelled at negotiations behind the scenes. He played a key role in the negotiations over the future of the Grand National at Aintree; he also browbeat Edinburgh Corporation into building the Meadowbank Stadium for the Commonwealth Games of 1970.

Beyond sport, Howell showed himself to be a doughty in-fighter on the right wing of the Labour Party. His first loyalty, however, was to his native city. His autobiography, published in 1990, was entitled *Made in Birmingham*. He lived his whole life there, and sat for a Birmingham seat for more than 30 years.

Denis Herbert Howell was born on September 4, 1923 and educated at Handsworth Grammar School. His father Herbert, a factory foreman, was sacked for being the only man in the plant to join the General Strike. Having started work at 15 as a clerk in a bicycle factory, Denis Howell devoted his spare time to the Clerical and Administrative Workers' Union. He joined the Labour Party in 1942.

He fought his first sporting crusade during the Second World War, when factories were working six days a week but Sunday football was illegal. To obviate this difficulty he established the "Birmingham Monday League, Sunday Section". Birmingham became the first Sunday League to be affiliated to the Football Association.

As a city councillor for 10 years from 1956, Howell established Britain's first smokeless zone and pioneered free bus travel for pensioners, paid for out of the rates. This scheme was at first declared illegal by the courts, but Howell fought back and eventually forced a change in the law. On the terraces, Howell was a keen Aston Villa supporter. He became a Football League linesman in 1951, the year he fought his first Parliamentary seat, at King's Norton. "Next time I'll vote Tory," someone shouted after he had four times flagged down a Spurs forward for offside. He refereed his first match in 1956.

By then he was an MP, having been elected for the All Saints Division of Birmingham at the General Election of 1955. At Westminster, he campaigned to improve conditions in mental hospitals, to reform the Sunday Observance laws, and to regulate estate agents. In 1958 he was appointed to the Albermarle Committee on the Youth Service, who produced a highly praised report.

He lost his seat by 20 votes in 1959 after boundary changes lost him 3,000 constituents. Out of Parliament, he joined a Birmingham plastics firm, and later became a consultant to Bagenal Harvey, the public relations organisation. Eventually he started his own firm, Denis Howell Consultants. He also became a director of Wembley Stadium.

Howell remained closely in touch with the Gaitskellite wing of the Labour Party, though his pro-European views clashed with Gaitskell's policy. On Roy Jenkins's recommendation he was appointed to round up union support. His "Victory for Sanity Group" eventually became the Campaign for Democratic Socialism, with Howell himself as vice-chairman. In 1961 he returned to Parliament as member for the safe Labour seat of Birmingham, Small Heath. He supported George Brown against Harold Wilson in the Labour leadership contest of 1963, and with William Rodgers set up the "1963 Club", which kept the standard of the party's right wing flying at monthly dinners. But this did not prevent Harold Wilson from giving Howell office in 1964.

After Labour lost the election in 1970, Howell became president of the Clerical and General Workers' Union. Though, in 1977, he joined Shirley Williams on the picket line at Grunwick, he was one of the first Labour MPs to descry the danger from Militant. Nevertheless, he refused to join the Gang of Four in leaving Labour. "I am not a quitter," he insisted. "I stand and fight. They are running away from the problems facing the Labour Party."

Howell's last great campaign was the attempt to bring the Olympic Games to Birmingham in 1992. He saw to it that Birmingham became the British choice, but, despite raising several million pounds and travelling the world to lobby for his cause, he was unable to convince the International Olympic Committee.

Howell was sworn into the Privy Council in 1976. He stood down from Parliament in 1992 and later that year was created a life peer. He married, in 1955, Brenda Marjorie Wilson; they had three sons and a daughter. In 1974 Mrs Howell and their 10-year-old son David narrowly escaped death when the IRA, who were conducting a terror campaign in Birmingham, booby-trapped their car. The bomb detonated when Mrs Howell turned on the ignition. Fortunately the gelignite had slipped off the exhaust pipe and exploded under the engine. David Howell, though, was killed in a motor accident 12 years later.

April 20 1998

GOTTFRIED DIENST

GOTTFRIED DIENST, who died in Basle aged 78, refereed the World Cup Final in 1966; he allowed England's controversial third goal, which set them on their way to victory over West Germany. The score stood at 2–2 after 90 minutes, the Germans having equalised only a few minutes before. As the teams drew breath, England's manager, Alf Ramsey, encouraged his players, telling them that the game was theirs for the taking, that they were playing the better football. "You've won it once," he said. "Now go and do it again."

Ten minutes into extra time, Alan Ball cut the ball back from the right touchline to Geoff Hurst, who was about 10 yards from the German goal. Hurst trapped the pass, swivelled, let the ball bounce twice and then lashed a shot over Hans Tilkowski, the German goalkeeper. The ball thumped against the underside of the crossbar and in the blink of an eye had bounced down on the goal-line. The English team were convinced that the whole of the ball had crossed the line, that it was a goal. The closest player to the ball, Roger Hunt, instantly turned away in celebration, rather than knocking the ball into the unguarded net.

The Germans, though, disputed the goal. All eyes turned to Dienst, and Wembley became very quiet. The Swiss referee had been in the worst possible position to judge, having been standing head-on to the goal. Unsure, he in turn looked at his Russian linesman, Tofik Bakhramov, who unhesitatingly pointed to the centre circle. The goal was good. Wembley erupted. The third of Hurst's goals in the 1966 final, four minutes from time, settled the matter and rendered the Germans' arguments about the other goal immaterial.

Gottfried Dienst was born into a German-speaking family in Switzerland on September 9, 1919. He refereed 1,224 first-class games and was one of FIFA's designated international referees. He retired in 1968 after taking charge of his last game, the European Championship Final between Italy and Yugoslavia.

June 10 1998

MAVIS STEELE

MAVIS STEELE, who died aged 69, represented England at bowls for 40 years in succession. She was a formidable figure. Standing head and shoulders above other players, she would follow her woods crisply up the green and stop, legs planted apart, hands on hips, daring one of her bowls to misbehave.

Her most successful days as a solo player came in the 1960s, when she won the national outdoor singles title three times. In 1973 she took silver in the world outdoor singles and in 1981 skippered England to the world fours title in Toronto. A year later, at the Commonwealth Games in Brisbane, she won bronze in the triples. Later, in 1989, she triumphed in the national indoor championships.

She first represented England in 1958, and a month before her death played for her country for the 40th season, when she was selected for the home international series, held in Llandrindod Wells. Altogether, she played 120 matches against the other home countries.

Mavis Steele was born at Kenton, Middlesex, on September 9, 1928. Her father was a county bowls player. When Mavis was 17 her mother persuaded him to introduce the shy girl to the game. Though she took her game seriously, and could be a brisk authority on its rules, her stern and matronly appearance concealed a generous heart. She was keen to see younger players come up, and though she was worried that professionalism might encourage gamesmanship, she approved of the use of coloured clothing to encourage spectators.

Though she never married, Mavis Steele was an advocate of mixed bowls. She insisted that playing against men at her own club in her early days had strengthened her game. Indeed, she played a vigorous, attacking game. Women's bowls remains an amateur sport, and Mavis Steele worked for 34 years as an office manager with Kodak. Within the game, she was president of the English Women's Indoor Bowling Association in 1990 and was chairman of the Umpires' Association. She had been due to marshal the umpires at the Commonwealth Games in Kuala Lumpur later in the year. She was appointed MBE in 1983.

July 9 1998

BILL SHANKLAND

BILL SHANKLAND, who died aged 91, was one of the most versatile sportsmen that even Australia has produced: as a rugby league player he was paid more than anyone else of his day; as a golfer he was once in contention to win the Open.

William Shankland was born in Sydney on July 25, 1907, the son of an accountant, and educated at the Christian Brothers' School. Though he had his father's head for figures and began to study accountancy, his life was soon being dictated by his sporting prowess. As a young man, he swam and boxed for Australia, and excelled on the track. He was a fine cricketer and once beat the baseball pitcher Johnny Newman in a cricket-ball-throwing contest.

His best game at this stage, though, was rugby. He toured New Zealand, South Africa and (in 1926) the British Isles as fly-half with the Australian rugby union side. Having converted to centre, he returned to Britain with the Australian rugby league team – the Kangaroos – in 1929, and became a favourite with the crowds for his strong running and tackling. He played in all four Tests and in all 25 matches on that tour, scoring four tries and kicking 17 goals.

Though the Australians lost the series, his talent did not escape the attention of English rugby league clubs: in 1931 Warrington signed him up. At a time when miners were getting £2 10s a week, Shankland was paid a £1,000 signing-on fee, and then £8 a week and £6 a match. He led the club to two championship wins, and three Wembley finals, though each time he finished on the losing side.

The first of these finals, in 1932, was against Huddersfield. "It was the first royal visit to a rugby league final," Shankland recalled, "and the Prince of Wales was guest of honour. Just before kick-off an equerry came to me and said, 'Shankland, only speak if you are spoken to.'" "I do actually know His Royal Highness," Shankland retorted. "I met him in 1929." "Only speak when you are spoken to," the courtier reiterated. It was therefore satisfying that the Prince made a beeline for Shankland. "So, we meet again," he said. "How's your golf?" "Fine, sir," Shankland countered. "How's yours?"

Before retiring in 1938, Shankland turned out 231 times for Warrington, scoring 71 tries and 70 goals. By now he wanted to become a first-class golfer, too, and had become assistant professional at Haydock Park. In 1938 he was appointed the professional at Temple Newsam, and in 1939 finished joint third in the Open at St Andrews with 294, only four strokes behind the winner, Dick Burton. For this he won £67 10s.

During the War, and up until 1951, Shankland played hundreds of exhibition matches for the Red Cross with Henry Cotton, Bobby Locke and Dai Rees, supported by such entertainers as Sid Field, Ted Ray and Bud Flanagan.

In the 1947 Open, Shankland was in a position to win on the back nine of the last round. But at the 16th he hit a bunker, took a six and finished fourth, two strokes behind the winner, Fred Daly. "Shankland makes a habit of doing well in the Open," *The Daily Telegraph*'s Leonard Crawley observed two years later.

In 1951, at Portrush, Shankland tied for sixth place with Bobby Locke and Peter Thomson. That year he became the professional at Potters Bar, where his assistants, Alex Hay and John Sharkey, profited from his teaching. Shankland played his last Open in 1955.

Well into old age he remained a buoyant figure, whose handshake gripped like a vice. (He once led a team out at Wembley carrying a rugby ball between his thumb and forefinger). His gruff manner, however, failed to conceal the kindest of hearts.

His death was in keeping with his life. On the morning of Sunday, September 6 he was fêted at Haydock Park Club; that afternoon he led out Warrington's great players at the club's centenary celebrations; on the Monday he slipped and fell, and never recovered consciousness.

He married, in 1929, Daphne Craig, who died in 1994; they had three sons, two of whom became professional golfers.

September 18 1998

FLORENCE GRIFFITH-JOYNER

FLORENCE GRIFFITH-JOYNER, the American athlete who died aged 38, was the outstanding female sprinter of her generation; she won three gold medals at the Seoul Olympics in 1988, and demonstrated a talent for self-promotion almost as great as her gift for running. Until her performances at the American trials in July 1988, there had been no hint that she was capable of some of the most sensational times seen on the track. She had won a silver medal in the 200 metres at the World Championships in Rome the previous year, though she was known principally for her idiosyncratic taste in running kit, which tended to garish colours and one-piece bodysuits.

Then, in the first heat of the trials, wearing a lime-green one-legged leotard, Florence Griffith-Joyner broke the world record for the 100 metres, knocking $^{16}/_{100}$ths of a second off the existing time of 10.76 seconds, a mark that had stood for four years. Because of a strong tail-wind, officials ruled that her time could not stand. She promptly showed it had been no fluke, crossing the line in her next race in 10.49 seconds, taking more than a quarter of a second off the record. In the previous 75 years of women's athletics, no sprinter had lowered the record by more than a tenth of a second.

In the semi-final and then the final itself, Florence Griffith-Joyner, wearing successively a yellow-striped black leotard and a white fishnet bodysuit, beat the previous world record holder, Evelyn Ashford, by a margin of first five, and then 10 feet. In four races, she had run the four fastest times in the history of the event.

In the two months before the Olympics, Florence Griffith-Joyner became the hottest property in athletics. Showing a sure grasp of the importance of image in a sport moving into the professional era, she was able to multiply by 25 times her fee for competing in events. She amply repaid the faith of her sponsors in Seoul. By now sporting talon-like fingernails painted with the Stars and Stripes, she destroyed the field in the 100 metres, recording the second fastest time in history to take the gold medal. Now almost visibly propelled by an invincible self-confidence, she broke the world record for the 200 metres in the semi-final, and lowered it again to 21.34 seconds, to win her second gold. She wore one red and one blue shoe for the race, slowing down as she passed the cameras to flash them the smile that went with her nickname "Cash Flo".

Florence Griffith-Joyner completed her tally of medals by helping the 4x100 metres relay team to gold. Forty minutes later, she ran the anchor leg of the 4x400 race, taking silver. Her overall performance was the second greatest by a woman track athlete in the history of the Olympics, beaten only by that of Fanny Blankers-Koen in 1948.

The spectacular – unprecedented – improvement in her sprinting inevitably provoked speculation that she had enhanced her performance with drugs, a suspicion that gained momentum when Ben Johnson, who had also blasted to gold from relative obscurity, was stripped of his medal for taking steroids. She vehemently denied the charges, though many inside the sport noticed a sudden masculinity to a physique that had hitherto been very feminine.

With the world at her feet, and with several dozen endorsements to her name (including a FloJo doll with 10 different outfits), Florence Griffith-Joyner unexpectedly retired from athletics in February 1989. She said she wanted to devote more time to writing and acting; sceptics pointed to the imminent introduction of year-round drug testing. Nevertheless, she was voted the Most Outstanding Amateur Athlete in America in 1989.

She was born Delorez Florence Griffith in southern California on December 21, 1959, the seventh of 11 children of an electrician and a seamstress. Her parents divorced when she was four, and she moved with her mother to the tough Watts section of Los Angeles. Though often obliged to survive on oatmeal, Florence Griffith set school records in sprints and long jump at Jordan High School. At home her mother exerted a tight discipline and made sure her children kept out of trouble. "Nobody did drugs; nobody got shot at," Florence Griffith later recalled.

At California State University, Florence Griffith was coached by Bob Kersee, who struggled to add technical skill – especially out of the starting blocks – to her natural ability. When Kersee moved to UCLA, Florence Griffith decided to join him, and showed impressive form against some of America's top runners. At the same time in 1980, she was beginning to show her flair for fashion, painting her long fingernails in rainbow colours. "We all *know* you're different," remonstrated an exasperated teammate. "Why do you have to *show* it?"

In 1983, Florence Griffith won the 400 metres in the national championships. Though no longer at UCLA, she continued to train with Kersee, and in the 1984 Olympics (in Los Angeles), she finished a quarter of a second behind her great rival Valerie Brisco to take the silver medal.

Bitterly disappointed, Florence Griffith more or less abandoned training for two years, and by 1986 was 60lbs overweight. Nevertheless, she asked Kersee to help her train for the 1988 Olympic trials. The regime he prescribed included work-outs in the small hours of the morning, her daytime hours being taken up with her work as a beautician. In her efforts to regain fitness she received much help and encouragement from her new boyfriend, Al Joyner, who had won the gold medal for the triple jump at the 1984 Olympics. They were married in Los Angeles in October 1987.

At the World Championships in 1987, Ben Johnson beat the world record for the 100 metres with a time of 9.83 seconds, and Kersee insisted that, if Florence Griffith wanted to win Olympic gold, she would have to emulate Johnson's speed out of the blocks. "If you want to run like a man," Johnson told her, "you have to train like a man, and weights are the main factor." In 1995 she was inducted into the USA Track and Field Hall of Fame. She had a daughter in 1990.

September 22 1998

RAN LAURIE

RAN LAURIE, who died aged 83, was one of the last of the great "Gentleman Amateurs" of rowing, though his belief that the activity was its own reward did not prevent him from enjoying many brilliant successes, culminating in an Olympic gold medal in 1948.

When Laurie and his fellow colonial officer and Cambridge rowing partner, Jack Wilson, returned home from the Sudan in 1948, Wilson had not touched an oar for 10 years. He had been severely wounded by an assegai in 1942. However, after only three months' training, the pair won the Silver Goblets at Henley so convincingly that they were invited to represent Great Britain in the first post-War Olympic Games, the rowing taking place at Henley itself. Known as the "Desert Rats", Laurie and Wilson crowned their distinguished rowing careers by putting on an outstanding exhibition of coxless pair-oared rowing to win the gold medal. After completing his service in the Sudan, Laurie realised a life-long ambition by qualifying as a doctor in 1954. He went on to spend 30 years as a general practitioner in Oxford.

William George Ranald Mundell Laurie was born at Granchester on June 4, 1915, almost within sight of the university where he was to establish his reputation as one of the greatest of Light Blue oarsmen. Educated at

Monkton Combe School, he rowed in the school eight in the Ladies' Plate at Henley from 1931 to 1933, as stroke for the last two years.

Going up to Selwyn College, Cambridge, in October 1933, he immediately made his mark as a Freshman, rowing there in the record-breaking 1934 Cambridge crew, with Wilson rowing seven. At Henley that year, Laurie stroked Leander to win the Grand and break the course record. He stroked Cambridge to easy wins in the 1935 and 1936 Boat Races, with Wilson at seven on both occasions, the 1936 victory being the last in a record run of 13 Cambridge wins.

At Henley in 1935, Laurie stroked his college eight in the Ladies' Plate, losing in the second round, but he also competed with Wilson in the Silver Goblets for the first time, winning a heat despite hitting the booms. However, he then withdrew because of Wilson's involvement with Pembroke in the Grand, which they won.

Wilson departed for the Sudan after the 1936 Boat Race but Laurie, who succeeded him as president of the CUBC, went on to stroke the Olympic eight who finished fourth in Berlin that year. The next year, Laurie joined Wilson in the Sudan Political Service, but the two contrived to arrange leave together in 1938 to compete at Henley where, with Wilson stroking, they represented Leander and won the Silver Goblets, equalling the record without being pressed. The pair, with Laurie stroking, also won the Stewards' Cup with ease.

Laurie was elected a Henley Steward in 1951 and was on the committee of management from 1964 to 1986. He was captain of Leander Club in 1936 and president from 1975 to 1980. He was chairman of the committee for the Duke of Edinburgh's Award, Oxford

Branch, between 1959 and 1969, and chairman of the Save the Children's Fund, Oxford Branch, from 1986 to 1989.

He was twice married, and had two sons and two daughters. His son Hugh, the comic actor, rowed for Cambridge in 1980. It was a proud moment when the same edition of *The Times* carried an account of Hugh Laurie rowing in the Cambridge trials on one page, and of his performance in a Footlights Review on another.

Ran Laurie was a charming and modest man whose attitude to rowing was encapsulated in the tribute he paid to Jack Wilson, who died in February 1997: "He was not only the greatest mover of a boat I have ever seen, but rowing was such fun to him that he made it fun for anyone who rowed with him."

September 28 1998

GORDON RICHARDS

GORDON RICHARDS, who died aged 68, was a skilful and successful trainer of steeplechasers; he saddled the winner of more than 2,000 races, including two Grand Nationals and most of the other great prizes in the jumping calendar. The Cheltenham Gold Cup and the Champion Hurdle eluded him, though.

Born in Bath (he always retained a West Country accent), Richards enjoyed his best years as a trainer at Castle Stable, Greystoke, in Cumbria. However, he knew disasters as well as triumphs. He lost a flamboyant chaser in Noddy's Ryde, and seven months before his death, on one of his last big-race days (he had cancer) shared a tragedy with the whole racing world when the brilliant grey One Man was killed at Aintree.

Another grey, Dark Ivy, was the subject of a film made by the BBC before the 1987 Grand National. Unforgettable shots were shown of Dark Ivy galloping past the towers of Greystoke on a foggy morning as part of the television introduction to the National. They stayed all too clearly in viewers' minds when the grey broke his neck in a dreadful, headlong fall at Becher's. The tragedy played an important part in the campaign which led to the remodelling of Aintree's most famous fence.

A timber merchant's son, Gordon Richards was born on September 7, 1930. He was at first apprenticed to J. C. Waugh and Ivor Anthony. When Richards started riding on the Flat, his great namesake, later Sir Gordon Richards, was still at the top of the tree. "We can't have this," said a nervous Clerk of the Scales when young G. Richards attempted to weigh out. "What's your other initial, boy?" Since Richards had none, and he was riding for J. C. Waugh, a "W" was inserted. For a long time thereafter he was known as Gordon W. Richards. Soon, though, he became too heavy for the Flat. He decided to move north and joined Major Renwick, a trainer in Northumberland. He had to give up as a jockey after taking a fall at Perth from Sea View, a cast-off from Arthur Stephenson.

Richards set up as a horse dealer and livery stable proprietor at Beadnell on the Northumbrian coast. Asked to begin training to help out a neighbour, he took out his first licence in 1964. One of the first horses to come into his care was Playlord, and he scraped together the money to buy him. Playlord subsequently won the

Scottish Grand National and other good races. Richards was always convinced that Playlord was doped when he ran so much below expectations in the Cheltenham Gold Cup. Cheltenham was rarely a lucky course for the trainer, though in 1998 One Man won the Queen Mother Champion Chase.

He set up at Greystoke in 1968, and was soon one of Arthur Stephenson's greatest rivals in northern steeple-chasing. Both achieved what was then the rare feat of saddling 100 winners in a season. It was at the dispersal sale after Stephenson's death that Gordon Richards bought One Man, the last great steeplechaser he trained.

Gordon Richards worked tremendously hard himself, and expected the same commitment from those he employed. He was always a critical, and often an outspoken, taskmaster to his jockeys. "Of course I listen to my staff and my jockeys," he once remarked. "There would be no point in having them if I didn't. But in the final instance they have to do as I tell them, or leave."

Yet the finest jockeys, including Ron Barry, Jonjo O'Neill, Neale Doughty and Phil Tuck, were eager to ride for him. Tuck once held the record for consecutive winners: nine, and all for Richards. Doughty rode Hallo Dandy to victory in the Grand National in 1984. Greystoke's other National winner, in 1978, was Lucius, ridden by Bob Davies.

The best hurdler Richards trained was the great all-rounder Sea Pigeon, though before his two Champion Hurdle victories a difference of opinion with the owner, Pat Muldoon, caused the horse's removal to Peter Easterby. It went on to win the King George VI Chase twice.

Richards was always a man of decided views and his pungent post-race comments were eagerly noted by the racing press. His fellow trainers also regarded him with the greatest respect. Gordon Richards was twice married and had a son and a daughter. His son, Nicky, took over at Greystoke.

October 1 1998

MARGARET JENNINGS

MARGARET JENNINGS, who died aged 89, was, as Margaret Allan, one of the select band of women racing drivers who made their mark in the sport in the Twenties and Thirties; she was one of only four women to hold the Brooklands 120mph badge. Her finest racing years came in the mid-1930s. In 1933 she made the first and best of three drives in the Monte Carlo Rally, first in a Rolls-Royce, and in subsequent years in a Triumph and an AC. She followed this with wins in three Junior Long Handicaps at Brooklands in 1933 and 1934 in a 4.5-litre Bentley. After these races she was asked to join a women's team with MG Magnettes.

The team promptly carried off the Morgan Trophy for third place in the 1934 Light Car Club Relay Race. Margaret Allan was then invited to join Cecil Kimber's first all-female Abingdon works team, driving 847cc MGs at Le Mans in 1935. Nicknamed "The Dancing Daughters", Margeret Allan and her co-driver, Colleen Eaton, covered 1,576 miles and took 26th place in a race dominated by the far more powerful Lagondas. They also qualified their team for the 1936 Rudge Cup, though they were subsequently withdrawn from racing by Lord Nuffield.

Margaret Allan's sporting career was now moving into top gear and in August 1935 she won at Brooklands, lapping the track at 119mph in Dudley Folland's Frazer-Nash. During her practice laps, a timekeeper found that she had broken the 1500cc Outer Circuit speed record set by Earl Howe at 127.05mph. But the time was not accepted, and a later official attempt ended in failure, with a broken top gear chain and a cracked engine head.

The next year she was invited to share Richard Marker's 6.5-litre Bentley, known as "Mother Gun". She raced successfully in it many times that year, easily winning the Whitsun Long Handicap at Brooklands. She averaged 115mph throughout the race, and completed one lap at 122.37mph, earning her the coveted 120 mph badge.

Margaret Mabel Gladys Allan was born on July 26, 1909 into the Scottish shipping family who ran the Allan Royal Mail Line. Her father was also the principal shareholder in a teetotal paddle steamer, an enterprise that tried to reverse the drunken reputation of other Clyde steamers. After Bedales, Margaret Allan began to take part in equestrian competitions.

However, in 1929 she bought a second-hand Riley 9 and then an open Lagonda. In 1932, Margaret Allan was offered a co-drive with Eve Staniland in the Monte Carlo Rally. Her own supercharged two-litre Lagonda was too highly geared for trials, so after Monte Carlo she was persuaded to make up a team for a novices' handicap at an Inter-Club meeting at Brooklands. She was a lap and a half in the lead when her engine blew up. While making the necessary repairs she met her future husband, Christopher Jennings, whose Riley had suffered the same misfortune.

Later that year she accepted the offer of a drive in the Alpine Trial in a 4.5-litre Bentley. When the car's owner had a smash on his way out to the rally, Margaret Allan substituted another car. With her brother as navigator, she tackled the course in a Wolseley Hornet. The Allans finished with the bonnet of their car on top of the luggage and the spare wheels held on by ropes, but Margaret Allan gained the Coupe des Alpes and also took the Ladies' Prize. Her brother never drove competitively with her again.

After her marriage in 1937, Margaret Jennings cut down on her racing. In 1942 she was recruited to work at Bletchley Park, in the Italian naval subsection, just as shipping intelligence became crucial to counter enemy convoys. After the war, she became motoring correspondent of *Vogue*; her husband was editor of *The Motor*. She was an honorary member of the British Racing Drivers' Club. She gardened at Carmarthenshire, but retained her dash. When she was over 80, *Autocar* magazine asked her to test drive three high-powered cars. In taking them off to the Welsh hills, she outpaced the editorial staff. Christopher Jennings died in 1982; they had a son.

October 29 1998

ARCHIE MOORE

In an immensely long pugilistic career Archie Moore, who died aged 84, held the light-heavyweight title for a decade. He was the only man to fight Rocky Marciano and Cassius Clay, and knocked out 141 opponents, more than any other boxer in the history of the sport. Moore might have been champion far longer, but he was not given a shot at the title until he was 39. Though he had been the leading contender for many years, he was the sort of fighter champions feared, a cagey, ringwise boxer with a fearsome punch.

By 1952 he had grown tired of waiting for his chance and wrote to 427 American sports journalists accusing the holder of the light-heavyweight crown, Joey Maxim, of refusing to fight him. He even offered to fight Maxim for a purse of one dollar. Maxim duly issued a challenge, and in a bloody bout Moore, wearing his customary knee-length trunks, took the title from him on a unanimous decision.

He successfully defended the title eight times, with his most difficult fight being against the Canadian Yvon Durelle in 1958. Moore was dumped on the canvas four times, three of them in the first round. "The first time he put me down I thought, 'Wow, this guy can hit,'" Moore recalled. But he got back up to batter Durelle into submission, and eventually knocked him out in the 11th round. It was his 127th knockout, a record, and brought him the award of Fighter of the Year.

Moore had less success when he tried to step up a division. In 1955, at Yankee Stadium, he fought Rocky Marciano for the heavyweight championship of the world. Marciano was 10 years his junior but "The Mongoose", as Moore was known, dropped Marciano for a count of four in the second round. By the eighth, Moore was exhausted and the referee tried to stop the fight. Moore, though, told him he wanted to go the only way a champion should, knocked out cold. Marciano granted his wish in the next round.

Moore had a second crack at the title in 1956 when, at 42, he took on Floyd Patterson, who was half his age, for the throne vacated by Marciano. He lost in the fifth round. Moore was stripped of his title in 1962 amid wrangling between the several boxing associations, and in almost his last fight later that year took on the swaggering young Cassius Clay, who beat him in four rounds. Nevertheless, Moore's ambition remained unquenched. "My career is like a river," he said at the time. "I would like to have it end in fulfilment, by flowing into the mighty ocean. I don't want it to dry up before it reaches there." He went on to have one more fight, a victory over Mike DiBase, before finally retiring, unbowed, shortly before his 50th birthday.

He was born Archibald Lee Wright in Benoit, Mississippi, on December 13, 1913. His parents separated while he was a baby, and he and his sister were brought up by an uncle, Cleveland Moore, whose surname he took. Young Archie grew up in St Louis, where he was soon running with street gangs and in trouble with the law. He bought his first boxing gloves with the proceeds from a pair of oil lamps he had stolen from home. At 14 he was sent to a reform school for three years, after which he emerged determined on a career as a boxer. He fought his first professional bout in 1936 as a middleweight and won the next 12 by knockout.

In 1940 he toured Australia, where he won all seven of his fights and discovered a way of rapidly losing weight. A considerable trencherman and naturally heavier than his fighting weight of 12st 7lb, Moore closely guarded his secret diet, which he claimed to have learnt from an aborigine. In his autobiography *The Archie Moore Story* (1960) he eventually revealed his method, which involved chewing but not swallowing meat so as to extract only juices.

By 1941, Moore was the fourth-ranked middleweight in the world when he entered hospital for surgery on an ulcer. While there he fell into a coma for five days and contracted peritonitis and pneumonia. When he was discharged, he appeared to have aged 10 years, and weighed only seven stones. Moore was noted even among boxers for his devotion to fitness, and he built himself back up to his peak with a regime that included hours spent walking on his hands and 250 press-ups a day.

Courteous, likeable, with gold-tipped teeth, Moore was also known for his honourable behaviour in the ring, never being disrespectful to his opponents or taking a dive in an era when it was common. He later revealed that he had been influenced by his aunt, who told him: "Take your rest, Archie, mind your trainer and bring no disgrace on your family by throwing fights."

After his retirement, Moore acted as a trainer to both George Foreman and Muhammad Ali, the former Cassius Clay. He appeared in several films, notably as the slave Jim in *The Adventures of Huckleberry Finn* (1960). Moore once listed his interests as jazz, ice cream and snooker; in 1956 he missed a flight to London for a title defence against Yolande Pompey because he was playing snooker in Harlem. *Boxing News* rated Moore as, pound-for-pound, the ninth best boxer of all time. He was married five times and had eight children.

December 11 1998

JOE DIMAGGIO

JOE DIMAGGIO, who died aged 84, was arguably the greatest baseball player of the 20th century; after his retirement he compounded his fame by marrying perhaps the only person of that period to outstrip him in the affections of the American people, Marilyn Monroe.

In 1934 DiMaggio, aged 19, was bought from a minor Californian team by the New York Yankees. His transfer made him the most discussed rookie player in the Major Leagues since the advent of Ty Cobb in 1905. DiMaggio himself had doubts about his prospects after modest performances in spring training. One day, however, the team were visited by Babe Ruth, who had left the Yankees two years before. Ruth could rarely remember names, and as he moved down the line he greeted each of his former team-mates with "Hiya, kid." When Ruth got to DiMaggio he looked at him and said: "Hiya, Joe." DiMaggio's confidence soared.

Before DiMaggio arrived at the Yankees the team had been under-performing for several years. After he began to play for them, they won the World Series nine times in the 12 seasons played between 1936 and 1951, the year DiMaggio retired. In that time the side also won the American League 10 times.

DiMaggio's game was distinguished by his powerful and, above all, consistent hitting, rooted in an unorthodox wide stance and a loose, easy swing reminiscent of "Shoeless" Joe Jackson, which he only unleashed at the last possible moment. In his first month as a professional, DiMaggio became one of only three players then to have hit two home runs in one inning. He went on to have a career average of .325, scoring 361 home runs, and in 1941 set a record of 56 consecutive hitting games (in which he made 91 hits), beating the former record of 42 games, which had stood since the previous century.

He was also a supremely elegant and reliable centre fielder who moved about the outfield with the grace of a cat. DiMaggio was renowned for one particular and regularly displayed piece of skill in which he would turn his back on a ball hit in the air, glide over to the exact spot where he calculated it would fall, then swing round just as it dropped into his outstretched hand for the catch.

DiMaggio was also known for his ability to overcome or ignore injuries which would have threatened the careers of other players. Even before he arrived in New York he had seen off a serious knee injury, and he played his first few games at Yankee Stadium with a severe burn to his foot, caused by over-use of a sun lamp. He later suffered from bone spurs in his heels, and from stomach ulcers, seemingly brought on by his time as a physical training instructor in the Air Force between 1942 and 1945. DiMaggio disdained to take pain-killers, confining himself to numerous cups of strong coffee.

DiMaggio was in person taciturn, even melancholy, though in public his inner diffidence was masked by greater self-assurance. It was this confidence that inspired his team-mates and made him so important to the Yankees that, in 1948, he became the first player to command an annual salary of more than $100,000. He had the knack of being at his best in important games, which he often dominated. In consequence he was three times voted the League's Most Valuable Player. And every year between 1936 and 1951, he was picked for the All-Star team.

Yet these triumphs never went to his head. Eschewing flashier recreations (and indeed all other forms of exercise), he relaxed by going deep-sea fishing. Even at his peak, he always retained a sense of his obligations. Asked why he seemed to give his all in every game he played, the "Yankee Clipper" replied: "Because out there is some kid seeing me play for the first time. I owe him my best."

Joseph Paul DiMaggio was born at Martinez, California, on November 25, 1914. His parents were emigrants from Sicily and his father worked as a crab fisherman. The eighth of nine children, Joe had two brothers who also became professional baseball players. Joe grew up and was educated in San Francisco, learning to play baseball on the city's wastelands. In 1932 he was recommended by his brother Vince as a fielder to a local minor team, the San Francisco Seals. In his first game he batted well but endangered the spectators with his wild throwing. Nevertheless, he was called back by the team the next season and broke the Pacific Coast League record by hitting safely in 61 consecutive games.

In 1951, DiMaggio retired from baseball, working first as a television commentator and later as a representative for several large frozen-food firms. His first marriage, to the starlet Dorothy Arnold, had been dissolved after five years in 1944. Then, in 1952, he was introduced to Marilyn Monroe, who was just starting to make her name in films. He was smitten, and as her studio were keen to raise her profile, they sent her on a blind date with DiMaggio. She had little idea who he was and was two hours late for dinner. Halfway through the meal Mickey Rooney came over and asked DiMaggio for his autograph. Only then did Marilyn Monroe begin to grasp the eminence of her modest dining partner.

They were married in January 1954, but the union was not a success. DiMaggio's only real interests were baseball and television – Marilyn Monroe later revealed that he had spent most of their honeymoon watching the one on the other – and he naively believed that his wife would gladly become a housewife. He was also a jealous and possessive husband who disliked both Marilyn Monroe's famous friends and her status as public fantasy. They were divorced after only nine months of marriage, the final straw being DiMaggio's rage at seeing his wife flashing her underwear at a crowd of gawping spectators as she filmed the subway grating scene for *The Seven Year Itch*. Nevertheless, DiMaggio remained protective of Marilyn Monroe, and in 1962 he was the second person to be told of her death. It was he who made the arrangements for her funeral, to which no Hollywood stars or members of the Kennedy entourage were invited. Afterwards, he sent two roses to her grave three times a week for the rest of his life.

In his later years, DiMaggio seemed to many to embody a lost golden age of American life, when sportsmen played on sunlit afternoons for the joy of the game. In the 1960s his reputation remained so potent that Paul Simon was able to use him as a symbol of America's passing innocence in his song "Mrs Robinson". Joltin' Joe has indeed left and gone away. Joe DiMaggio was survived by a son from his first marriage.

March 9 1999

LORD KILLANIN

THE 3RD LORD KILLANIN, who died in Dublin aged 84, was president of the International Olympic Committee from 1972 to 1980, a period during which the Olympics were subjected to unprecedented pressures. Killanin took over as president from Avery Brundage, just after the outrage at the Munich Olympic Games, when 11 Israeli athletes were murdered. Though the Olympic Games at Montreal in 1976 were a great success, Killanin faced a boycott of African and Asian athletes who walked out of the Games in protest against the participation of New Zealand, who had continued to play rugby against South Africa. He also had an argument with the Canadian Government over the admission of Taiwanese athletes into Canada.

A jolly man, plump and rubicund, with a fine head of hair and side whiskers and a penchant for pipe smoking, Killanin strove in vain to maintain the Olympic ideal of Baron de Coubertin, who saw the Games as transcending international tensions and hatreds. Killanin faced another boycott in 1980, when President Carter advised the American Olympic Association not to send a team to Moscow after the Russian invasion of Afghanistan. Killanin could not prevent the American withdrawal from the Games, and found it hard to forgive Carter. "Despite the efforts of certain politicians to use the Games at Moscow for political expediency," he reflected in 1981, "I believe that they, in the end, were the losers. The victors were the Olympic Movement."

It is true that Killanin, with his good humour and patience, managed to prevent a complete collapse of the Moscow Games. No one could have accused him of not working hard at his job; he travelled hundreds of thousands of miles each year, earning the soubriquet "Pope of Sport". However, his hope of keeping politics and sport apart was unfulfilled.

He had more success in redefining "amateur", having had the vision to see that the Olympic Movement could not survive if the old standards were not brought up to date. Gradually, he persuaded the Olympic Association that top-class competitors had to spend so much time away from their jobs and families that it was reasonable for them to receive financial aid or compensation. He therefore simplified the laws on amateurism, and reduced the chances of a reaction by placing a limit on the age of members of the IOC.

When he retired as president in 1982, the problem of athletes using drugs to enhance their performances was already causing difficulties. Killanin considered it was the greatest threat to the future of the Olympic Movement. In his book, *My Olympic Years* (1983), he also drew attention to the political and financial manoeuvring behind the Games.

He was born Michael Morris on July 30, 1914, the son of Lieutenant-Colonel George Morris, of the Irish Guards, who was killed in action in the same year. His ancestors had been in Galway since medieval times. Young Michael succeeded his uncle as the 3rd Lord Killanin in 1927, when he was still at Eton. As a boy he boxed, swam and rowed, but had no eye for ball games (save rugby), nor any love of shooting. He continued his education at the Sorbonne in Paris, and at Magdalene

College, Cambridge, where he was president of the Footlights and literary editor of *Varsity Weekly*.

On leaving Cambridge in 1935 he obtained a job,
through the influence of Lord Castlerosse, with Lord
Beaverbrook, as a reporter on the *Daily Express*. Subsequently, he transferred to the *Daily Mail*, and at the
coronation of King George VI was the only reporter to
type his story wearing Coronation robes. Subsequently, in
1937, he reported the war between China and Japan. On
his return to Europe, Killanin became assistant political
and diplomatic correspondent to the *Daily Mail*. He also
wrote a political column in the *Sunday Dispatch*.

In 1938 Killanin volunteered and went on to serve
throughout the War in the Queen's Westminsters (King's
Royal Rifle Corps). By 1943 he was brigade major of the
30th Armoured Brigade; and for his part the next year
in the Normandy invasion he was appointed MBE. After
the War Killanin turned to film production, and in
1952 was associated with John Ford in making *The Quiet
Man*, which featured John Wayne as an Irish-American
boxer. He produced a number of films, including *The
Rising of the Moon*, *Playboy of the Western World* and
Gideon's Day.

When the Four Province Films Company was wound
up, Killanin returned to writing. He had already published a life of Sir Godfrey Kneller, the 18th-century
portrait painter, in 1948; and while he was on the *Express*
had edited *Four Days*, about the Munich Crisis. Now,
with Professor Michael Duignan, he published *The Shell
Guide to Ireland*. *My Ireland*, a personal impression, was
published in 1987. Lord Killanin took on a number of
directorships, including Chubb Ireland and Gallaher
(Dublin), of both of whom he was chairman. Other

chairmanships included Bovril (Ireland), Lombard & Ulster Banking Ireland and Ulster Investment Bank.

Killanin's connection with the Olympics began in 1952, when he became Ireland's representative to the International Olympic Committee. He became a member of the eight-man committee and vice-president of the IOC in 1968. In that position he was involved in some of the organisation's more controversial decisions, including, in 1972, the expulsion of the Austrian skier Karl Schranz from the Winter Games. There was also an unsuccessful attempt to keep the Rhodesian team in the Games despite a boycott by Black Africa.

Lord Killanin was a member of the Irish Turf Club and the Irish National Hunt Steeplechase Committee. In 1982 he was appointed chairman of the Irish Government Commission of Thoroughbred Horse Breeding. For 23 years up to 1984 he was honorary consul for Monaco in Ireland. Lord Killanin married, in 1946, Mary Dunlop, daughter of Canon Douglas. They had three sons and a daughter. The eldest son, Redmond Morris, born in 1947, succeeds to the peerage; he has been a film executive. The second son, "Mouse" Morris, is a well-known trainer and former jockey.

April 26 1999

SIR ALF RAMSEY

SIR ALF RAMSEY, who died aged 79, managed the England football team to World Cup victory in 1966; his qualities of determination and motivation were as important as any player to a triumph that none of his successors has matched. Ramsey quickly made his mark after his appointment in 1962. Unlike his only predecessor, Walter Winterbottom, Ramsey was able to insist that he, and not a selection committee, should pick the England team. He also made a rod for his own back by predicting with characteristic certainty that England would win the forthcoming World Cup.

This he proceeded to do by building a team of outstanding footballers bonded by an indomitable camaraderie. Unlike Winterbottom, Ramsey was a team man, with utter loyalty to his players. In return he expected discipline and commanded respect. He had little time for individuals who indulged themselves on or off the pitch, notably recidivist drinkers like Jimmy Greaves and Bobby Moore. When seven players broke curfew once on tour, they returned to find their passports on their beds. The threat brought them to heel.

Ramsey made England a side built on defence, and one who were hard to beat. He employed the same tactics he had used successfully as manager of Ipswich, eschewing conventional wingers in favour of a midfield packed with energetic, hard-running players. However, with England this was an expediency forced on him relatively close to the World Cup by an absence of gifted wingers, rather than (as many thought) by a suspicion of attacking footballers. Indeed, his winning side were distinguished by the quality and subtlety of their play in the last third of the field. Crucially, Ramsey also persuaded Bobby Charlton to move in from his favoured position on the left wing to a more central role, dominating midfield.

As the tournament approached, the press doubted the team's chances after a series of ordinary results. Ramsey was deeply sensitive to criticism, perhaps a legacy of childhood taunts that related his strong, dark looks to gypsy stock. He could appear aloof and graceless, and a fear of betraying his lack of formal education made him a linguistic contortionist in the presence of journalists.

Yet he was unbending when it mattered. His judgement was tested on three crucial occasions in the competition itself. First, when pressured by FIFA to drop Nobby Stiles after a dreadful tackle on Simon in the game against France, Ramsey stood by his toothless workhorse, believing him to be hard but fair. Ramsey's notorious criticism of later opponents Argentina as "animals" was based less on their hard play than on their spitting at England in the tunnel afterwards. His faith in Stiles was rewarded when he smothered Eusebio out of the game in the semi-final against Portugal. Ramsey also had to decide whether to recall popular favourite Greaves, now recovered from injury, for the final against West Germany. He persisted instead with the untried Geoff Hurst, a gamble that would pay off spectacularly.

Lastly, he was faced with a team who believed they had surrendered the initiative when Germany equalised just two minutes from the end. With extra time to play, Ramsey pointed across to where the Germans lay exhausted on the pitch. Drawing as much on the spirit he had forged as on the tireless running of Alan Ball and George Cohen, he said: "You've won it once – now go and do it again. Look at them. They're finished." It was a masterpiece of motivation. As Hurst cantered on to Moore's long pass some spectators ran on the pitch. As his shot flew into the net and the final whistle blew, the England bench and the entire nation erupted in joy –

except for Ramsey, who remained seated, impassive, feelings in check, his promise kept.

Alfred Ernest Ramsey was born in Dagenham, Essex, on January 22, 1920. His father was a small-holder who dealt in hay and straw. Young Alf's first experience of football was in kickabouts with his three brothers as they walked to school. He came late to professional football, having pursued his ambition to become a grocer on leaving Becontree Heath School. He signed amateur forms for Portsmouth before joining Southampton after playing against them while stationed there as a sergeant in an anti-aircraft unit in 1943. He served briefly in the Middle East, captaining the Palestine Services XI, before returning to the Dell and converting from centre-forward to right-back.

Ramsey's playing style reflected his character. Lacking natural advantages of pace or height, he became a deliberate, stubborn player of great intelligence and positional judgement. He thrived on pressure, and cultivated an aura of calm that made him a natural choice to take important free-kicks and penalties. Ramsey won his first international cap in 1948 while still in the Second Division, surprising the senior England player, Stanley Matthews, with shouted instructions on when to hold and release the ball.

Ramsey lost his place at Southampton after injury, but was snapped up by Tottenham. He became an integral part of the side whose push-and-run tactics brought them the Second and First Division titles in consecutive years between 1949 and 1951. His influence brought him the nickname "The General", while he learnt much from the Tottenham manager, Arthur Rowe. Ramsey was dedicated to self-improvement, as was later shown by the elocution lessons that stranded his vowels halfway to Mayfair, and he never forgot a footballing lesson.

He won 32 caps as an England player, three of them as captain in the absence of Billy Wright, and scored three penalties. He played in the historic 1950 defeat by the United States, and his last game was the 6–3 rout by Puskas's Hungarians in 1953. That year his weak back-pass cost Spurs a place in the FA Cup Final.

In 1955 he was appointed manager of Ipswich, an obscure team wallowing in the Third Division South. By 1957 they had become the division's champions. In 1961 they won the Second Division title and, emulating Tottenham, captured the First Division championship the following year. Ramsey had taken the club from oblivion to unimagined glory in six years. Operating on a shoe-string budget with largely superannuated players, his success was based on innovative tactics taken from abroad. He withdrew his wingers into midfield, forming a hard-working defensive screen that prompted the opposing full-backs to push up, leaving space in which Ipswich poured passes.

Ramsey exerted extreme self-control, but was not without emotion. As Ipswich celebrated their title in 1962 John Cobbold, the patrician brewer who owned the club and whose mien Ramsey strove to acquire, found his manager alone in the stand, reluctant to show his feelings in public. Wordlessly, Ramsey removed his jacket and ran a private, joyful lap of honour.

Other teams took only a season to get the measure of Ipswich, and the side were struggling when Ramsey was offered the England job in October 1962. He was not the first choice and was never to enjoy good relations with the Football Association. He particularly felt the lack of an appropriate financial reward after his World Cup success in 1966. When one official approached him during a tour, saying brightly, "Aren't we doing well?", Ramsey snapped: "What do you mean we? The players are doing well. You're just here for the cocktails." It was this mutual dislike that ensured his eventual downfall.

After 1966 Ramsey began to lose his touch. As ever, the team found it harder to win abroad than at Wembley, losing a bad-tempered semi-final of the European Nations Cup to Yugoslavia in 1968. In 1970 the side lost 3–2 to West Germany in the quarter-final of the Mexico World Cup, having been 2–0 up. Many observers felt the match turned on Ramsey's substitution of the ageing Bobby Charlton, though goalkeeper Peter Bonetti was responsible for two of the goals conceded.

After England lost again to the Germans in the 1972 quarter-final of the European Championships, critics began to question Ramsey's tactical acumen and his sentimental loyalty to players. When England failed to qualify for the World Cup after a match against Poland in which they contrived to miss several dozen chances, Ramsey was summarily sacked by the FA in May 1974. Despite a superlative record in which he had won 69 of his 113 games in charge, and lost only 17, he was not consulted again in any capacity by the FA. He never fully recovered from this shabby treatment.

Ramsey retired from football to Ipswich, where he concentrated on his golf and watching his favourite Westerns. He emerged briefly to manage Birmingham City for six months in 1977 before resigning because of ill-health. He was technical director to the Greek club

Panathanaikos in 1980. He published a ghosted, rather selective autobiography in 1952, *Talking Football*. Alf Ramsey was knighted for his services to football in 1967. He married, in 1951, Vicky Answorth; they had a daughter.

Bryon Butler writes: So many memories but one endures above all. It is the picture of Alf Ramsey just before quarter past five on July 30, 1966, sitting on a wooden bench and looking as if he had toothache. His black eyebrows were like little glowering clouds, his lips pursed and shoulders hunched. He seemed alone.

Around this solitary man was a mighty crowd celebrating a seismic moment in the history of sport. England had just won the World Cup and the country who set football rolling 100 years before could claim, at last, to be its undisputed champions. But Ramsey, the architect of the success, was always true to himself. At the apogee of his distinguished career, when any excess of emotion would have been pardonable, he still managed to look self-conscious, taciturn, calculating and bloody-minded. He said England would win the World Cup and he had delivered. What was all the fuss about? A little later, on that sunny afternoon, he allowed himself to be photographed kissing the trophy but only because he had been persuaded that it was his bounded duty.

This, however, was Ramsey: a Dagenham man, the son of a hay and straw dealer, who became a knight of the realm. He could be friendly and likeable on his own terms, and especially after a few gin and tonics, though a part of him was always roped off and any attempts to trespass into private corners were waspishly rejected. He felt deeply but wore his dignity like a bespoke suit of armour. He took football and life (which were much the same thing to him) too seriously to have a conspicuous sense of humour.

Popularity, for Ramsey, was the small beer of success and so was publicity. He regarded the press, by and large, as ticks on his back. "Hello, Alf, d'you remember me?" smiled one welcoming scribe at a faraway airport. "Yes," replied Alf. "You're a ****** pest."

Yet, paradoxically, Ramsey generated great affection and loyalty among people he cared about and many of those he worked with. He was a player's man and the Class of '66, above all, thought the universe of him. They respected his knowledge, experience, strategies, constancy, discipline and determination, but they also respected him as a man without daring to take him for granted. "Cheers, Alf, see you next time," said Gordon Banks after one victory. "Will you?" replied Ramsey.

Ramsey's standards and values counted for something. He frequently used the word "gentleman" in football team talks and was able, precisely, to make his players understand what was expected of them. Outside the dressing-room, however, he often committed assault and battery on the English language. His accent was cut-glass East London – vowels from his youth, aspirates from an elocution teacher – and his delivery and thoughts were sometimes in opposition. But, when it mattered, he made his point. When he likened Argentina's footballers to "animals" in 1966, he meant it.

He was also defined by small things. His tie-knot was always perfect, his shoes mirror-bright. His rare "Maybe It's Because I'm A Londoner" was a show stopper and he loved cowboy films. Once, during the 1970 World Cup, he agreed to do a BBC interview with me at 11.30 a.m.

and I found him outside the studio at 11.27 a.m., waiting patiently for the half-hour to come round.

No purpose is served in wondering if any other man of his time could have engineered English football's finest triumph. Ramsey, as a young chap, had wanted to be a grocer and he was not even the Football Association's first nomination to succeed Walter Winterbottom as England's football manager in 1963. But he was the chosen one and the strands of his life prepared him meticulously for the job of guiding a team of his choice to six victories in 19 days at Wembley in the high summer of 1966.

As a right-back for Southampton, Tottenham's "push-and-run" champions and England (32 caps, 1949–53), he was so polished and influential he was known as "The General". As manager of Ipswich Town (1955–63), he guided this homely club, astonishingly, to the championship of the Third Division South, Second Division and First Division, in only five years. He recharged the careers of players believed to be past their best and employed the tactics which flummoxed all opposition. Ramsey stitched a collection of remnants into a quilt of quality. Ramsey the player gave everything he had and, as a manager, he expected no less from others. He demanded full control when the Football Association approached him and thus the old convention of selection by committee passed into history. In any case, Ramsey had little regard for the older men of Lancaster Gate and believed their most important job was "looking after cocktail parties".

Not everyone believed in Ramsey's England. Don Revie, manager of Leeds and the man destined to follow Ramsey, even wrote in the *FA News*: "If England win the World Cup, it would be the greatest thrill of the season for me, but sadly I cannot see them doing so."

Everyone recognised, though, that the home of the game would never have a better chance of victory and Ramsey duly turned great expectations into conviction and then into fulfilment. He shaped his side and strategy slowly and by trial and error, the director of a classic piece of theatre which picked its way scene by scene towards a compelling climax: England 4, West Germany 2.

Ramsey ruled; yet things would never be the same again. England were beaten 3–2 by West Germany in the quarter-finals of the 1970 World Cup in Mexico, but should Ramsey have sent on Colin Bell and Norman Hunter for Bobby Charlton and Martin Peters when England were 2–0 up? Ramsey's face showed no more emotion in defeat than it had done in his moment of triumph four years before. He formally reported to the FA that, given the same challenge again, he would pick the same men and play the same way. No one knew it would be 12 years before England played in the finals of a World Cup again and by then Ramsey was long gone.

Even old admirers, in the end, crossed to the other side of the floor to join Ramsey's old foes. Ramsey was accused of everything from tactical suicide to contempt of the footballing public. His "wingless wonders" were even said to have damaged the morale of English football. The decision to sack him was announced on May 1, 1974. "English football indebted to Sir Alf, loyalty, dedication, integrity" etc., etc.

Ramsey had been England's football manager for 11 years and his record spoke for itself: played 113, won 69, drawn 27, lost 17, goals for 224, against 99. His salary was around £7,000 a year, his 1966 World Cup bonus £5,000, his pay-off £8,000 and his pension £1,200 a year. However, Ramsey's legacy is something beyond measure. He was the man who, during the summer of 1966, came closest of all to convincing the nation that football is something more than just a game.

May 1 1999

GENE SARAZEN

GENE SARAZEN, who died aged 97, enjoyed a career as a professional golfer that spanned the eras of Harry Vardon and Jack Nicklaus; he himself was one of the greatest players in the history of the game, and the first to win all four "major" championships: the American and British Opens, the American PGA and the Masters at Augusta.

Sarazen won the American Open for the first time in 1922, finishing ahead of Bobby Jones and Walter Hagen. Four weeks later he carried off the PGA title, and then – in great pain from his appendix, which was removed immediately afterwards – beat Hagen, the reigning British Open champion, in a challenge match. The next year, 1923, Sarazen retained his PGA title, but performed disastrously when he crossed the Atlantic to compete for the first time in the Open. Caught in a gale lashing in from the sea at Troon, he failed even to qualify. Undaunted, he vowed to return until he won – "even if I have to swim the Atlantic". He finally achieved victory, with a record low score of 282, at Prince's, next to Royal St George's, Sandwich, in 1932. This was the last Open in which Harry Vardon played.

Earlier that year, Sarazen had won the American Open

again at Flushing Meadow, New York. He needed only 100 strokes to complete the last 29 holes, turning a deficit of seven into a winning margin of three strokes. These and other triumphs brought him £25,000 in 1932, making him the highest-paid sportsman in the world, some compensation for large losses on the stock market. "I don't want to be a millionaire," he once said. "I just want to live like one."

Sarazen's success was partly due to a method of bunker play he had pioneered. This derived from some flying lessons he had taken, for he was a keen amateur pilot, along with his friend Howard Hughes. As he pulled back the stick on take-off, the nose of the plane went up and the tail down. This made him think, he recalled, "that maybe if I put some lead on the back of a niblick to make the sole a little lower, the club would bounce up when it hit the sand instead of digging in". So the sand iron made its appearance. Until then players had used a niblick from the bunker, and even Hagen and Jones struggled. Sarazen practised with the club until he could almost guarantee to get down in two from a bunker. At the Open he hid his club under his coat at the end of each day's play; and took it back to his room at night in case some official took it into his head to ban it. Finally, though, he did not greatly profit from his invention; Wilson, who made his clubs, had the rights.

Sarazen always remained loyal to the Open, insisting on the prestige of the event after the Second World War, when very few Americans entered. "What's wrong with you?" Sarazen demanded of them in 1953. "Not one of you can call yourself a great player until you have been to Britain and won the Open." Arnold Palmer would eventually take heed.

Though Sarazen was several times in contention for both the American and British Opens after 1932, his last great triumph was at Augusta in 1935. Bobby Jones had inaugurated what was at first called the Augusta National Invitational in 1934, when it was won by Horton Smith. However, it was the drama of Sarazen's victory that helped to establish the event – rather against Bobby Jones's inclination – as the Masters. With four holes to play, Sarazen was three strokes behind Craig Wood. At the par five 15th he found himself in a dubious lie some 220 yards out. Ignoring the advice of his caddie, who recommended a three wood, Sarazen took a four wood and holed out for an albatross. Tied with Wood after 18 holes, he won the 36-hole play-off the next day by five strokes.

The son of an Italian immigrant, Gene Sarazen was born Eugenio Saraceni at Harrison, New York, on February 27, 1902. At 10 he began to caddie for members at the Apawamis club at Rye, New York. In 1916 he developed a lung complaint, and for four or five days seemed to be at death's door. "These priests would come in and pull the curtain round," he remembered. "They figured I was going to go." After recovering, he decided that his original name was better suited to a violinist than a professional golfer, and having consulted a telephone book to assure himself that the new nomenclature was unique, began to call himself Gene Sarazen.

Four years later, in 1920, when he played his first American Open, he was still pushed to break 80 for a round. Apart from his suspect health, he seemed too small, at 5ft 4½in and with tiny hands, to keep up with the long hitters. He practised with a weighted driver to tone up the muscles in his shoulders and arms, until he was known as "the pocket Hercules of the links". Even so, the short game remained the basis of his success.

Sarazen was not sentimental about the great players of the past; he thought that Bobby Jones was better than Harry Vardon; that Ben Hogan was better than Bobby Jones; and that Jack Nicklaus was better than Ben Hogan. Yet the length of his own career suggests that there was no unbridgeable gulf between the champions of the past and today – especially when it is remembered that the equipment used in his youth was far inferior. "We were lucky if three balls in every dozen were even round," he recalled.

In 1960, aged 58, Sarazen had a first round of 69 on the Old Course at St Andrews in the Open, and then followed up with a 72. In 1973, aged 71, he returned to Troon for the Open, 50 years after his first appearance. There, in the first round, at the eighth hole (the Postage Stamp), he caused a sensation by holing in one, which put him on the leader board. In the next round he drove into a bunker at the same hole, and then holed from the sand. Alas, age eventually caught up, and he failed to make the cut. He played at Royal Birkdale in 1976, but having lost his ball at the ninth, announced: "That is the end of the Open for me."

As late as 1978 Sarazen, with 12 other former champions, filed a suit against the PGA for restoration of playing rights. In 1991 he was still playing a nine-hole curtain-raiser with Sam Snead at the Masters, and in 1992 he marked his 90th birthday with nine holes (which he was still capable of doing in 40) at the country club at Marco Island, Florida.

In recent years it became a tradition that Gene Sarazen should drive off from the first tee at the beginning of the Masters. In 1998, when he was 96, he was joined by Sam Snead, aged 85. "Get that left shoulder tucked under your chin, Gene, and make a full turn," advised Snead when he took a practice swing. Sarazen duly sent his drive whistling 160 yards straight down the middle. "God damn it," he told Snead, "if someone had told me that 80 years ago, I'd have been a hell of a player." His wife of 62 years, Mary Catherine, predeceased him.

May 14 1999

VIOLET WEBB

VIOLET WEBB, who died aged 84, was part of the sprint relay quartet who became the first women to win Olympic medals for Britain at athletics, taking the bronze in the 4x100 metres at the 1932 Games in Los Angeles. Athletics for women had entered the Olympic programme in 1928, amid some controversy; Baron Pierre de Coubertin, founder of the modern Olympics, was strongly against women taking part in sport. "This does not mean that they should not participate in any sports," he opined, "yet not in public. At the Olympic Games their primary role should be like in the ancient tournaments – the crowning of the (male) victors with laurels."

As a result of a very limited women's involvement – they were invited to compete in only five events – the British female athletes decided to boycott the Amsterdam Games in 1928, the first year they were eligible to enter. Four years later they relented and, at Los Angeles, Violet Webb and her team-mates constituted the first British

Olympic women's athletics team. "People thought it was terrible that we should want to compete," Webb remembered. "But that was just stupid. Athletics was my life, so I just did it."

The journey to Los Angeles was first by ship to Canada; other passengers included the Prime Minister, Stanley Baldwin, and the Cabinet. The athletes then continued by special train. "When it stopped, we got off and ran up and down the platform. I hurdled a few dustbins." In Los Angeles, the women's team stayed at the Chapman Park Hotel, while the male athletes were installed in the first purpose-built Olympic village, complete with a high wall to keep out female competitors. Webb managed to glimpse such film stars as Jimmy Durante and Mary Pickford.

She reached the final of the 80 metres hurdles, finishing fifth. Then, when sprinter Ethel Johnson injured her leg in the heats of the 4x100 metres relay, Webb was called in as replacement for the final and ran the second leg. The British team won the bronze medal in 47.6 seconds; the Americans took the gold. "When you see people standing on the rostrum and you see their tears, I can understand that," Violet Webb said later. "If you're proud of your country, you do feel that way."

One of seven children, Violet Webb was born on February 3, 1915, in Willesden, North London, and educated locally. Her father Charles Webb was an athlete, and seeing the potential in young Violet, he built her a flight of eight hurdles which were kept at Paddington recreation ground. Fashioned from wood, the hurdles did not fall over if an athlete struck them. "They were formidable," Webb recalled. "I jumped high over them, as it hurt when you hit the solid barrier. I broke my arm on those awful hurdles once. It didn't deter me – I just went straight back again."

She joined the Ladies' Polytechnic Club in Regent Street, where she excelled. At her first international, against Germany in August 1931, she won the 80 metres hurdles and the relay, bringing her to the attention of the Olympic selectors. After the 1932 Olympics, Webb competed in the Women's World Games (at first known as the Women's Olympics until the International Olympic Committee objected), which had been started in 1921 by the Frenchwoman Alice Milliat in response to the lack of women's involvement in the Olympics. At the last Women's Games in 1934, Violet Webb was invited to take the Olympic oath on behalf of all the competitors. She also competed in the 1936 Olympics in Berlin, where she remembered the arrival of Hitler at the Olympic Stadium. "You'd have thought God was coming down from Heaven."

There she finished fourth in the semi-final of the 80 metres hurdles. Independent observers judged her to have finished third, which would have meant a place in the final, but the officials disagreed. Undeterred, she came back to equal the world record of 11.7 seconds at a post-Olympic meet in Wuppertal. Soon afterwards, she retired and married Harry Simpson. They had two daughters, one of whom, Janet, went on to international honours, competing in three Olympic Games between 1964 and 1972. At the Tokyo Games she emulated her mother by winning a bronze in the relay.

May 29 1999

RUTH LAWRENCE

RUTH LAWRENCE, who died aged 77, refused along with two other Jewish women swimmers to take part as members of the Austrian team in Hitler's 1936 Olympic Games; their stand earnt them a lifetime ban by the Austrian Swimming Federation. She was born Ruth Langer in Vienna on May 21, 1921 and educated at local schools. At the age of 14, she broke the Austrian records for both the 100 metres and 400 metres freestyle, and so was certain of selection. As the Austrian sports officials judged it preferable to be represented by three Jewish girls than by no one at all, Ruth and two team-mates had to make a choice between doing their final training in swimming pools where notice boards banned "dogs and Jews", or incurring the wrath of the Austrian Swimming Federation by refusing to travel to Berlin.

The three swimmers made their decision after the World Federation of Jewish Sports Clubs, headed by Lord Melchett, recommended that Jewish competitors refuse to take part in the Olympics. The recommendation cost the Dutch world record-holder, Willi den Ouden, a certain medal for breaststroke. For the Austrian girls, the cost was an immediate ban – and the removal of the names of all Jewish swimmers from the Austrian record books. However, Ruth Langer's swimming career was not over. She escaped from Austria to England after the Anschluss of 1938 by dyeing her hair blonde and carrying a false baptismal certificate. The next year she won a British long-distance championship, covering the distance from Kew to Putney in record time.

In 1995 the Austrian Government officially reinstated her name in the record books and finally sent her an apology. Her place in history, though, had already been secured by a special display in the Holocaust Museum, Washington DC. She had also been filmed for Steven Spielberg's Shoah archives. She married, in 1943, John Lawrence; they had a son and a daughter.

June 2 1999

KEN OLIVER

KEN OLIVER, who died aged 85, was Scotland's most successful racehorse trainer and one of the great characters of the racing world. In a career lasting half a century, Oliver trained five winners of the Scottish Grand National, saddled the Aintree runner-up three times (though without winning the race), and in all trained almost 1,000 winners.

An irrepressible enthusiast, rotund and with an impish sense of fun, Oliver – known throughout racing as "The Benign Bishop" – was the oldest licence-holder in Britain at the time of his death. In the 1960s he perfected a method of bringing horses up to fitness by working them up the hills of the Borders in several sharp canters – thus unknowingly employing interval training 30 years before it became common practice.

Oliver will perhaps be best remembered, though, for the horse Wyndburgh, a perennial Grand National runner-up. Wyndburgh was second in the National in 1959 and 1962, racing in the colours of Oliver's wife Rhona, and had been second in 1957 when trained by her. The result was particularly cruel in 1959, when Wyndburgh was the unluckiest of losers, coming in a length and a half behind Oxo. But for the fact that the jockey, Tim Brookshaw, suffered a broken stirrup iron at Becher's Brook on the second circuit, more than a mile from the finish, Wyndburgh could well have won.

James Kenneth Murray Oliver was born on February 1, 1914 on the family's 400-acre farm of Hassendean Bank, near Hawick in the Borders, where he was brought up with his three elder sisters. From Warriston Preparatory School, Moffat, he went on to Merchiston Castle, Edinburgh. There his academic record was undistinguished – maths was the only subject in which he did not come last. He excelled at sport, though, playing for both the first XV at rugby and the first XI at cricket, as well as being an accomplished tennis player. On leaving school, he decided in 1932 to join his father Douglas in the family livestock auctioneering business of Andrew Oliver & Son at Hawick, which had been founded three generations earlier by his great-grandfather and was the oldest such firm in Britain. Oliver progressed from office boy to selling pigs, before graduating to cattle and sheep. During the late summer the market was a busy place, with some sales bringing in as many as 30,000 sheep in a single day.

Foxhunting was always a passion in the Oliver household, but after a nasty childhood incident with an unruly Shetland pony, it was only as a young adult that Ken Oliver discovered the thrill of the chase with the Duke of Buccleuch's Hunt. It was a short step from there to point-to-pointing. In the spring of 1935, at the age of 21, he made his winning debut on a one-eyed horse called Delman. "I think we only had one eye between the two of us coming to the first two fences," he recalled. "Mine were tight shut."

Oliver soon acquired several decent horses, with whom he won; this suggested to him the idea of holding regular sales of bloodstock. In September 1937 he inaugurated the Kelso Horse Sales, to encourage the breeding of bloodstock in the Borders, something to which Oliver felt farmers, with their experience of breeding livestock, would be ideally suited.

During his pre-War days in the Territorial Army, Oliver found himself in the "Gentleman's ride", under one of the greatest trainers, Major Joe Dudgeon. With the onset of War, Oliver was commissioned into the Yorkshire Hussars, with whom he served in North Africa and Sicily before being invalided home. While still in Italy he had come up with the idea that the family firm should set up an estate agency. On his return he persuaded his father that this would prove to be sound business. He was correct, and soon the firm was selling farms and estates all over Britain, as well as frequently supplying the new owners with livestock.

Soon after the War, Padge Berry, from Wexford, sent Oliver a horse named Johnnie Walker. Though first impressions were not very favourable, Johnnie Walker proved to be an exceptional horse of great intelligence: when told it was necessary, the horse would take itself off to the blacksmith's to be shod. Oliver rode Johnnie Walker to third place in the Aintree National. Later, tragically, the horse broke its back at the open water at Manchester. "I lost a very dear friend that day," said Oliver. "I cried for a fortnight."

Oliver's long friendship with Padge Berry was to result in countless horses being sent over from Ireland, many of them winners. One of these was Sanvina, who walked off a train at Denholm, near Hawick, at 11 o'clock one night in the late Forties. "I couldn't see much to like about this bag of hones that I'd been advised to buy," said Oliver, "but I did have to run to keep up with her as she walked me the two miles home in the dark." In 1950 he rode Sanvina to victory in the Scottish Grand National.

In the late 1950s Oliver teamed up with his second wife, Rhona Wilkinson, herself a talented trainer, and together they fostered a string of jumpers with the stamp of old-fashioned chasers, interspersed with the tiny light-boned type that Sanvina and her offspring produced. Over the years, Oliver horses made their mark at the Cheltenham Festival, but it was at Wolverhampton in 1968 that Oliver achieved the remarkable feat of taking five horses down from the Borders to the Midlands track and winning with all of them.

Many great horses came under his charge, among them Arctic Sunset, Even Keel, Drumikill, The Spaniard and High Edge Grey. In 1962 Oliver and his good friend Willie Stephenson resurrected the Doncaster Bloodstock Sales with an investment of just £100 each. The sales are now one of the most important trading places for quality horses.

Away from racing, Oliver, a keen gardener, became a director of the Royal Highland and Agricultural Society of Scotland. He transformed both the light horse section and the flower section at the society's annual show. An enthusiastic golfer, he was a member of the Honourable Company of Edinburgh Golfers at Muirfield, and played on his local course at Minto. He was appointed OBE. In the late 1980s Oliver underwent a successful triple bypass operation – "One for blood and two for Tio Pepe." Ken

Oliver's first marriage, to Joan Innes, was dissolved; he married secondly, in 1958, Rhona Wilkinson. He had a son and a daughter.

June 19 1999

MALCOLM MARSHALL

MALCOLM MARSHALL, who died in Barbados aged 41, was one of the West Indies' truly great fast bowlers. "I am a fast bowler," he said in an interview in 1993. "This is my job. I love cricket and am a keen professional. I am a man who wants to do the best for himself and his team every time I go to work." No one could have doubted that he did exactly that.

Malcolm Denzil Marshall was born on April 18, 1958, in St Michael, a small parish in the middle of Barbados. His father, a policeman, died in a motorcycle accident before Malcolm's first birthday. At the local school he attended, teachers found young Malcolm a model pupil, and a team man even then. He loved cricket, batting especially; outside school, his grandfather Oscar Welch bowled at him in the parks and on the beaches. He took to bowling after once waiting four days to bat in the school playground. Finally, he decided to take action, bowling as fast as he could. By the end of break-time that day he was batting.

As he grew up, he became an avid follower of Hampshire's fortunes in the pages of the Barbados newspapers; and so it was most appropriate that after two years in first-class cricket he should come to play for Hampshire in 1979.

E. W. Swanton writes: Of the formidable array of modern West Indies' fast bowlers, none was either faster or more highly rated than Malcolm Marshall. In a career for Hampshire between 1979 and 1992, all the foremost English batsmen faced him and a poll among them would probably vote him as the greatest of all.

Of the 11 West Indian fast bowlers who have taken more than 100 Test wickets, only Courtney Walsh (playing in more Tests) has narrowly exceeded Marshall's 376 wickets, and none has taken them less expensively than his average of 20. Over the international scene, only three others, the New Zealander Sir Richard Hadlee, Kapil Dev of India and Ian Botham of England (all enjoying longer Test careers), have more wickets to their name. Of the 11 fast bowlers mentioned, only Sir Garfield Sobers was a manifestly better bat. Marshall made six hundreds, including the first for Hampshire against Lancashire and Clive Lloyd, his Test captain, against whom he tended to add a yard or two of speed.

Marshall was not a conspicuously tall man in the mould of Ambrose, Garner and Hall, but slight with the build of an athlete. His great speed derived from perfect rhythm and a flexible wrist. The delivery came as a flowing continuation of his approach, and the ball tended to skid through lower than when propelled by the giants.

A wispy beard and shining eyes gave him a daunting aspect and there were times when his reliance on the bouncer, as in the case of his fast-bowling contemporaries, though ignored by the umpires, was frankly intimidating. Usually he kept a full length, so that the ball tended to move either way, before pitching or after.

Off the field he was geniality itself, with a cheerful Bajan humour and a mode of speech which grew, it was said, "liltingly rushed". His captain and close friend Mark Nicholas could be persuaded to give a highly comical imitation of Marshall-speak. Marshall was fond of soul music and a good man at a party; next morning, though, he was punctilious with his exercises in preparation for the day's work.

Coming in 1979, aged 21, from Barbados sunshine in his first match for Hampshire he took nine wickets despite his introduction to snow. In 1980 he made the first of four visits to England with West Indian touring sides. In 1982 he touched the heights for Hampshire, taking 134 wickets at 15 runs apiece, 44 more than anyone else. He bowled 822 overs, also more than the next man. One of his captains said it was often hard to wrest the ball from him. He just loved bowling. Against England at Headingley in 1984, he broke his left thumb when fielding and so had to bat one-handed. Typically, he chose the occasion to return his best figures in a Test, seven for 53.

Having completed his Hampshire career he went, in 1993–94, to South Africa directly apartheid had been lifted and captained Natal, signing off with a flourish and a batting average of 60. In his career he took 1,524 wickets at 18 runs each, and made 9,863 runs with an average of 24.

In the summer of 1999 Marshall underwent a serious operation for cancer, but was finally overwhelmed by the illness. He married only a few weeks before his death.

November 6 1999

LEON STUKELJ

LEON STUKELJ, who died aged 100, won an Olympic gold at Amsterdam in 1928 for a sensational routine on gymnastic rings, including the standing cross – head vertically downwards, feet aloft, arms outstretched horizontally – still seen as one of the most difficult exercises in the sport. Stukelj, who lived to be the world's oldest Olympic champion, exercised to the end of his life on rings suspended in the bedroom doorway of his house at Maribor in his native Slovenia. He won six Olympic medals: golds for horizontal bars and overall gymnastics in Paris, 1924; gold for rings and bronze for overall and team at Amsterdam; and silver for rings at Berlin, 1936.

Leon Stukelj was born on November 12, 1898, in Novo Mesto, Slovenia. He was educated at the local grammar school and read law at university. Stukelj took up gymnastics at the age of eight, because "there was no other sport to do", as he recalled on his 100th birthday. He was self-taught, and when the world championships were staged in the Slovenian capital in 1922, he managed to win three first places, in rings, horizontal bars and parallel bars. He went on to win 14 top-three places in four world championships. But there was no aggression in his style, according to one of his closest colleagues: "His aim was perfection, much more than victory."

For the Paris Olympics in 1924, Slovenia provided the whole of the Yugoslav gymnastics team. Though the national federation paid their rail fares, competitors had to find and pay for their own lodgings. "There was only cold water for washing," Stukelj recalled. His biggest regret at those Games was that, because of clashing schedules, he could not watch Paavo Nurmi, the great Finnish runner.

In those days the overall programme included rope climbing, which he found particularly tough. After competing in that event, the Slovenian team went to have dinner in the centre of Paris, the judges still busy calculating the results. Returning later to their lodgings, Stukelj was told by another competitor that he had won. He and colleagues leapt into a taxi to go to the offices of *Le Matin* to confirm the news. On his return home he was decorated by King Alexander and went back to the legal practice he had established.

For the Amsterdam Games of 1928, the team took their own sets of bars, the last time it was permitted, to avoid unfamiliar apparatus. Stukelj remembered applauding the 100 metres swimming gold won by Johnny Weissmuller, who went on to play Tarzan.

Yugoslavia could not afford to send a gymnastics team to Los Angeles four years later. Stukelj decided he would make one last Olympic attempt at Berlin in 1936, though he was by then 37. Gymnastics, which had been a sport for all in 19th-century Germany, had by then become more muscular and aggressive, with strict rules on compulsory exercises. It was, Stukelj complained, much less elegant. Nonetheless, at Berlin, he succeeded in taking the rings silver medal by a tiny fraction ahead of the German favourite (the event being won by a Czechoslovak). "The organisation in Berlin was excellent," Stukelj recalled, "but the sea of swastikas was very depressing." Yet he considered the German crowd in the Olympic Stadium to be scrupulously fair. At the Olympic village he was able to meet the champion of all champions, Jesse Owens, and they exchanged autographs.

By now Stukelj was a high court judge. When German troops occupied Slovenia at the start of the War, they requisitioned his house to use as their headquarters, and imprisoned him as a suspected partisan. Freed at the end of the War, he was then accused by the Communist Government of having been an anti-partisan. Stukelj was demoted to a lowly clerical post. He lived long enough, though, for his house to be returned to him after the fall of Communism.

In 1992 Stukelj was featured on a series of Olympic postage stamps. Celebrations for his 100th birthday were attended by sporting dignitaries from around the world. He was survived by his wife of 66 years, Lydia, and by their daughter.

November 10 1999

INDEX

Index